1963

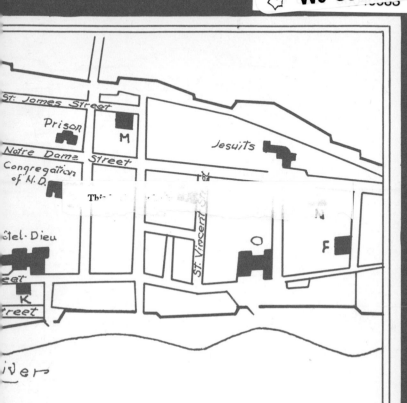

St. James Street
Prison
M
Jesuits
Notre Dame Street
Congregation of N.D.
Th...
N
Hôtel·Dieu
O
F
...eet
K
...reet
...iver

A- Gaultier
B- Madame You
C- Le Verrier
D- Fonblanche
E- Lapalme
F- La Corne
G- De Cuisy
H- Thaumur

I- General Hospital
J- La Vérendrye
K- Marie Louise Lajemmerais
L- Clemence Lajemmerais
M- Timothy Silvain
N- De Ramezay
O- De Vaudreuil
P- Market Place

HANDS TO THE NEEDY

Jesus said: I am the way, and the truth, and the life.

JOHN xiv:6

BLESSED MARGUERITE D'YOUVILLE

HANDS
to the
NEEDY

BLESSED
MARGUERITE D'YOUVILLE
APOSTLE TO THE POOR

by

SISTER MARY PAULINE FITTS,

G.N.S.H.

Garden City, New York

DOUBLEDAY & COMPANY, INC.

1958

Nihil Obstat: George T. Donnelly, S.T.D.
                Censor Librorum

Imprimatur: Bryan J. McEntegart, D.D.
                Bishop of Ogdensburg

Ogdensburg, New York. February 14, 1949

Nihil Obstat
Signed and sealed: Nicolaus Ferraro, S.R.C., Adsessor
                    Fidei Sub-Promoter Generalis
                    Rome. April 26, 1958

In obedience to the decree of Pope Urban VIII and other Sovereign Pontiffs, the writer declares that the graces and other supernatural facts related in this book, as witnessing to the holiness of Servants of God other than those beatified or canonized by the Church, rest on human authority alone and are not meant to anticipate the judgment of the Holy See, to which the writer is entirely submissive.

To the
ETERNAL FATHER
for the Grey Nuns

PREFACE

SINCE the original publication of this biography of Mother Marguerite d'Youville in 1950, the Cause of her beatification advanced so rapidly, by Divine Providence, that it is now appropriate to reissue the book in order to signalize the ceremonies that call her blessed.

When the Cause was introduced in the Sacred Congregation of Rites in Rome in 1890, Pope Leo XIII, then gloriously reigning, honored the Servant of God with the title "Venerable." On March 17, 1953, after the preliminary procedures had been completed, a Preparatory Congregation of Cardinals declared the Cause ready for discussion in General Congregation. Two years later, on May 3, the Feast of the Finding of the Holy Cross, His Holiness, Pope Pius XII, declared the heroicity of her virtues, calling her "Mother of universal charity." Official recognition, as miraculous, of the two cures attributed to her intercession has finally brought the process of beatification to a triumphant end. A review of her life is therefore in order.

For those who read French there is no lack of material on the life of Mother d'Youville, from the first personal sketch written before 1790 by her son, Father Charles Dufrost, to the scholarly biography published by Madame Albertine Ferland-Angers in 1945. For English readers, however, the sources are few. Besides pamphlets and articles, there are only two biographies in English: a partial translation, now out of print, written in 1895 by the Reverend D. S. Ramsay, of South Shields, England; and a short life by Mother Mary G. Duffin, S.G.M., published in 1938.

This present biography is the first complete account in English of the life of Blessed Marguerite d'Youville, the first native North American foundress of a religious community for women. It is in no way a translation, except in the case of documents, letters, and direct remarks of the foundress herself, which are reproduced with as much fidelity as possible to the original French. There are no interpretations in any way contrary to facts; where readability or artistic effect has required details, these have been supplied only in accordance with truth and inevitability.

Many sources, both archival and published, have served in this work; these are acknowledged fully in the general bibliography. It is a pleasant obligation to express gratitude for the use of the archives and for sisterly courtesies extended at the Motherhouse of the Grey Nuns of Montreal. Sincere thanks are due also to the Grey Nuns of St. Hyacinthe, the Grey Nuns of the Cross, the Sisters of Charity of Quebec (Grey Nuns), and the Grey Sisters of the Immaculate Conception, for generous co-operation in supplying information about their respective communities. For the privilege of providing this life of Mother d'Youville, the writer is deeply thankful to her own community, the Grey Nuns of the Sacred Heart.

Above all, this biography is a prayer that, through the intercession of Blessed Marguerite d'Youville, "Mother of universal charity," the kingdom of the love of God may cover the world.

S. M. P.

January 25, 1958.

CONTENTS

CONTENTS

FOREWORD

ONE of the most regrettable features of the study of the history of the colonization of this continent as conducted in American schools is the almost complete neglect of the foundation and development of French Canada. The average American youth knows very little indeed about the French settlements that were made in eastern Canada except for a few poetic notions that come to him with the story of Evangeline and possibly the name of Samuel de Champlain. In spite of all this neglect there is a history here that should be of enormous interest to all Americans and most particularly those who share the faith that has been the brightest jewel in the precious heritage of these stalwart people. Not very different from our own country, this half a nation has its own national heroes and heroines. The story of their lives, their fervor, and their fame has too long now awaited full publication. Surely their exploits should long before this have found expression in English.

Sister Mary Pauline has described in the pages that follow the life of one of these great national heroines, Mother Marguerite d'Youville, who reflected in herself so many of the qualities that are even now characteristic of that country and that people. In the accomplishments of the great foundress one can see the blessed blending of a natural inclination for charity with that particular divine inspiration which is the work of grace in the soul.

Mother d'Youville faced what seemed to be insurmountable obstacles and nearly certain defeat, and yet, almost in the same way as the young nation and its people to which she had dedicated her life, she triumphed by a miracle of persistence and determination. She had the rare privilege of being not merely the foundress of one of the great religious congregations of the New World, *les Soeurs Grises,* or the Grey Nuns, but also the mother of two priests. No one could have foreseen that the young widow left with two children at the age of twenty-nine would take over, as an adventure in charity, the enormously indebted Charon Hospital and begin there with the aid of other pious women a work which would in two centuries extend to three continents. Her fixed resolution in the midst of misunderstanding, deception, and even outright corruption reveals at a glance that here was no ordinary woman but one in whom the sublime endurance of the greatest of saints had found a true home.

Her work was not at all the ordinary work of a hospital of that time, but she considered her particular calling to be a dedication to labor among those afflicted ones who were not welcome elsewhere. This truly divine charity placed her interest among the epileptic, the lepers, those bearing contagious diseases, and most particularly those declared medically incurable. It was this special devotion to the most unfortunate among all human beings that provides the full explanation of her extraordinary goodness. In poverty and even in persecution no one was abandoned. Though adversity might arise on every side, as so often it seemed to do in those uncertain days, her life was moved by a faith stronger than steel and by a fortitude beyond all assailing. Truly her inspiration lay beyond the stars, for her destiny was heaven.

Here in our own Archdiocese of Boston, we have felt for more than half a century the comforting hand of the Grey Nuns—the order that she founded, still continuing in their special and complete fervor the extraordinary work of Mother d'Youville. But here too even the task accepted by these valiant women is not the more ordinary hospital work of the nursing sisters who are themselves in our tradition angels of kindness and mercy. The Grey Nuns, bearing still the indomitable spirit of their foundress, make the special object of their interest and efforts those ill ones who in the opinion of medical science are beyond the power of man to heal. To these incurables, to these lives from which it would be so easy to see all hope vanish, the daughters of Mother d'Youville bring by their ministrations new life, new hope, and even joy. The Holy Ghost Hospital for Incurables is not at all, as one might think, a house of dolor and despair; it is, through the unforgettable inspiration of Mother d'Youville and *les Soeurs Grises,* a very real home of happiness.

Today, in a world so different from that of Mother d'Youville, a world which does not take easily to sacrifice, at an hour when men are beginning to see charity, and especially difficult charity, as less a personal and more a societal obligation, I find especially timely this powerful and moving story of one of the great Catholic women of North America. I feel sure that in that life, love, and devotion the women of our day may find a model for imitation. I do not share the opinion of those who merely admire the glorious accomplishments of those religious and national heroes and heroines whose very names rightly inspire reverence; for I am persuaded that we must be sure that in this hour in which we live we bring a similar greatness, aided by their inspiration, to the pressing problems of our times.

Mother d'Youville has a true claim to greatness because she answered so successfully, under God, a vibrant challenge of her times. She may lay further claim to greatness at every moment that her story and example call new names to sanctity and success. This powerful and moving biography by Sister Mary Pauline makes that call more compelling. May God speed its precious message.

✠ MOST REVEREND RICHARD J. CUSHING, D.D.
ARCHBISHOP OF BOSTON

I

THE WAY

*Make the way known to me wherein I should walk: for
I have lifted up my soul to Thee.*

PSALM 142

CHAPTER ONE

THIS THE LAND

CHRISTOPHE LAJEMMERAIS, looking down at the tiny baby girl cradled in her young mother's arms, must have forgotten that his soldier heart had hoped for a son. "She will be named Marie," he whispered. "Marie, for the Blessed Virgin—and for you."

"And Marguerite," she added softly, "for your mother."

The next day, Sunday, October 16, 1701, the bells of the little parish church of St. Anne joyously announced the baptism of this child. Marie Marguerite, destined by Divine Providence to be the mother of many daughters who, as Grey Nuns, should rise up to call her blessed, entered on this day into the kingdom of God's grace.

At Varennes, Quebec, where she was born, there was more than gorgeous beauty in this autumn of 1701. There was peace, and there was promise. To the inhabitants of the little white village that spread itself comfortably along the south bank of the blue St. Lawrence, about twenty miles below old Ville-Marie, the crown of the year was more splendid than ever. When before had the maples seemed so golden, the graceful elms and mighty oaks so radiant and so red? When before had great white clouds gleamed with gold sunlight in October skies so blue? And there, far across the upper bank, losing themselves in the distant

3

Laurentian foothills, stretched fertile fields, resting and relaxed, promising production for many years to come.

Yet autumn had been beautiful many times before; but there had been no peace. For more than sixty savage years the five great nations of the Iroquois had fought the settlements of the white men and the little Huron villages in the rich Laurentian valley. From that fateful day in 1609, when Champlain's men, venturing up the Richelieu River, had fired upon a party of surprised Iroquois, the vindictive hatred of these Indians had fed itself on the massacre of the French.

Not for long had the red men themselves fought without guns. From the Dutch traders moving up the Hudson they had received firearms for furs, thus beginning an alliance deadly to the French. Then the French in turn had supplied their Huron and Algonquin allies, bitter enemies of the Iroquois, with muskets and powder. The massacres north of the great St. Lawrence had become so frequent and so savage that the smoke of battle and the blood of the habitants had blotted out the beauty of all seasons of the year.

By 1642 the situation had become desperate. In the fall of that very year, Father Isaac Jogues and René Goupil, accompanied by a band of Hurons on their way back from Quebec to Ste. Marie, had fallen into the hands of the Iroquois, to be kept in tortured captivity for nearly a year. René Goupil had been martyred then, but Father Jogues, with the help of the Dutch, had escaped to France, only to return voluntarily to the Iroquois themselves in 1646 for his own martyrdom.

For the four hundred or so French villagers in missions or trading posts strung along the St. Lawrence from Huronia to Quebec, the little colonial garrison of three hundred soldiers was inadequate protection, even with the aid of Indian allies. By this time the Dutch were giving the Iroquois more guns and ammunition than the French could possibly supply. And the fur trade flourished in proportion.

If the additional traffic in firewater, as the Indians too aptly named the white man's brandy, compensated for the lack of firearms by inflaming the ferocity of the savages, the advantage was not only slight but temporary. All too soon the Indians preferred firewater in return for their furs; nor were the French traders too patriotic to discourage their craze for liquor and the lure of greater wealth for themselves. After all, was it not to their interest to satisfy the policy of the powerful Company of Merchants in France, which held the fur monopoly?

Accordingly, richly laden canoes, passing to and from Quebec, had fallen more and more easily into the snares of treacherous Iroquois lying in ambush along the waterways of trade. Great swarms of painted warriors had crossed the St. Lawrence, cutting off Quebec. Swinging west into the land of thousands of Hurons in the summer of 1648, they had savagely attacked their scattered villages, burned their shaggy bark huts, tortured and slaughtered their victims with diabolical cruelty, or dragged them off to a captivity of unspeakable horror.

This was the land and the era consecrated by the blood of the first Jesuit martyrs in Canada: big Father Antoine Daniel, missionary at old Ste. Marie, who, twelve years before, had wrapped his arms in hearty welcome around the newly arrived Father Jogues; heroic Father Jean de Brébeuf and Father Gabriel Lalemant, who were horribly tortured to death when the little Huron villages of St. Ignace and St. Louis were left in ashes. With them had perished the Huron nation.

With the destruction of their Indian allies, the French had found themselves standing alone, their missions wiped out, their fur trade ruined, the Iroquois danger more threatening than ever.

The Company of Merchants had then been dissolved. Because of its consuming interest in the fur trade, it had neglected colonization and the greater problem of defense. Richelieu had organized instead the Company of One Hundred Associates to encourage settlement in Canada as well as to develop economic interests favorable to France. Nevertheless, settlers had come only too slowly. There were plenty of reasons why the comparatively comfortable villagers of the Old France should not venture into the New.

For twelve more terrible years the heart of Canada struggled for life in the compact triangle formed by Montreal, Three Rivers, and Quebec. Now it seemed that the end had come.

It was not the end; it was the turning point.

During these desperate years courageous leaders had repeatedly appealed to the mother country for aid. Among these leaders, one of the most distinguished was Pierre Boucher, Governor of Three Rivers. In 1661 Governor General d'Avaugour had commissioned him to the court of France to expose the tragic state of the Canadian colony. At the request of the King, Louis XIV, he had composed and published an account of the customs and advantages of New France. This work, the first description of Canada, he was wise enough to dedicate to the great Colbert, then minister in the royal government.

There is no doubt that the representations of Pierre Boucher played an important part in drawing to the attention of the Royal Court the imperative needs of the colony. Today, almost three hundred years later, a statue of this eminent leader, called the Father of Canada, adorns the front of the Legislative Palace of Quebec. But the highest distinction of this noble Catholic statesman is that he was the great-grandfather of Marguerite d'Youville, apostle to the poor.

Louis XIV and Colbert, impressed by the economic possibilities of the struggling colony represented by Pierre Boucher, had acted to improve the state of affairs. In 1663 they had dissolved the Company of One Hundred Associates, drawing their loose and scattered powers under royal control. Then the King had appointed a Superior Council of officials to govern New France.

Of these, the most important were the Governor General, responsible for defense and political relations with the Indians; the Intendant, charged with the regulation of trade, industry, and internal or local affairs; and the Bishop, devoted to the religious life of the colony, schools and hospitals, and the spiritual well-being of the Indians.

There was disruptive overlapping of responsibilities among these three higher officials and sometimes serious disagreement in their management of colonial affairs. Particularly were they at odds with regard to the sale of intoxicating liquor to the Indians as a means of fostering the fur trade. This traffic, encouraged by some officials and bitterly denounced by others, continued for many years to be a real blight on the colony. In one grave matter, however, they were all in accord: the Iroquois menace must be removed.

Without delay the Superior Council had issued a call for troops; without delay six hundred seasoned soldiers, veterans of the magnificent Carignan-Salières regiment, under the command of the distinguished Marquis de Tracy, had been dispatched to New France. They brought with them not only the power of arms but also the more exhilarating power of pomp and prestige. Having landed in Quebec, they had paraded in splendor through the narrow streets of the city to present themselves to the Governor General for service to the colony. The bells of the cathedral had rung out joyously over the land, and in all the churches the *Te Deum* had praised God in thankful relief.

Joined to these seasoned troops, trained colonial soldiers and ready volunteers made a formidable array of thirteen hundred men to march against the Iroquois. Nothing like it had ever been seen before. By waterways and through deep forests they advanced into the lands of the five nations between the St. Lawrence and the Hudson. The Indians scattered like autumn leaves in the wind. In the following year, sadly defeated, they crept to Quebec, pleading for peace.

So there was peace for almost twenty years. Many of the soldiers of the Carignan-Salières regiment settled along the St. Lawrence. They brought new blood, new strength. They mingled with the sturdy habitants who had long lived close to the soil. They refreshed the gay social spirit of New France.

One of the officers of the regiment, René Gaultier de Varennes, a nobleman of the Order of St. Louis, for his exceptional services was granted a fine seignorial estate on the south bank of the river, about twenty miles from Montreal, between Boucherville and Verchères. Here, in days of peace and plenty, he built his great white manor house and fostered paternally the village of Varennes. Above all, he thought it a privilege and a grace from God to donate a section of his land for the foundation of the little parish church of St. Anne.

Pride and joy swelled the hearts of his habitants when he brought among them as his bride the beautiful Marie Boucher, daughter of the distinguished Governor of Three Rivers! Many days of joyful festivity followed this union of brave hearts and noble names! Had not Pierre Boucher been lifted up in New France as a model of faith and patriotism when he consecrated to God his own great seigniory at Boucherville?

Proudly, too, these good people rejoiced a year or two later when René Gaultier succeeded to the governorship of Three Rivers!

Many other settlers like René Gaultier de Varennes contributed to the development of the colony, under the wise and efficient government of such leaders as Count Frontenac, the fighting Governor; Talon, the first great Intendant; Bishop Laval, saintly, farsighted, fearless in his denunciation of the liquor traffic. It was a breathing space that these men made possible for New France, a precious time for repairing the ravages of war and for developing the resources of peace.

But it was only a breathing space. As the years of peace dwindled, the times became adverse. The successors of the great Frontenac did not conciliate the Indians. Friction continued until the flame of war was again enkindled. A new generation of Iroquois had grown up in the land of the five nations between the St. Lawrence and the Hudson. In their veins ran the proud, hot blood of their fathers who had bowed to defeat in 1667.

Moreover, the English had in the meantime supplanted the

Dutch in the New World. They had won the support of the Iroquois not only through fur trading but also through the ready sale of liquor. A further bond of alliance, and a much more effective one, was a common hostility to the French; for there had been many bitter years of war between England and France. The English did not hesitate under the circumstances to incite the Indians against the French whenever there was an opportunity to do so.

Once more savage bands of red men began to move toward Canada, to appear with terrifying suddenness on the banks of the St. Lawrence. Once more the peaceful habitants knew uncertainty and dread.

To make matters worse, war between England and France was fully resumed in 1689. The Indians were further strengthened by the English in their common hope of driving the French out of the country altogether. Savage border raids became more frequent and frightful, culminating in a shocking massacre of more than two hundred men, women, and children at Lachine, on the western end of the island of Montreal.

It was not necessary this time for the colonists to appeal to the mother country for aid. Louis XIV was not willing to lose the colony that had become economically valuable. Frontenac, having been recalled to France, was hurried back to Quebec to take over until 1698 the control of military operations and the conciliation of the Indians. Once more seasoned troops were dispatched across the Atlantic to defend the French settlements and to uphold the glory of the Empire.

Ten years of cruel border warfare again turned the little white villages along the St. Lawrence into armed garrisons in constant danger of attack. Soldiers quartered on the farms became part of the life that they were there to defend.

History is proud to record many deeds of heroism during these years. One of the most thrilling was the defense of the seigniory of Verchères, adjoining Varennes, by Madeleine, aged fourteen, the daughter of the house, assisted by two soldiers and her two younger brothers, their parents being absent on business. When a band of hideous, war-whooping Iroquois suddenly attacked the little garrison, the young girl herself took command and with heroic daring and persistent firing completely deceived the Indians as to the strength of the little fort. Such was the caliber of these colonists.

It was not until the Treaty of Ryswick was signed in 1697, ending hostilities temporarily, that any real progress was made in overcoming the Iroquois once and for all. For three years after that agreement the French in Canada were able to concentrate all their forces against the savages.

Finally, in September of 1700, the proud chiefs of the five nations were forced to admit defeat. In the presence of Governor General de Callières, they signed the Great Peace of Montreal, freeing the colony forever from the terror of organized Iroquois attack.

Once more the colonial manors became scenes of gay social festivity. Grateful habitants, young and old, thronged into the parish churches to thank *le bon Dieu* for the blessings of peace. It was good, the farmers thought, to sheathe their swords and to hang up their muskets and powder horns. It was good to gaze across the St. Lawrence at the rich lands lying there, waiting for cultivation.

At Varennes sorrow had struck during the years of war, for René Gaultier had died on June 4, 1689, leaving to his brave and gracious widow, Marie Boucher, the care of their growing children.

The attention of this family of Varennes had been drawn not a few times during the war to the exploits of a fine young Breton gentleman who had come to Canada with the French troops in 1687.

This distinguished young officer, Christophe Dufrost de Lajemmerais, born at Médréac in the diocese of Saint-Malo in Brittany on December 21, 1661, had passed his youth on the beautiful estate of his parents. As a younger son, he had

10

followed ancient custom, entering military life. When a call for troops was issued at the outbreak of hostilities in New France, the young ensign, then aged twenty-six, left his native land to fight the Iroquois under the command of Denonville.

His first assignment was to Niagara, at the head of the lakes, where his courage, ingenuity, and coolness in danger favorably impressed his superior officers as well as his fellow soldiers. In the following year Frontenac himself commended the bravery of young Lajemmerais in his annual report. Many times had he risked being captured and burned alive by the savages.

It is not surprising that this outstanding young officer was soon made a lieutenant, the second highest rank that could be attained by men of the colonial troops. In this capacity he led many attacks against the Indians. While commanding the fort at Cataraqui, where Kingston now stands, he had opposed remarkable alertness and courage to the craftiness of one of the Iroquois chiefs. It was at a critical time, for negotiations between Frontenac and the five nations were then under consideration. His success on this occasion strengthened the cause of the French and weakened the morale of the Indians, much to the Governor General's satisfaction.

After the war Lieutenant Lajemmerais, like many of his associates who did not belong to the seignorial system of New France, elected to remain with the military forces retained as permanent protection for the colony. Moreover, since peace had come at last, he felt that the time was now opportune for marriage.

The young Breton officer had already been looked upon with favor by the members of the Gaultier family. Here was a gentleman, they thought, after the pattern of their own hearts. Here was one—nor were there many in those postwar days—worthy of their lovely daughter, Marie-Renée.

It is true that Christophe Lajemmerais was now forty years old, and Marie-Renée but half that age. It is a tribute to his excellent qualities, to his integrity above all, that this personable young woman, the granddaughter of Pierre Boucher of Boucher-ville, had favored him. It is a greater tribute that her deeply religious family had taken him to their hearts in spite of the difference in their years. At a time when men far outnumbered women of marriageable age, she and her family could easily have chosen otherwise.

On Sunday morning, January 10, 1701, after Holy Mass, Christophe Lajemmerais presented himself at the manor house of Varennes. Here, according to custom, he formalized his betrothal to Marie-Renée Gaultier de Varennes and became acquainted with the terms of the marriage contract proposed by her mother. By these terms her dowry was to be a large section of the paternal estate adjoining the property on which stood the little parish church. This land would be the site of their future home.

The beautiful marriage ceremony was performed in the church of St. Anne on Monday, January 18, 1701. The whole village rejoiced as the brave and handsome Lieutenant Lajemmerais and the graceful Marie-Renée, properly accompanied, proceeded separately to the church to meet before the altar and there to be united in marriage by Father St. Claude.

This was the happiest event in the whole season of festivities that lay between Christmas and the first day of Lent; the happiest, in fact, since peace had begun. In songs and dances, in games and abundant feasts, the proud and delighted people of Varennes expressed the joyful sentiments of their hearts.

But there was work to be done, a home to be furnished, and, before many months, a cradle to be prepared.

It was on Saturday, the fifteenth of October, that the first child of this happy union was brought into the world.

This was the autumn of 1701, beautiful, peaceful, and full of promise.

CHAPTER TWO

AND THESE THE PEOPLE

IT WAS back to a home already built on the strong foundations of piety, righteousness, and honor that Marguerite was brought by her godparents after her baptism. Immediately, in a little ceremony cherished by custom, she was laid in the arms of her great-grandfather, Pierre Boucher of Boucherville, to receive his patriarchal benediction: "My little one, may God bless thee as I bless thee!" In that home the roots of faith grew deep.

Pierre Boucher, the founder of his family in North America, though now in his eightieth year, was still the inspiring guide of his community, and particularly of the seigniory at Varennes. He had devoted all his life to the service of his people in Canada. As a disciple of the Jesuits, as a soldier in the ranks of the militia, as an interpreter of the Indian languages and, finally, as Governor of Three Rivers, he had performed many far-reaching services. In 1659 he had built the first chapel at Cap de la Madeleine, from which hallowed spot a replica of the miraculous statue of the Blessed Virgin was brought to Ottawa for the Marian Congress of 1947.

In consequence of his mission to the court of Louis XIV to expose the wretched state of affairs in New France, he had not only been given an estate on the St. Lawrence, but had also been raised to the rank of the nobility, the first Canadian to be thus honored.

In 1669 Pierre Boucher had left Three Rivers to give all his time to the founding of his seigniory at Boucherville. It was his Christian desire "to have a place in this land consecrated to God, where the people could live in peace, making open profession of belonging to God." There were land grants to be made to his tenants and yearly rents of produce or money to be determined; there was a mill to be built, and a wine press, and ovens for the use of his people. Most of all, there was the parish church to be constructed, and plans to be made for their religious services, as well as for happy social gatherings from time to time. All these things had been done somehow, in spite of Iroquois warfare. Yearly, on St. Martin's Day, his habitants had brought their rents; and yearly, on the first day of May, they were his happy guests, partaking of his bountiful refreshments, sharing with him and with one another their joy and contentment.

Until his death in 1717 at the age of ninety-five, this fine old gentleman took a zealous interest in the political, social, and religious affairs of his people. Not only did he freely dispense both charity and good counsel; he gave splendid example as a strong Catholic leader, the best type of the landowning class. The poor he loved with special tenderness, aiding them often to the limit of his own means, or tactfully helping them to better their condition themselves. He was fond of reminding his family that Jesus Christ could always be found in the person of the poor.

The salvation of his own soul, however, was his deepest concern. In 1668 he composed a rule of life that revealed his strong spirit of faith, his principles of self-discipline, his appreciation of the need of constant effort in doing the will of God. This rule was treasured by the members of his family as a guide to a true Christian life, all the more precious because it was put into practice by him whom they all venerated. As if his piety and patriotism were too ardent to be contained even in a lifetime measuring

14

almost a century, he bequeathed an expression of both in a spiritual testament of enduring edification. For many years the members of every French Canadian family read this testament once a year on their knees as a profession of love for God and country.

Pierre Boucher's wife, Jeanne Crévier, who survived him ten years, died in 1727 at the venerable age of ninety-three. She too was a model of virtue and patriotism, of maternal devotedness as well as of gracious refinement. For the women of her day it was no small matter to maintain domestic peace and order while bringing up large families in the fear and love of God.

Of their fifteen children—a number typical of the best French Canadian families—one, Nicholas, became a priest. Geneviève, one of their daughters, entered the Convent of the Ursulines in Quebec in 1694 and was professed under the name of Mother St. Pierre. After almost three quarters of a century of devoted religious life as subject or as superior, she died in 1766, only five years before her grandniece, Marguerite d'Youville.

The last letter that Pierre Boucher wrote to one of his sons contains in its concluding sentences a simple summary of the qualities of this exemplary father, as well as of his lifelong teachings.

Tell your sister at Varennes that I say good-by to her and to all her children, whom I love and whom I have always loved. To her and to them I give my blessing. I urge them all to live in the fear of God and to love one another as God and rectitude demand.

One of the children to whom Pierre Boucher refers in this letter of affectionate farewell was his namesake, Pierre de Varennes de la Vérendrye. Many years later this grandson gained great renown as the pioneer explorer of western Canada. Acting in the interests of France, he set out from Montreal in 1731 with a large expedition of hardy woodsmen, among them his three sons and a nephew, Christophe Lajemmerais, the youngest brother of Marguerite.

15

As a good Christian, having at heart his own spiritual well-being as well as that of his men, La Vérendrye took with him a young Jesuit chaplain. Here in action was the spirit of Pierre Boucher. Five years later this priest and the explorer's eldest son, Jean-Baptiste, besides nineteen companions, were brutally killed by the Sioux Indians as they set out to get provisions for the journey farther west.

In spite of incredible difficulty and danger, La Vérendrye and his men pushed on, reaching the Red River at the point where it branches into the Assiniboine. Here the intrepid leader turned north to the forks of the Saskatchewan, having directed his sons to continue westward.

The heavy cost of supplies and the expense of constructing forts at strategic points along the way put La Vérendrye into considerable debt. Fur trading now and then failed to yield enough income to meet his obligations. The merchants of Montreal, unwilling to wait for their money, and the authorities in France not inclined to provide funds, La Vérendrye was called before the courts and forced to give up further explorations. It seemed that only failure should be his reward for years of hardship and peril endured for his country. Further representation of facts before the French court, however, brought him final recognition. The King granted him special honors, but it was too late. He died in Montreal on December 6, 1749.

To his son, another Pierre, fell the honor of looking for the first time upon the majestic peaks of the Rocky Mountains.

Another distinguished lineal descendant of Pierre Boucher was Archbishop Alexandre Taché. This great prelate spent nearly half a century in Manitoba, from 1845 to 1894, shaping the destinies of the Canadian West once discovered and explored by his intrepid relative, La Vérendrye. As a missionary he was tireless in apostolic labors among the Indians and the métis, those half French and half Indian inhabitants of the Red River region; as a statesman he controlled the archrebel, Louis Riel, and his followers, thus making possible the passage of the

Manitoba Act; as a writer he produced works of classical excellence and unquestionable logic. The influence of this eminent Archbishop is still felt in Canada.

It was in an atmosphere charged with the virtues that made such men as these that Marguerite spent her childhood, under the direct influence of her exemplary great-grandparents of Boucherville, and of their sons and daughters. Their piety was real, expressed in steady fidelity to the commandments of God and of the Church. They loved God above all things and their neighbor as themselves for love of Him. They were happy in keeping alive their spirit of faith through the beautiful devotions and ceremonies of the Church, through joyous celebrations of religious feasts and holydays, of which there were many. They were devoted to their country and to their king. They thrilled to the splendor of courtly ways and to the imposing dignity of brilliantly uniformed soldiery. To sacrifice themselves for God and country was an ideal dear to their hearts. They loved honor and truth, courage and fortitude, goodness, serenity, and peace. And courtesy was in the air they breathed.

They were not rich, these men and women of piety and patriotism, not rich at all in worldly goods. Their seigniories had been vast enough in the beginning, but grants and inheritances to many sons and daughters had through the years reduced individual holdings to small farms barely productive of a living. Secondary sources of income were limited. There were few industries. Fur trading had its disadvantages, although many of the Boucher men devoted their lives to it. Salaries for military service were never very large nor very dependable.

In such circumstancs thrift, ingenuity, diligence, the wise use of time, the yet wiser use of natural resources were virtues of fundamental value. These people could not be too leisurely, too comfortable, but they could always be very gay indeed. No matter how small their homes might be, they were clean and compact and colorful. Rugs and furnishings were bright; so were the copper kettles that reflected the flames of their fireplaces.

There was always the family spirit, the warm atmosphere of home.

At Varennes the little Marguerite was not long a novelty, for the family cradle was never empty for long. She was only fourteen months old, scarcely able to find her way on her own small feet, when her brother Charles arrived, two days after Christmas in 1702. The little girl was wisely guided by her parents into this new relationship and taught how to love her baby brother with a protective, helpful love. Then came a baby sister, Marie Clemence, born on January 26, 1704. Less than two years later, on September 13, 1705, another little girl, Marie Louise, took her place in the swiftly growing family. The next year, on October 29, came Joseph, a welcome boy, destined, like his brother Charles, to be chosen from this favored family to serve God in the priesthood. Little Christophe, the last of them all, was born on December 6, 1708, some months after great sorrow had shrouded their home.

Early in June of 1705 Lieutenant Lajemmerais was promoted to a captaincy, the highest rank that could be attained by a soldier of the colonial troops. His fidelity to duty, his spirit of self-sacrifice, his prompt willingness to undertake any assignment desired by his commanding officers had kept him in a favorable light at military headquarters. His merit was accordingly rewarded.

What thankful rejoicing there was at Varennes! By this time three of their babies had arrived to share the family income. To provide for them on a lieutenant's modest salary had become somewhat difficult. Real money was needed for a family that did not raise on its own land all the necessities of life. Family prestige and military honor could not provide all these.

To French Canadian hearts, however, both family prestige and military distinction were highly important. Now Captain Lajemmerais could erect the village flagstaff before his own home; he could wear a sword; he could have a special pew in the parish church. How happy he and his family must have been when they attended Holy Mass the next Sunday in their new glory! How very bright the Captain's sword! How like a citadel the family pew! Little Marguerite's dark eyes must have shone with joy as she looked up at her distinguished father and caught her mother's glance of loving pride.

There was greater security in the Lajemmerais home during the next three years. As each new baby arrived, Marguerite's position as the eldest became more responsible. Generous and affectionate by nature, intelligent beyond her age, she learned quickly how to help her young mother in the little details of family life. At first she could rock the baby's cradle gently; she could carry small burdens; she could run errands. Always she remained close to her mother, who loved her dearly and taught her precious little lessons that she could pass on to her younger brothers and sisters. She must have been a sweet comfort as she tried in tiny ways to lighten her mother's increasing burdens. It may have amused her soldier father to see her assume maternal manners with little Charles or baby Marie Louise, imitating her mother's directive tones or her loving caresses.

Yet if her elders smiled, Marguerite took her duties very seriously; so did the little ones whom she helped to guide. To them she was a dear and important person, very close to them, indeed, almost their own size, but so much wiser! It was easier to tell her their little troubles or secrets than to tell their mother, who was often ill and always busy, or their father, who was many times absent on military affairs.

They loved to have her take them to the little church of St. Anne next to their home. She would carry the youngest in her small, strong arms. The others would follow close, hand in hand, stepping carefully down the narrow stairs, walking in their very best manner across the yard and through the little door that Grandfather Gaultier de Varennes had cut in the wall between his property and the church grounds. Once at the door of God's house, they would remember to be very silent; to take holy water lightly from Marguerite's finger tips because they could

19

not reach the bowl themselves; to tiptoe softly up the aisle, looking straight ahead; and then to genuflect reverently on one little knee. After that, close together in a row, they would kneel on both knees, fold their hands for prayer, and tell the little Boy Jesus of their own dearest love.

When all the details of their pious visit had been precisely fulfilled, and the door of St. Anne's had been quietly closed behind them, they could tumble gaily down the stairs and run as fast as their solid little legs could carry them through the garden gate, across the yard, and into the freedom of home.

Marguerite was now almost seven years old. As her mother's little assistant in the home, she seemed much older. Tall for her age, strong, perfectly healthy, singularly thoughtful, she gave an impression of confidence and poise unusual in one so young. While she always kept the sweet docility of childhood, she gradually acquired a serious sense of responsibility. The dignity that she observed so keenly in her elders she herself assumed, not in proud imitation but through a reasonable belief that it was best because it was characteristic of those whom she dearly loved.

The completeness with which Marguerite yielded to the excellent formative influences of her environment may be considered as a natural preparation for her later surrender to the dispositions of Divine Providence. From the dawn of reason she took into her heart and soul all that was good and beautiful and true. She appreciated the importance of being a good example to her little brothers and sisters; therefore, she took the best possible example from those older than herself. Fortunate for her that those examples were of the best!

Fortunate, too, that the courageous endurance of the trials of life was a virtue of prime importance to them all; for now came the first test of the lessons that she had already learned.

On the first day of June in 1708 her beloved father died. This blow, so unexpected, so heartbreaking, so serious in its effects on the lives of his bereaved, strengthened Marguerite as great souls always are strengthened by adversity. This was the first station on her way of the cross. Quietly she kept the younger children apart while the last sad ceremonies were performed. Tenderly she helped her mother to make adjustments to their unbelievable loss, folding away familiar clothing, removing remembrances too poignant.

"Never fear, dear Mother," she would comfort over and over. "I am here to help you."

This was her spirit: to help—always to help.

The adjustment was far greater, however, than her childish efforts could help to effect. The salary of Captain Lajemmerais had been large enough to keep his growing family in comfort, but not sufficient to provide savings for the future. Now suddenly his wife and children were without an income.

This was a tragic time—a time of insecurity, of humiliation, even of destitution. It was a time of depending upon others for the needs of the children, of seeking revenue from every possible source, of drawing upon all the treasures of faith and of character for the endurance of trials never dreamed of before. The greatest sorrow of all was an event that should have brought instinctive joy to the poor mother's heart—the birth of a little son six months after his father's death. Alone in grief that only God could fathom, she received this child into her arms, naming him Christophe in tender memory. Marguerite, only seven years old herself, was his godmother. It was this Christophe who accompanied La Vérendrye into the distant West many years later.

Madame Lajemmerais had come of a large family to which she might now have turned in her great need; but each member of it had his or her own problem of subsistence. All could help the poor; all did so, because sympathy was in their very hearts; but no one could long support another growing family. Some friends and relatives gave as much practical aid as possible, while others tried to interest government authorities in their behalf.

Governor General de Vaudreuil, whose charming wife was a

21

close friend of the Varennes family, personally appealed to the Minister of the Marine.

Captain Lajemmerais died this summer. He has left a wife and six children in destitution. It is a shame to see this family forsaken and unable to subsist unless you have the charity to help them. As you will reassign her husband's company only next year, it will help them very much if you will kindly let them receive his salary until that time. We beg this of you in their behalf, for we are deeply concerned by their most wretched state.

The Intendant Raudot also strongly represented the little family's great need. "Madame Lajemmerais is utterly destitute," he explained, "and is left with six children. We beg you to grant her Berthier's pension, which has been open since his death."

In spite of these and other appeals, it was not until 1714, six years after her husband's death, that Madame Lajemmerais received aid from the government. She was then given a pension of fifty crowns—less than sixty-five dollars—the amount usually granted to an officer's widow.

This long delay in allotting relief was not due to indifference or neglect. Many French Canadian families at this time were depending on government subsidies for their existence. Communication between mother country and colony was slow and uncertain; formalities were many and complex. There was too much organization, and there was not enough money. Financial affairs in France were at low tide as a result of many years of warfare. It is therefore not surprising that the Lajemmerais family waited a long time for aid. Under the circumstances it is surprising that government aid reached them at all.

In the meantime, Marguerite's mother proved the worth of her heritage. Trusting always in God, she made the most of the little that was left to her. She had her land put into cultivation, raising wheat, maize, beans, potatoes, and peas sufficient for subsistence. The mills and other general advantages of the Varennes seigniory were always at her disposal. Berries were plentiful on their land. It was both profitable and healthful for the children themselves to help in the work involved; natural exercise in good, fresh air kept them strong and well. Moreover, each child learned in a practical way his own importance in the well-being of the family through his contribution to the support of all.

Madame Lajemmerais did more: she put into immediate use the skill in fine embroidery and other needlework which she had learned from the Sisters in Quebec, as well as from her own mother. Besides keeping her little sons and daughters neatly dressed, spinning, weaving cloth, making their garments herself, she added a small sum now and then to her revenue by making dainty handwork for her neighbors. They loved fine decorations on their colorful clothing. As she worked on these in the quiet hours of the evening, Marguerite remained near, her eager fingers following her mother's stitches and designs. The day would come when she too would be able to help.

Never during these years of adjustment did the brave mother neglect her most important duty, that of rearing her children in the knowledge and practice of their religion. She taught them their prayers as soon as they were able to speak; she saw to it that they learned by heart the lessons that the parish priest gave them. By her own love and example they became devoted to the Blessed Sacrament dwelling so near their home, drawing from this devotion a deep reverence for the holy priesthood. In time, two of her sons themselves became priests, and her three daughters were one day to be mothers of priests. Strong indeed was the faith of this brave mother.

Friends and relatives were interested not only in the general welfare of the family. In a very special way they were interested in Marguerite. She was now ten years old. Her unusual intelligence, her charming manners, her remarkable attention to the needs of her mother and the young children inspired them to agree that in some way she should be given the advantage of an education with the Ursuline Sisters in Quebec, such an education as her grandmother and her mother and her aunts had received. How could this be done?

It was easily done. Very little influence was needed. A daughter of the family of Pierre Boucher would be welcome in the convent school where his own daughter, Mother St. Pierre, was exemplifying in the cloister the virtues that he had always manifested in the world; where other children and grandchildren of this great man had left enviable records and very pleasing memories.

Marguerite's mother, accustomed as she was to sacrifice, eager as she was to have her dearest first-born receive the beautiful advantages that she herself had been given, yet found it hard to part with the child who had meant so much to her in the difficult years that were past. But there was no question of holding her back from opportunities that now lay before her through the kind generosity of others.

Marguerite herself, knowing only this beloved home, living only for her mother and her dear little brothers and sisters, could be resigned to the necessary separation only when she understood what it would later mean to them. She could teach them all that she learned. She could help them more than ever.

CHAPTER THREE

INTO A WIDER WORLD

TO BE resolutely resigned to separation from home and loved ones was one thing; to be separated from them was quite another when the time actually came. It was exciting, of course, to Marguerite's normal, childlike heart to be the center of a new interest in her little world. It was delightful to have a trunk of her own, to see it filled, a little at a time, with new jackets and dresses of her mother's making, with pretty kerchiefs, knitted stockings, shoes with real embroidery. How kind were the relatives and friends who gave her little presents, and how interesting their stories of the good Sisters at Quebec and of the happy days that they had spent there themselves!

It was no new experience to talk over business matters with her mother; but this business matter was different: all details would be carried out far from her mother's wise guidance. She was used to affectionate admiration from her brothers and sisters, but there was wistful bewilderment in their eyes now as they followed her preparations to go away from home. She could not think about it too much. It was something to be done for the good of all, and she must do it.

But when Marguerite, one fine day in late July of 1712, turned at the gate and looked back at the beloved little group in the doorway, her aching heart knew for the first time the exquisite

25

pain of being set apart by God for some purpose beyond her present comprehension. All the way to Quebec, beautiful and fascinating as the trip was, that little picture remained in her mind: tall Charles, who would now have to be his mother's assistant, ably seconded by Marie Clemence; Marie Louise, not trying in the least to keep back her tears; little Christophe, not quite four, clinging to Joseph's hand but trying to be as brave a soldier as his father had been; most of all, her mother's steady smile.

There was no time for grief, however. There was no need for fear, either, for Marguerite was safely in the care of relatives traveling on business. But to go from Varennes to Quebec, a distance of nearly one hundred and fifty miles, was a test of endurance in 1712, especially for a child not yet eleven years old. The journey had to be made by canoe, following the blue St. Lawrence all the way. One had to take one's place carefully in the little craft and remain almost motionless among the other passengers and all the supplies day after day, sometimes for as many as fifteen at a stretch.

It was a relief to make a long stop at Three Rivers, there to be met and feasted by those who knew Pierre Boucher and René Gaultier, each governor in his own time of that historic town. No child could fail to be impressed by the importance of relationship to these noble patriots. Surely one would resume the difficult journey with a lighter heart!

It was a beautiful experience, too, to be swept along on the calm, majestic waters of the great river, sometimes between high, precipitous cliffs, sometimes along low and level shores, where clusters of white, steep-roofed houses like those of Varennes reminded Marguerite of home, and tall church spires like St. Anne's reminded her of God. It was like being carried in the Everlasting Arms through the dark night, or in the open, sunny day.

Finally the great bluffs and battlements of Quebec signaled the end of the long journey. Quickly the passengers landed on

the shore edge of the Lower Town, where grey wooden tene-
ments, such as Marguerite had never seen before, huddled in
irregular groups. Passing with their baggage through narrow,
winding streets, they ascended graded slopes and uneven stairs
to the yet more straggling highways of the Upper Town. Here
at last, beyond rows of high stone or wooden houses with steep
roofs and inevitable dormer windows, the tired travelers came
to the Convent of the Ursulines.

Set far back from the highway, within an enclosure of tall,
wooden palings, this plain, three-story convent, the first institution of learning for women in North America, was a monument
to the valiant virtues of its foundress and first Superior, Mother
Mary of the Incarnation.

Born in France of middle class parents, married at seventeen,
widowed two years later but left with a baby son who grew up
to become a Benedictine priest, this woman, irresistibly attracted
to a holy life with God, had entered the Ursuline Convent in
Tours in 1631, as soon as her son no longer needed a mother's
care. Her religious life might have continued until her death In
the happiness and secluded peace which she found at Tours had
not Father Le Jeune, Superior of the Jesuit missions in Canada,
appealed to France for teachers to instruct French and Indian
children in Quebec.

Another young widow, Madame Marie Madeleine de la Peltrie, a lady of deep piety but thoroughly of the world, was the
first to respond to the appeal with enthusiasm and money. But
nuns also were needed, and application was made to the Ursulines. Mother Mary of the Incarnation, accompanied by Madame
de la Peltrie, was chosen to lead the small group of nuns who
left their native land in 1639 for the unknown mission fields of
New France.

Quebec welcomed them with a grateful heart, but Madame
de la Peltrie and her Ursuline companions had no time to lose
in celebrations. Immediately they began to solicit funds for the
construction of a convent in which to do their work.

By 1642 the convent was finished. Now in earnest began the education of French girls in the colony and the very difficult task of civilizing and Christianizing the little Indian maidens who were brought to them.

Then, in the dark night of December 30, 1650, the building burned to the ground.

Undaunted by this disaster, Mother Mary of the Incarnation and her Sisters, aided by Madame de la Peltrie, set themselves to the immense task of constructing another convent, of which they took possession on Pentecost in 1652.

This convent henceforth shared vitally in the troubled history of New France. It was always a center of French culture and learning, where wellborn ladies, distinguished military officers, and government officials could in times of peace find co-operation and counsel. In times of war it served also as a refuge, as a hospital, and even as a fort. Here at last, many years later, when New France was no more, the body of Montcalm was buried, in a shell hole under the chapel. Here was, and is, the spirit of French Canada.

It was this convent to which Marguerite Lajemmerais presented herself, and in which, on August 9, 1712, according to the annals of the institution, she was formally registered among its boarders. As she was embraced by her grandaunt, Mother St. Pierre, how glad the child must have been to see someone belonging to her!

Mother Mary of the Incarnation and Madame de la Peltrie had long since received their eternal reward; but their spirit, their teaching, their fine traditions of gentle courtesy, thoroughness, and simple piety continued to live in the school that they had founded with truly valorous zeal. Here was the heritage shared by Marguerite, to which Divine Providence had led her.

The biographer of Marguerite d'Youville cannot overestimate the significance of the training that she was given at the Ursuline Convent in Quebec. From the gentle Sisters there she received the only formal education that she ever had. It must have been their example which later inspired to a very important extent her own ideal of the perfect nun. With no others had she close and personal association. Under their guidance, in an atmosphere still fragrant with the virtuous example of Venerable Mother Mary of the Incarnation, whom, as a valiant woman herself, Marguerite would one day so closely resemble, she "advanced in wisdom, age, and grace." Theirs was a creditable achievement.

In the annals of this convent Marguerite is recorded as one of the most distinguished pupils of her time. She was sincerely pious, gentle, straightforward, and intelligent. Realizing that she could not long enjoy the privilege of being trained in this school, she made the most of the two years granted to her. She fulfilled her duties faithfully and promptly; she prepared her lessons painstakingly, remembering that she was learning not only for herself but also for the younger children who were waiting at home for these treasures of mind and heart.

Far from envying or criticizing gay companions who gave less time and attention to their studies, Marguerite candidly faced the facts of her own life and worked harder than ever. "These girls are more fortunate than I," she would comment. "Their years are not limited here. But I no longer have any father, and my poor mother is anxiously waiting for me to return home."

One of the nuns, Mother Mary of the Angels, having the discerning heart of a true teacher, felt that the remarkably strong and serious qualities of this child would someday be tested by great suffering and used in some special work for God. Wisely she counseled her to read *The Holy Ways of the Cross* by Abbé Boudon.

This was severe and ascetic reading for a child of twelve, but Marguerite's intelligence was not the kind to be satisfied with easy sentimentality. She had already met suffering face to face. She was yet to become intimately acquainted with it. It was a provident attention on the part of her heavenly Father to give her in the pages of her reading the example of His Divine Son.

Someday, when she found herself on the Holy Way, she would remember the spirit in which He had followed it before her. Mother Mary of the Angels was a keen instrument in the hands of the Divine Planner.

Spiritually the most important event of Marguerite's life at the Ursuline Convent was her First Holy Communion. Neither she nor anyone else has left any account of this first intimate union of her soul with Christ. Reflective by nature rather than effusive, she spoke little and thought much. To her, deeds, not words, were of prime importance. A child intelligent and far-seeing enough to grasp the intrinsic value of a single lesson in reading or writing would not be likely to miss the greater spiritual significance of her first reception of the Body and Blood of Christ. To her long preparation for this happy event she undoubtedly gave attention as wholehearted as that which she devoted to daily lessons in the practical arts.

It is much more important that for the rest of her life she faithfully sustained her union with Christ by frequent reception of the Holy Eucharist. Because of the increasing gentleness and fortitude of her personality, those about her might hear unuttered but unmistakable words: "I live, now not I, but Christ liveth in me."

There was another important spiritual influence at the Ursuline Convent which in its effects remained always with Marguerite. This was devotion to the Sacred Heart of Jesus. Even before 1675, the year of the great revelation of the Divine Heart to St. Margaret Mary, Mother Mary of the Incarnation had zealously fostered this devotion among all with whom she had contact. It was in the chapel of the convent at Quebec that the first solemn celebration of the feast of the Sacred Heart was held in North America on June 18, 1700, with all the splendor and magnificence that the love of the Sisters could create. Henceforth the devotion was a vital part of the religious atmosphere there.

To Marguerite, warmhearted and generous, this devotion had

an abiding appeal; it brought her closer to the human Christ Who loved all men so much.

Some years later, when the Confraternity of the Sacred Heart was started in Quebec, she became a devoted, lifelong member. In 1749, the year in which the Confraternity was established in Montreal in perpetuity, at the General Hospital of the Congregation which she had in the meantime founded, she planned a chapel specially dedicated to the Sacred Heart. This chapel she succeeded in building a few years before her death. To crown her dedication, the Sacred Heart was solemnly enthroned in 1945 as Eternal King in the original Motherhouse of the Grey Nuns at Montreal.

Now, more than two centuries after the enkindling of Marguerite's devotion by the Ursulines of Quebec, it is the privilege and special mission of the Grey Nuns of the Sacred Heart, one of the branches of her vast Congregation, to keep alive her love.

But perhaps the most enduring proof of her devotion—surely the most personal—was her having a representation of the Divine Heart set on the silver crucifix which every Grey Nun wears over her own heart. Thus uniting all her spiritual daughters forever in a common love, the great foundress may have prayed, in the words that arose from Christ's own burning Heart, "That they may be one, as we also are!"

Marguerite's two years at the Ursuline Convent were short in extent, but centuries long in effect. All too soon they came to an end, for Madame Lajemmerais could not afford to leave her eldest child in Quebec any longer, even with the help of relatives and friends. There were still five younger children to be educated.

Early in the summer of 1714 Marguerite again traveled the lovely St. Lawrence. How different now were her thoughts and emotions as she left Quebec and began the long journey to Varennes! While her heart swelled with joy at the prospect of being soon again with her family, she was sorry to leave her teachers and companions. They, too, grieved to lose the company of the serene and unselfish child who had won their love and admiration.

To the little family awaiting her arrival with tense eagerness, the sight of their beloved Marguerite was somewhat of a surprise, a surprise which by no means restrained the wild exuberance of their welcome. Though she was not yet thirteen years old, she seemed at least fifteen. Not only had she grown taller and more maturely beautiful; she was even more self-reliant, more capable. Little Christophe, not yet six, was shy of this precious stranger until in a few moments he caught the spirit of his gay and delighted family. It was a glad day for them all.

It was soon evident that Marguerite's convent training had developed her numerous practical skills, besides remarkably co-ordinating the inherent qualities of her character. Clearly understanding the obligation which that training had laid upon her, she lost no time in taking up her duties at home with generous and loving devotedness.

The first of these duties was the alleviation of her mother's many burdens. To her wishes Marguerite gave perfect obedience. Thus she not only fulfilled her own duty to a wise and self-sacrificing parent, but also gave to the younger children an example of respect that fostered harmony and peace. Madame Lajemmerais, still a young woman herself, soon felt that she could place full confidence in this rare and capable daughter.

In the months that followed, Marguerite proved worthy of her mother's trust. She possessed a natural aptitude for household management, for cleanliness and order, for discipline and peace. Physically strong and healthy, she was able to assume many domestic duties, thus relieving her mother of tasks that she long had borne almost alone.

Even now she manifested that special skill in making all means serve her ends which in later years was to prove a valuable asset in her work for the poor. She was ingenious in making a little go a long way. She never wasted anything: neither words nor acts; neither time nor money; neither the foods that comprised their simple meals nor the hand-woven cloth that made up their garments. She had a sure sense of the fitness of things, and simplicity was its essence.

It was eminently fitting, for example, that she should act as a second mother to the younger children, for she had received greater advantages than they, and her mother trusted her completely. They in turn readily accepted her position among them. While she never lost the dignity and reserve natural to her, she won their confidence by sincere and affectionate interest, by entering into their spirit, by being all things to each one. They trusted her judgment for the solution of their little problems; they knew that she would treasure inviolate the secrets of their hearts. When she corrected their faults, as sometimes she had to do, they understood that behind her firmness there was a deep and abiding love which sought only their good. They were always happy in her company, with a happiness that somehow united them more closely. Never, in the years to come, did Marguerite lose her gift of harmonizing diverse personalities without drawing them inordinately to herself.

Little Christophe might have the place closest to his sister when they all clustered around her for a fascinating story about Quebec, but quiet Charles, his dark eyes already reflecting the gleam of the Holy Grail, knew that his own place in her heart was secure and personal. So felt Joseph, and the two little sisters, Clemence and Louise.

But the time had come for something more serious: the education of these children.

Many a time, kneeling in the quiet chapel of the Ursuline Convent, Marguerite had dreamed of her two little sisters in this beautiful place. If only they could enjoy these advantages, she had thought. Often, while she was learning the gentle arts of embroidery and lacemaking, she had pictured her sisters beside her, their little fingers skillfully weaving dainty designs with the pretty silk threads. Sometimes she would imagine how appealing the lessons in religion would sound in Clemence's soft tones.

How they both would profit by the gracious ways of the Ursulines! So ladylike and sweet already, they would improve so beautifully!

One day, while discussing with her mother the possibilities of lessons for the children, Marguerite recalled her dreams.

"Do you think, Mother," she asked, "that we could manage to send Clemence and Louise to Quebec? If the Sisters were pleased with me, as they said, would they not take them too?"

"We might manage with one at a time, Marguerite," answered Madame Lajemmerais reflectively. "It would be a pity, though, to separate them. They have always been together."

"I know, but the Sisters are so kind that they would not be too lonely. Let us try to make arrangements, Mother. God will help us."

Madame Lajemmerais agreed. In due time arrangements were made through the generosity of the Ursulines. In October of that very year Clemence was received at Quebec. In 1718 Louise took her turn. They also were taught the rudiments of learning and the polite accomplishments of young girls of their age. Were they, like many younger children, frequently reminded of the excellence of an elder sister and urged to follow in her footsteps?

In the meantime, that elder sister herself undertook the education of her brothers. In their busy days of struggling for subsistence, it was not always easy to find time for lessons. Marguerite, habituated already to thoroughness and order, made the most of valuable moments free from other duties.

To Charles and Joseph, studious and quiet boys even then drawn to the priesthood, these moments were welcome and absorbing. But Christophe the adventurous, loving the great unexplored, was not so easily attracted to unknown fields of learning. He was going to be a trapper someday, he would dream in the midst of a lesson in numbers; he was going to find out what those lands were like far beyond the mountains; he was going to fight the Iroquois, like his father! Then Marguerite, laying a compelling hand on his wooden sword just as he thought

34

to draw it against a ferocious red man, would recall him unmistakably to the less thrilling present.

Teaching these boys was not the only duty that Marguerite
took upon herself in these days of meager comfort. She began to
put to economic use some of the practical arts that she had cultivated at the Ursuline Convent. She learned that in the large
families of the neighborhood there was much sewing to be done.
She could do it quickly and well. She could embroider beautifully, too, and make lace which was delicate and lovely. No
matter how homely the garments of these French colonial
women, there could always be a place for trimming. Who would
not be honored to have the fine handiwork of Marguerite Lajemmerais on blouses or sashes or full, gathered skirts? There was
plenty to do in order to add a small sum now and then to their
income. After all, her mother's pension of fifty crowns a year
could not go far.

It was on the nineteenth of April in 1717, when Marguerite
was in her sixteenth year, that her great-grandfather, Pierre
Boucher, died at the paternal home in Boucherville. The whole
community grieved at the loss of the venerable old man who
had inspired five generations of his people. At his funeral grateful habitants crowded into the small parish church or knelt in
the open roadway to offer their last homage and their prayers
for his soul. Marguerite, standing beside her mother as his body
was reverently laid beneath the floor of the church, prayed that
she would never forget the teachings and example of this man
of God.

So the full years passed. Clemence returned from Quebec, glad
to relieve her sister in duties that had multiplied during her
absence. It was right and just that the younger girl should now
take her turn in the affairs of the home, for someday she and
Louise would have their own homes to keep. Besides, it was time
that Marguerite should be free to enter more fully into the gay
social life of the village.

These were joyous times for the people of the old regime in

Canada. Each season sparkled with its own type of merry-making. With "the frolic wind that breathes the spring," came maple-tapping days and luscious confections of snow and sugared sap to reward one's labor. There were gay community gatherings at the manor houses on May Day, "the maddest, merriest day" of the year, with feasting from morning till night on meat pies and great bowls of stew, roasted mutton, pork, and veal, tarts and sweet cakes, white whisky and wine. Spirits were high and happy when the fiddler's tunes filled the air and the dancing began, not to end until both musician and merrymakers were exhausted.

In the summer days there were long hours together in the planted fields, with lazy laughter and good-humored gibes to relieve the labor, and leisurely draughts of cold, sour milk to relieve the heat. In the mellow sunset magic of a cool evening came quiet walks on the banks of the beautiful river, or canoe rides, or mirthful conversations and lively folk songs on a neighbor's front step.

It was in the long winter season, however, between the harvest moon and Ash Wednesday, that lighthearted merriment was unconfined. Traditional ceremonies, rollicking folk songs, graceful quadrilles and games enlivened harvest festivals until deep winter set in. Then, on light snowshoes or in swift toboggans and carioles, hilarious surprise parties flocked from house to house for a dance here, a feast there, and everywhere utter abandonment to carefree laughter and fun.

Holidays and religious festivals always meant merry celebrations. Baptisms, birthdays, and weddings were gay occasions. Even Sunday Mass was invariably followed by gatherings on the church steps to exchange bits of good-natured gossip or admiring comments on the newest fashions.

From all these social activities Marguerite Lajemmerais by no means kept aloof. Like every other normal and attractive young woman, "she liked good company and the pleasures of life," wrote Father d'Youville Dufrost, her earliest biographer.

Though she was not worldly, the world had many attractions for her; and she certainly had no intention of giving up these attractions for the spiritual treasures of the cloister. She was too candid, too simple in her attitudes not to enjoy the good things of life as long as they were good.

Serious and reserved by nature, Marguerite was also endowed with a sweetness of personality that made her a delightful companion in a group. She could enter into the joys of others as well as into their sorrows. She sincerely liked everyone, and everyone was intuitively aware of that fact. She possessed the faculty of drawing out the best in those around her. At the same time, she was neither soft nor complacent; she would never sacrifice principle for the sake of conciliation. Though her natural modesty and moderation would keep her from throwing herself too vivaciously into the spirit of merrymaking, her presence in lively company would encourage happiness rather than subdue it. The respect which she unconsciously inspired kept merriment from getting out of bounds.

Personality was not Marguerite's only asset. "She was one of the beautiful persons of her time," wrote Father Dufrost. At eighteen she was above average in height, of perfect form and features. Soft, dark brown hair framed a clear, rosy countenance. Her dark eyes could deepen in sympathy or sorrow, or sparkle like stars. Her soft lips parted often in a lovely smile, but never in loud, ungoverned laughter. Her movements were graceful; her manners, gracious. She was now a woman to love and to be loved.

In the gay group of friends with whom Marguerite could frequently be found was a young gentleman of excellent lineage and comfortable means, whose name her biographers have discreetly withheld. Between Marguerite and this young man congeniality grew into friendship and then quickly into the happy semblances of love.

They had much in common: family prestige and noble traditions; high ideals; culture, refinement, and similarity in tastes.

To these people a good name was indeed better than great riches. It was a perfect match, thought relatives and friends as they watched the beautiful Marguerite and the aristocratic unknown. Two fine families would unite to preserve the proud spirit of Varennes.

To Marguerite the alliance was a happy prospect. She would be the honored mistress of a good, substantial home; for her and the family that God might be pleased to send the future would unfold in comfort, security, and peace. She felt herself to be truly loved; and she, never halfhearted in anything, gave her love in return.

Then the blow fell.

Madame Lajemmerais, now thirty-eight years old, suddenly married a young medical practitioner, Timothy Sullivan, who tactfully changed his name to Silvain in an effort to conform at least to French pronunciation.

A newcomer to Montreal, Timothy Silvain was already the object of widely unfavorable comment. Though he had acquired some knowledge of medicine and was really trying to make himself useful in a town then lacking a physician, he had at the time no professional certificate of any kind. It is true that several years later, in 1724, the King of France granted him an honorary license upon the recommendation of Governor General de Vaudreuil. In the same year he received a decree of naturalization.

At the time of his marriage, however, his aggressive manner and his violent temper had already embroiled him in unpleasant legal proceedings; and the judiciary records of Montreal starkly testify that many times before his death he was brought before the courts on account of his rash and disorderly conduct.

All Varennes was shaken in surprise and shock. To think that Marie-Renée Gaultier, respected widow of Captain Lajemmerais, would entrust her life, her family, and her name to a foreigner of doubtful reputation!

The family of Marguerite's unknown recoiled in pride. Refusing outright to admit Timothy Sullivan, even indirectly, to their ranks, they discouraged any further alliance with the family into which he had been received. Whether or not the young aristocrat attempted to think for himself is not recorded. At any rate, upon the innocent Marguerite a cruel humiliation was laid. Let no one probe into her womanly heart. Outwardly she kept her serene reserve, the shield of the thoroughbred. Too well balanced and kind to allow personal feelings to alter public relations, she continued as much as possible to be both normal and neighborly. It was her secret.

But to future generations what a happy misfortune!

It seems not to have occurred to the critics of Madame Lajemmerais' second marriage that the poor mother probably saw in this alliance an opportunity to provide for the further education of her three sons. After years of struggling against poverty she may have thought it an opportunity of some promise. It would not have been unlike her to sacrifice herself for them, to prefer their future security to her present prestige.

The fact remains that Timothy Sullivan, or Silvain, provided faithfully and generously for his stepchildren. Madame de Vaudreuil claims that he even deprived himself of the necessities of life in order to do so. Charles was sent to the seminary in Quebec, where he was ordained to the priesthood on April 14, 1726. Joseph, having followed him there, was admitted to Holy Orders on October 21, 1731. Christophe was given all the assistance he needed to join the colonial troops and, later, to share the adventures of his distinguished uncle, La Vérendrye.

Even the last will and testament of Timothy Silvain is a revelation of qualities unsuspected by his critics, or at least unacknowledged by them. He left everything he had to his wife and her children and grandchildren; he directed that all his debts be paid; he asked pardon for the wrongs that he had done; and he provided that a thousand Masses be offered for the eternal rest of his soul. He may have been a blunt instrument in the hands of God, or perhaps too sharp a one; but he evidently served the Divine Plan.

Varennes could not see into the future, however. It could not or would not, readily accommodate itself to the changed circumstances of its most distinguished family. For all concerned, the marriage of Madame Lajemmerais demanded adjustments to new interests and to very different problems. Within two years the new family of Timothy Silvain agreed with him, though unhappily, that they should move to Montreal.

For Marguerite the decision was momentous. As she raised her eyes in quiet farewell to St. Anne's cross outlined against the grey-blue sky, did she think of One Who long before had gone from Nazareth to Jerusalem?

CHAPTER FOUR

MONTREAL AND MARRIAGE

LIKE Paris in the Old France, Montreal in the New was built on an island in the midst of a great river. Situated at the confluence of the St. Lawrence and the Ottawa, more than six hundred miles inland from the sea, the island of Montreal, about thirty miles long and ten miles wide, was destined inevitably to enthrone the queen city of Canadian commerce. For business advantages no city could have had a more favorable location.

But no other city in the New World ever had a more religious foundation. Conceived in the zealous heart of saintly Father Olier, founder of the Society of St. Sulpice in Paris, as a center of mission work for the Indians of Canada, it became the objective of the Society of Notre Dame de Montreal, which he also established. This Society, acting through Paul de Chomedey de Maisonneuve, purchased the island of Montreal on August 7, 1640, from Richelieu's Company of One Hundred Associates.

In the same year a delicate young woman, Jeanne Mance, daughter of the King's attorney, learned for the first time of the great and beautiful country called Canada, and of the religious women, Madame de la Peltrie and the Ursulines, who had just gone there for the faith. Immediately she also dedicated herself to the glory of God and the establishment of religion in New

France, in a kind of lay apostolate devoted principally to the care of the sick.

Not long afterward, Jeanne Mance and her two companions met the valorous Maisonneuve and his forty in Quebec, where they spent the winter of 1641 in final preparations for the settlement at Montreal.

Madame de la Peltrie, to the distress of the Ursulines, now overgenerously insisted on accompanying Jeanne Mance in order to devote herself in greater danger to a more difficult apostolate. Suffice it to say that before many months had passed she saw her mistake and returned to Quebec, there to continue until her death the mission for which she was adapted. Mother Mary of the Incarnation was more than relieved.

To all attempts to dissuade Maisonneuve and his brave companions from venturing into dangerous Indian territory—the Iroquois had already established the village of Hochelaga on the island—the intrepid leader had only this to say: "It is my duty and my honor to found a colony at Montreal; and I would go if every tree were an Iroquois."

Danger seemed to dissolve before such determination. In a small sailing vessel, two rowboats, and a barge, the pioneers left Quebec on May 8, 1642.

Ten days later, in the brilliant sunshine of a cool spring morning, they glided into shore. There before them, desirable beyond their dreams, the level land stretched far back to the foot of the majestic mountain that Cartier, more than a hundred years before, had named Mount Royal.

Maisonneuve, as governor of the new foundation, was the first to land. Then came Jeanne Mance, the invincible strength of her spirit shining through her physical frailness. In a few moments all were on shore. Falling to their knees, they gave thanks to God. They dedicated this beautiful place to the Blessed Virgin Mary, naming it Ville-Marie in her honor, in accordance with the suggestion previously made by Father Olier himself. This was the name it bore until 1705, when both the city and the island became officially known as Montreal.

At once the men hurried to erect an altar, which Jeanne Mance and the other women lovingly decorated with bright wildflowers. Nature and grace seemed to unite to create a setting of extraordinary beauty as Father Vimont, the Jesuit chaplain, consecrated this foundation with the Holy Sacrifice of the Mass. Then, turning to the reverent worshipers kneeling there in silent, heroic trust—noble men and women, soldiers, artisans, farmers —he said to them: "You are a grain of mustard seed that shall rise and grow until its branches overshadow the earth. You are few, but your work is the work of God. His smile is on you, and your children shall fill the land."

The little foundation of Ville-Marie flourished in spite of suffering, hardship, terrifying Indian attacks. During the twenty-two years of Maisonneuve's governorship many little wooden homes were constructed; the wooden stockade that first surrounded their settlement was replaced by stone walls; a small chapel was built over the first altar; the Iroquois were repeatedly and successfully repelled.

Above all, Jeanne Mance founded Hôtel-Dieu for the care of the sick; Marguerite Bourgeoys, another French gentlewoman of heroic virtue, established the Sisters of the Congregation in 1658 for the education of young girls; Father Olier, never able to satisfy his own immense longing to labor in Canada, sent four Sulpicians in 1657. Since that date the Fathers of St. Sulpice have devotedly ministered to the spiritual needs of the city. To their guidance Marguerite Lajemmerais later entrusted the affairs of her soul; and to all Grey Nuns in Montreal since her time the Sulpicians have given faithful and consistent spiritual direction.

By 1678 Father Vimont's "mustard seed" had taken deep root, and its branches had begun to overshadow the city. On October 28 of that year saintly Bishop Laval canonically established the parish of Notre Dame in the center of the city, entrusting it to the Sulpician Fathers, whose seminary adjoined the church grounds on Notre Dame Street. It was in this venerable church, many years later, that Marguerite Lajemmerais found sanctuary in her sorrow and the source of all her joy.

With the "White Peace of 1700," bringing to an end the wars with the Iroquois, Montreal entered an era of rapid prosperity. The ravages of the great fire of 1695, which had destroyed Hôtel-Dieu and the mortal remains of the beloved Jeanne Mance, had been repaired. For a generation or more the city spread out along the two main streets, Notre Dame and St. Paul, and in between, on streets whose names read like a litany of the saints—St. Joseph, St. Peter, St. Francis Xavier, St. Nicholas, St. John.

But if gold must be tried by fire, so must cities. Once again, in June of 1721, purifying flames raged unchecked in the strong winds that swept the little town at the foot of Mount Royal. More than one hundred and sixty of the small wooden homes in the western end were burned to the ground.

Montreal was slowly raising itself from the ashes of this fire when Marguerite and her family arrived. The work of reconstruction had begun; strong dwellings of Montreal granite, white and grey, were replacing the frail wooden houses of the past.

Timothy Silvain's home on St. James Street, at the northern edge of the town, had escaped the recent conflagration, but it was now too small to accommodate his new family. Madame Gaultier de Varennes solved the problem of residence by giving them a large and comfortable house that she owned on St. Vincent Street, in the most fashionable and important section of the town.

From the high front windows of their new home they could admire the beautiful gardens of the Governor General's mansion, which faced St. Paul Street. Beyond, on Notre Dame Street, on a slight elevation, stood the noble château of Claude de Ramezay, the eleventh governor of Montreal, and one of the most upright gentlemen of the time. In his substantial mansion frequently assembled the most illustrious leaders of the period, as well as the most afflicted poor, and even the Indians so often and so cruelly betrayed by the masters of the liquor traffic. Rich and poor found genial welcome here.

Now in our day this venerable home is a treasury of priceless relics, collections of historical works, and portraits of important individuals, including the only known picture of François d'Youville, who married Marguerite Lajemmerais.

Here, in 1721, was the bright center of the social and political life of Montreal. Within the circle of its immediate influence stood the old Varennes home on St. Vincent Street. There was no need for wealth as an introduction to this circle; in that day and age a noble name was of far greater value than money.

As a matter of fact, the newcomers were neither unknown nor unwelcome in this environment. Governor General de Vaudreuil cordially received them when he returned to Montreal from his official residence in Quebec. His wife, whose friendship with Marguerite's mother dated from their school days together at the Ursuline Convent, was pleased to welcome them as her neighbors. Governor de Ramezay, who had become acquainted with the late Captain Lajemmerais during the Iroquois wars, when both men had served under Denonville, manifested toward them an interest in which sympathy played a characteristic part.

Moreover, many relatives had already settled in Montreal. Pierre Boucher is said to have claimed as many as one hundred and fifty living descendants in his own day! Some of these—uncles, aunts, cousins of the Lajemmerais family—were now respected and important persons in this city of about three thousand souls. The advent of the family from Varennes was the signal for a merry round of house-to-house parties. These people were never found wanting in the glad obligations of hospitality.

Marguerite, while continuing her many duties as second mother in the home, nevertheless entered normally and graciously into the program of social festivities planned by relatives and friends. She was interested in the pleasures of city life. The gentle spirit of moderation which at Varennes had kept her from an excessive display of worldliness now also nicely balanced her natural desire to appear well and to be highly regarded and admired.

To this beautiful young woman, honored both for her name and for the integrity of her character, the distinguished families of Montreal soon opened their doors. She added grace to their social gatherings. Ambitious parents, considering her qualities, cultivated aspirations for their marriageable sons. The future looked bright indeed.

The first summer that the Lajemmerais family spent in Montreal, besides being an introduction to social affairs, was a revelation of extraordinary commercial activity. From May to September the city rocked with the clamor of trade. Crafty Indians, in great fleets of canoes, each loaded with eight or nine hundred pounds of furs, came down the St. Lawrence to sell or barter their wares to the merchants of Montreal. White traders from inland posts—tough, hardy woodsmen—pushed their long, flat-bottomed *bateaux,* heavy with pelts, among the Indian vessels moored to the shore.

In the open market places or in the streets closest to the river's edge, they all pitched their brightly decorated tents and laid out great piles of rich supplies, shouting at one another in noisy, goodnatured competition. For many gala weeks the trading went on, in the midst of solemn Indian councils, ceremonious smoking of the peace pipe, and continued drinking of fire water. Heavy sales meant wild revelry. Only too often the Indians and their money were soon parted, for other merchants with brandy for sale furnished an ugly side to the triangle of trade in the city of Montreal.

When the summer orgy of trading, spending, and drinking was at an end, Indian and white trappers took solemn account of gains and losses, shrugged more or less lightheartedly at both, and started back for their forest homes, laden with supplies for another year. The city settled back into accustomed ways of life.

To the discredit of Governor General de Vaudreuil, it must be said that he countenanced the unscrupulous exploitation of the Indians' passion for liquor in connection with the fur trade. Moreover, deaf to Governor de Ramezay's spirited protests, he defended and fostered it as a matter of economic policy and even as a source of personal income.

For years, from the time of his appointment as governor general in the year 1703, he had maintained his own private system of getting furs from the Indians without using money at all; he gave wine and brandy instead. But, he argued, if he did not use this medium of exchange for the beaver skins which meant prosperity, the British settlers in New England would do so. Though by his method he succeeded in keeping the precious pelts out of the hands of the New Englanders, he eventually kept them also out of the hands of the merchants of Montreal, who had their own economy to uphold. The situation was well on the way from bad to worse.

In the summer of 1722 Governor General de Vaudreuil was no more disturbed than ever by the city merchants' complaints that the market had not brought enough profit. If the valuable beaver skins went to France instead of to England, ought not the merchants to be satisfied? After all, had he not recently been awarded the Grand Cross of St. Louis for his vastly progressive services to Canada?

That summer his mansion was as usual the setting for a brilliant series of stately receptions, elaborate dances, and sumptuous dinners. Charming Madame de Vaudreuil played hostess in truly Parisian style; she had once known the splendor of the Court of Versailles.

Marguerite Lajemmerais, often a guest at these social affairs, not only aroused interest with her beauty and her gracious manners, but also caused considerable speculation as to her future. Certainly it was time that she should contract a good marriage, thought the gay socialites of her circle, time that she should think of taking her place among the exemplary matrons of old French Canada.

In those days it was not uncommon for interested elders to make marriage arrangements, to which the young people involved would customarily agree with good grace. Therefore, it may have been Governor General de Vaudreuil himself who first suggested that François d'Youville, his own confidential agent, handsome, rich enough, and eligible, would be a suitable match for lovely Marguerite. It may have been her mother. The young gentleman himself may have taken the initiative. Neither of the parties concerned the most has left a record on this point. At any rate, Marguerite gave her consent, "more through reason than through inclination," wrote her son, Father d'Youville Dufrost. She realized that it was her duty to marry. Besides, François d'Youville had much in his favor: wealth, good looks, and a certain amount of inherited prestige.

His father, Pierre You, a native of La Rochelle, France, had been a brave and highly trusted companion of La Salle in hardship and adventure, in dangerous missions against the Iroquois, and, above all, in explorations of national importance. His greatest distinction was that he had been a co-signer of the document by which La Salle, on May 13, 1682, formally claimed Louisiana for France. For his share in this deed Pierre You was raised to the glamorous rank of a Discoverer, created an officer, and authorized to add "de la Découverte" to his name. This title was inherited by his eldest son, Philippe, but François, as a younger son, was distinguished only by the simple surname, d'Youville.

In 1693, while on a mission to the post which is now called Chicago, Pierre You married Elizabeth, an attractive Indian of the Miami tribe, who presented him with a daughter, Anne Marie, in the following year. Whatever happened to Elizabeth is not recorded, but You shortly afterward returned to Montreal with Anne Marie. He must have been conventionally free in 1697, for on April 19 of that year he married Madeleine Just, a wealthy widow.

Thereafter, with her assistance, he became a man of consider-

able property. Besides several city lots, he acquired valuable
land at the upper end of the island of Montreal where, from
1704 onward, he maintained a profitable, if illicit, fur-and-liquor
trade. The distance of this post from the city enabled him to
evade certain ordinances which might otherwise have restricted
his gains. His wife and their children made their home permanently in Montreal, in a large house facing the Market Place,
between St. Louis and St. Paul streets.

Pierre You de la Découverte was unfortunately the type of
man who could be of discreet service to higher officials inclined
to act outside the law. He became confidential agent to Governor
General de Vaudreuil in the latter's private trade on the island
of Tourtes, west of Montreal, where the Sulpician Fathers were
doing their best to support a mission for the poor Nipissing
Indians. According to the standards set and approved by the
Governor General, Pierre You was an extraordinarily successful
agent.

At his death in 1718, his younger son, François d'Youville,
who had been assisting him, stepped gracefully into his place
not only on the island of Tourtes but also in the confidence of
the Marquis de Vaudreuil. Indeed, this high official was personally interested in the young man. He had keenly observed his
progress throughout his early childhood and during his school
days at the Sulpician Seminary at Quebec. Especially did he
recognize the young man's business qualities.

To those who saw only the surface of things, the engagement
of the Governor General's protégé to Marguerite Lajemmerais
was an alliance of fairytale proportions: a handsome prince and
a beautiful princess destined, so it would seem, to live happily
ever after.

Midsummer business matters demanded a short engagement,
for François d'Youville had obligations on the island of Tourtes.
For reasons deemed sufficient, the customary banns of marriage
were set aside, and plans were made at once for a brilliant
wedding.

In those days of detailed and elaborate formalities, the settlement and signing of the marriage contract was an affair of social magnitude.

Early in the afternoon of August 11 relatives and friends began to assemble in the Varennes mansion on St. Vincent Street. Marguerite's grandmother, Madame Gaultier de Varennes, received the happy group with all the exquisite courtesy of the old regime. Assisting her was the serene Marguerite, whose own mother and Timothy Silvain, the new master of the house, stood beside her. Clemence and Louise were there, attractive young women themselves now, thrilled with the good fortune of their sister, and not a little conscious of their own importance on this shining occasion.

Soon and solemnly there arrived important guests, Madame You de la Découverte, a rather sharp-faced old lady, leaning with rare dependence on the arm of her son, Francois d'Youville.

He was a picture of proud elegance in his azure velvet dress coat and breeches, light blue taffeta vest enriched with silver lace, heavily embroidered silk stockings, and silver-buckled shoes. Jewels sparkled on his fingers as he made sure of the soft black velvet ribbon on his powdered wig. Bending low over the hand of his betrothed, lovely in her simplicity, he caught whispers of praise and approval in the gay conversation around him.

Then, in all his official splendor, came Governor General and Madame de Vaudreuil, Governor and Madame de Ramezay, the King's lieutenant and his lady, Governor de Longueuil of Three Rivers and his wife. Military officers in magnificent uniforms of black and white velvet, with buttons of gold, moved in stately contrast among ladies and gentlemen in gorgeous gala dress.

At last Christophe Laurent, their legal adviser, having won a sufficient degree of silent attention, solemnly read aloud the long contract which had previously been arranged by the parties concerned.

By this contract Timothy Silvain and his wife promised to give Marguerite, by her own will and consent, to François d'Youville for his true and legitimate wife, and to have their marriage solemnized and celebrated according to the regulations of the Holy Roman Catholic Church.

Madame You de la Découverte agreed to furnish to her son, within a year of his marriage, the sum of four thousand pounds, besides three thousand pounds for the common use of husband and wife.

On Marguerite personally a dowry of six thousand pounds was settled, besides her share in joint property amounting to a full thousand pounds in jewels and household goods. Best of all, she was given a completely furnished bedstead valued at two hundred pounds, a gift that could be the joy of any bride's heart.

These were magnificent terms. While expressions of surprise mounted from murmurs to excited congratulations, all witnesses signed their names to the formal document.

The Governor was the first to sign: "De Ramezay" was all he wrote. But the young groom-to-be, with an elaborate flourish, stretched "Francois Youville de la Découverte" across the page, assuming for the occasion his elder brother's prerogative. On the line below, Marguerite's signature was firm and complete, each letter clearly formed. It gives an impression of integrity, simplicity, strength of purpose; it seems to signify her interior realization of the full meaning of her acceptance and her intention to abide thereby "till death."

The next morning, in the presence of relatives and friends, the promise of the contract was sealed by a nuptial Mass in the Church of Notre Dame. Father Priat, Vicar General of the Bishop of Quebec, received the marriage vows. As he invoked the benediction of God upon the young couple kneeling before him, Marguerite's soul must have absorbed the sustaining grace of the blessing: "May she marry in Christ . . . may she pass her days true to the troth she has plighted . . . may she be respected for her seriousness and venerated for her modesty;

51

may she be well versed in heavenly teachings and in all things may she be approved and innocent."

After the wedding reception François d'Youville brought his wife to his mother's home on the Market Place, between St. Louis and St. Paul streets. Located in the commercial heart of Montreal, this house was a total contrast to the fashionable mansion on St. Vincent Street, in the social center of the city. A plain, two-story building of grey stone, it combined accommodations for two small shops on the ground floor with living quarters on the second, which Madame You was now called upon to share with Marguerite.

Four narrow windows on the second floor framed strange and varying sights in the Market Place. There were rough, open counters where habitants exposed their wares twice a week; there were the King's stores commanding patriotic preference; there were jostling crowds of citizens, merchants, soldiers, painted Indians, and plain, shaggy woodsmen; there were instruments of public penance for offenders against the law—the pillory, the iron collar, the torture wheel, and even the dreaded gallows.

There were many noises in the busy street—heavy tramping of soldiery, persuasive shouts of trade, the ruffle of drums announcing a proclamation by the heralds of the King.

Life on the Market Place promised to be very different from all that Marguerite had experienced in the dear and quiet past. Had she not pledged herself, however, "for better or for worse"?

Yet upon this very house which she was now entering, Divine Providence had once bestowed a saving grace. In the terrible fire of 1721, while great sparks from blazing buildings nearby were falling upon the roof of Madame You's dwelling, that lady had promised many Masses for the souls in Purgatory if her home were saved. It was saved. The wind changed, and the fire stopped in its course.

CHAPTER FIVE

THE BITTER YEARS

THE LARGE, high-ceilinged bedroom facing the Market Place was very beautiful in the eyes of the young bride who entered it so proudly on August 12, 1722. The brightness of the late afternoon sun gave a special glory to the great four-poster feather bed that dominated the softly carpeted room. With its canopy and cover of ruffled, beribboned light green serge, it merited honorable mention among the items of Marguerite's bridal dowry. Six wooden chairs, upholstered in silk and wool brocade, stood gracefully here and there. Beside a pretty folding table with its array of water bottles and glasses waited a large, comfortable armchair, stuffed with straw and wool and covered with a rich blue material. Five pieces of beautiful tapestry hung on the walls and—to the delight of a truly feminine heart—a little mirror in a gold frame.

Having been second mother in her own family for so many years, Marguerite confidently expected to be at least second mistress in this home on the Market Place to which her husband had brought her. She had had rich experience in homemaking; she was skilled in the management of household affairs; her own mother had trusted her completely. Now, like every other good young wife, she looked forward to the happiness of using

53

her womanly aptitudes in a free, creative spirit. She had much to give to this house that was to be her home.

Not many days had passed, however, before she realized that she had been sadly mistaken in her expectations. Madame You, though now more than sixty years of age, had no intention whatsoever of surrendering the least part of her authority in this house; nor, to make matters worse, did François d'Youville require her to do so. Perhaps he understood, if he cared at all, that her apparent jealousy of a much younger woman could not at this late date be overcome by him. There seemed to be no question at all of adapting this establishment to the presence of his wife, much less to her personality and powers. She was simply there; and it was evidently her duty to adapt herself to whatever she found.

As a matter of fact, Marguerite found nothing at all even remotely related to her past experience. Her mother-in-law was no more like her own mother than a stone is like bread. The simple openhearted interest in domestic affairs, which in her own home had been lovingly accepted and encouraged, now met with sharp rebuffs. Instead of the mutual confidence and shared responsibility that she had always known, she now encountered faultfinding and petty domineering.

Both these ugly aspects of human relationship were new to her. There had of course been frequent reproofs in the large family at Varennes; there had been just authority, duly respected by younger members. Carping criticism, however, and arrogant disregard for the rights of others had been unknown. She had never before had to submit to cutting, even coarse remarks. She knew no answer but silence to such attacks— silence that only aggravated them.

Marguerite's personal charm and her innate refinement had no appeal for Madame You. The lovely qualities of her character that had endeared her to other people made no impression here; for her mother-in-law neither knew nor cared to know the language of high ideals and noble birth. To this woman, who had actually sued her own son-in-law for the meager support of his dead wife's little child, only money could speak. Marguerite knew the value of money; she knew the meaning of poverty. Now, in this home where there was wealth enough but nothing else, she learned the mean and shabby restrictions of niggardliness.

She was obliged to give up all the little social pleasures to which she had lately been introduced by relatives and friends. Visits to her own mother had to be curtailed. She could not invite anyone to the house in the Market Place. Madame You forbade customary refreshments to those who came, refusing even the simplest signs of courtesy and good will. What a bitter contrast to the happy hospitality of the home on St. Vincent Street, where, only a few weeks before, gay, laughing friends had gathered!

In a short time Marguerite found herself confined entirely to the depressing company of her mother-in-law. Day after day the minimum of peace and harmony demanded a constant sacrifice of her own tastes and inclinations and the continual satisfaction of her querulous companion's wishes. There was no sympathy, no affection on the part of the older woman to alleviate the loneliness and pain of the younger. Selfishness and greed had ruled so long in Madame You's heart that consideration and understanding now had no place.

The suffering brought upon the young wife by her mother-in-law was nothing in comparison with that inflicted by her husband. Within a few days of his marriage to her he showed his true character—crude, selfish, indifferent. He made no effort whatever to support his bride in the difficult circumstances of life with his mother. To the hurt surprise on her face at his mother's first cutting words, he returned only a careless smile. He did not help her to arrange their large front bedroom, principally for his comfort. Gone was the courtly young gentleman of their marriage contract day! Gone was the reverent bridegroom who had promised to cherish the bride! Through the easy ways of convention he had acquired a wife who would please him and keep his fine clothes in order. That was all she meant to him.

Marguerite, however, understood her marriage vows. Her sense of duty, always one of her strongest traits, kept her faithful to the grave obligations that she had knowingly assumed. Though she was disappointed and hurt, though she wept bitter tears many, many times, she never wavered in her duty to her husband, nor in her affectionate efforts to please him.

Moreover, she never addressed the slightest reproach to him, however much he deserved it. When, only a couple of weeks after their marriage, his restlessness became acute and he suddenly went off to his property at the western end of the island of Montreal on business which he did not explain to her, she made no protest. No matter how long he remained away, this time and the many times of the future, she found no fault. Nor did she ever mar the brief pleasure of his unexpected return by complaints of her suffering through his absence or because of his mother's unkindness. Whatever the anguish in her loving heart, she kept it there and continued to perform her duty with a brave and generous spirit. There is no record that he ever appreciated the fineness of her return to his indifference.

Nevertheless, it must have been for Marguerite the climax of personal pain and wounded pride that her husband remained away from home when their first child, François Timothée, was born on May 21, 1723. Dangerously frail and delicate, the baby was baptized that very day, with old Madame You and Timothy Silvain as godparents. But the poor mother went down alone into the dark valley; alone she experienced the joy of looking upon her son. One would think that in the heart of even the most indifferent father the birth of a first child would inspire interest and consideration. Yet on this occasion François d'Youville gave his wife no sign of appreciation or regard, no tender word of love; and his baby boy no welcome.

It was business all too dishonorable that kept him on the

island of Tourtes when his little son was born. This was now late May, the beginning of the fur-trading season, and it was his business to keep the Indians from reaching Montreal with their rich beaver skins.

Since the death of Pierre You de la Découverte in 1718, François had been even more successful than his father in serving Governor General de Vaudreuil's private interests in the fur trade. At the time of his marriage his reputation was already under a dark shadow. Confident of the Governor General's protection, arrogantly scornful of public opinion, and overelated, perhaps, because of his distinguished marriage, he threw aside whatever precautions he had hitherto been pleased to observe and gave himself over to the worst features of his highly dishonorable business. Historical records tell a very sad tale.

As early as June 17, 1705, the French Minister in Versailles had complained to Governor General de Vaudreuil of the "notorious Découverte," who at that time was selling brandy to the Indians at outrageous rates and illegally getting furs from them. Despite De Vaudreuil's clever defense of his agent's tricks, the Minister suggested that a more trustworthy servant should be employed. No attention was paid to the suggestion. On the contrary, the Governor General increased his patronage, extending it later to his agent's son, with sad and disgraceful results.

On the tenth of July, 1723, a few weeks after the birth of baby François, a delegation of resident Nipissing Indians from the island of Tourtes went to Montreal. Presenting themselves before the Governor General, they read to him a solemn and most emphatic appeal:

O Father, we come to tell you that we cannot pray to God because Youville, who has set up trade on the island of Tourtes, gets us drunk every day, and makes us drink up the value of all our furs, so that we are miserable and naked, without even shirts or clothes of any kind to cover us, or firearms to hunt with. Every morning he comes into our cabins with wine and brandy, saying, with reference to the Marquis de Vaudreuil, "You have a good father; he wants you to drink his milk," and he always gets us drunk to the full value of the pelts, so that the good missionary, who makes us pray to God, always finding us thus senseless, told us that he would not teach us any more. So we make this strong appeal to you, O Father, to tell you that we want to pray to God, and that if you do not send Youville away from the island of Tourtes, we do not want to go there any more.

A few days after this pathetic appeal, which spread like fire among the people of Montreal, Father Gondalie, the Vicar General, formally called on De Vaudreuil to complain of François d'Youville's infamous treatment of the Indians. This important prelate was accompanied by Father Priat, the pastor of Notre Dame, who had married this D'Youville and Marguerite Lajemmerais less than a year before.

And yet nothing was done. Secure in the protection of his employer and patron, D'Youville continued his demoralizing violation of the law, both civil and divine; and the Governor General went so far as to claim in a letter to the Secretary of State on September 29 that the King had in the year 1716 granted him the right to trade on his island! "There are only two in this country who have this right," he boasted, "all other grants including only the right to hunt and to fish." How smoothly De Vaudreuil could take things for granted where his own advantage was concerned!

The moral welfare of the Indians was not the only issue involved; the commercial prosperity of Montreal was also at stake. The upright Governor de Ramezay, convinced that his immediate superior officer would not relieve the situation, respectfully submitted stark facts to the Secretary of State in Versailles, in a letter of October 15, 1723:

About three months ago I had the honor to represent to him [the Marquis de Vaudreuil], with all the respect and submission possible, that all the townsmen and merchants of this country were complaining of him because of the infamous trade that the said Youville is carrying on at the island of Tourtes, by keeping there not only the resident Indians but also the Ottawas and those who are coming for trade to

58

Montreal, so that the merchants and citizens being deprived of trade, honest people are defrauded.

I have the honor to tell you, Sir, that before the Marquis de Vaudreuil set up his post on the island of Tourtes, one hundred Indian canoes, or eighty at the very least, would come here every year. There would be a kind of open market; the merchants would sell their commodities; the habitants, their wares, so that everybody would profit. This year, not four canoes came down to Montreal, the said Youville having kept them all at the upper part of the island, using for this purpose a sergeant and six soldiers, who are kept busy examining all canoes and forcing them to go to the island of Tourtes, where they trade them only wine and brandy, as they have been doing for years, and for which trade merchants have complained to the Merchant of the Marine—to no avail, since no one has appealed to the Court.

This letter reveals the unhappy fact that even in France the name of François d'Youville was in disgrace. How bitterly the people of Montreal despised it his poor wife had to learn. Imagine her humiliation when, stepping out into the Market Place that summer with little François in her arms, she had to face sneers and reproaches from the merchants and citizens whom her husband had basely defrauded. Now she understood his business on the island, his long absences from home. Now she knew why he was not even interested in his little son.

Yet it was not for the effect upon her own happiness and good name that Marguerite grievously deplored her husband's iniquitous conduct. To her most Christian heart, the state of his soul was her gravest concern. True love desires the goodness of the beloved. Realizing already the utter futility of words, the faithful wife tried by prayer, patient example, and every good work to turn her husband from his dishonorable ways into the peaceful paths of upright living. To no avail.

It was not financially necessary for François d'Youville to continue on his base course, even if it had not been completely wrong for him to do so. His own patrimony was sufficient for a comfortable living for himself and his family, had he known how to use it. His avarice, however, if not inherited, at least inspired and developed by parental example, blinded him to the morally evil nature of his ways and even to the goodness of his wife. In any case, she was powerless against the influence of his mother, who stood like a rampart before her example.

Already in the depths of sorrow and shame because of the crushing revelations of her husband's conduct, Marguerite now had to bear another grief, greater than any she had ever known —the death of her baby son on August 17, 1723. Not even the shield of her maternal love and care, not even her desperate pleadings to the Eternal Father could keep the dark shadow from snuffing out his life. With infinite sadness the young mother surrendered the tiny babe—the only joy of her married life. The little crib, so recently added to the big front bedroom, was filled with baby garments and put away.

The wheels of government, particularly slow in early eighteenth-century France, had not yet turned on Canadian affairs involving François d'Youville when Governor de Ramezay died in 1724. While the city mourned, De Vaudreuil and his agents increased their gains.

Into the midst of the unspeakable anguish that now filled Marguerite's heart came another little François, born on September 21, 1724. Again the father was absent! The baby was baptized the next day by Father Dulescoat, the godparents being his uncle Philippe and his aunt Clemence. How tactfully the young mother apportioned the little honors attending the birth of her children! But never did her consideration on these occasions, or on any others, win the heart of her mother-in-law.

Within a year, on September 3, 1725, Marguerite's first little girl was born, whom she named Marie Madeleine Ursule, in sweet tribute to her teachers in Quebec. As usual her husband was on the island of Tourtes.

A month later, however, he was sharply recalled to Montreal by the sudden death of his patron, Governor General de Vaudreuil.

This event, in a particular sense a turning point for young D'Youville, meant a complex adjustment for the people of French Canada. As their leader since 1703, De Vaudreuil had become a part of their lives, and, in the manner of humanity in general, they now recalled the best that could be said about him.

He had encouraged agriculture, commerce and education. He had fortified Quebec against the English and constructed strong walls around Montreal. Even though he had many children of his own, he had adopted Esther Wheelwright, a little English girl who had been snatched from her home in Maine by the Abnaki Indians, and he had sent her to be educated at the Ursuline Convent in Quebec.

It is a point of special interest that this ward of the Marquis de Vaudreuil entered the novitiate of the Ursulines in 1712, the very year of Marguerite's admission to the boarding school, and that she pronounced her vows two years later as Sister Esther of the Infant Jesus. An excellent religious, she was elected the first Superior of the convent after the conquest of Canada by the British in 1760.

After the death of the Governor General, D'Youville, like many others, found himself without official protection. The arrogance of impunity became reckless scorn for the power of public opinion. No longer agent at Tourtes, from which unhappy island the Nipissing mission was removed in 1726, he continued in distant forest posts his debauching type of trade.

In the meantime, Marguerite's maternal heart again knew the pain of loss. On August 26, 1726, baby Madeleine Ursule died at the age of one year. Little François, only two, had seen his mother cry before, but never quite like this. It was small comfort that on December 16 of that year another baby girl, Louise, was born, for she lived less than three months. For the birth of this child, François d'Youville was not only at home for the first time on such an occasion but also signed the baptismal

61

record that day. The island of Tourtes no longer claimed his attention.

There seemed to be a slight ray of hope now that the father's heart might be touched by the appeal of his home. Surely the affection of the little son named for him would meet some response; surely the frailty of baby Louise would awaken the protective instinct of his manhood. These miracles might have come to pass if his mother had not died just then, leaving to him his unrestricted patrimony.

Now he entered into a worse phase of his life. Free from the necessity of making money, thoroughly indifferent to his home except as a place where his material needs were satisfied, he gave himself up to the excesses of an utterly dissipated life. Using his wealth as an opening wedge, he now entered into gay social circles only too glad to profit by his prodigality. Drinking, gambling, and dancing filled his wretched days while he remained in Montreal. Occasionally he interrupted his revelries to pursue his not entirely abandoned fur trading interests.

For his wife he now had no concern whatever. He was as indifferent to her sufferings as if she were a person totally unknown to him. If she had hoped that after his mother's death he would take a normal, manly interest in his home and family, she was cruelly mistaken. He did not even provide for them. For his own selfish pleasures he squandered all his inheritance and every cent that he could take from their common fund. The time came when the poor mother had to resort to difficult and constant work in order to provide necessities for her little ones. This was the very depth of her sorrowful life.

Yet it was not even her husband's utter indifference to the needs of his children that hurt her personally the most. It was the intangible violation of her finest feelings, the careless rejection of those delicate gifts of the heart that cannot be described with the frail substance of words. The recognition of a lack of sympathy was hard enough to bear; but almost intolerable was the final realization that in his soul there was nothing akin to hers, that between them there could never be that spiritual union which is the essence of perfect wedlock. Nevertheless, she accepted this painful disillusionment, protecting in faith, hope, and charity the integrity of her own marriage promise.

It was in 1727, after five tragic years of her marriage had passed, that Marguerite became a member of the Confraternity of the Holy Family, established at Notre Dame Church. The Holy Family! Entering spiritually into the blessed company of Jesus, Mary, and Joseph, in their home at little Nazareth, she found new strength for the life that God willed her to live in her own home in the Market Place.

Now at last, realizing fully that only in God could she find support and consolation, she put herself under the spiritual guidance of Father Dulescoat, a saintly Sulpician of the parish of Notre Dame. "Make the way known to me wherein I should walk," she prayed to the Eternal Father, "for I have lifted up my soul to Thee!" This was the turning point in Marguerite d'Youville's life.

Under the guidance of Father Dulescoat she learned how to sanctify the sorrows of her life, and, in learning, she became strong to suffer yet more. Though she had always been faithful to the practice of her religion, she now gradually developed a deeper and more constant piety. Having failed to find the good, the beautiful, and the true in the transient treasures of the world, she now sought them in the things of God.

Yet the strong active qualities of her character had to be exercised; passive love was not for her. Father Dulescoat, inspired by God, said to her one day, "Be consoled, my child! God destines you for a great work; and you will raise up a house that is falling into ruins."

Marguerite did not understand these prophetic words. At the time it was only her home, her home falling into ruins, that concerned her. Yet she rejoiced to believe that God had work for her to do, and she knew in her heart that with His grace she would do it, when and where He willed.

From this time on Marguerite remained serenely and valiantly in her home, fulfilling her duties, pouring out on little François, the one child left from four, all the tenderness of her motherly heart. To her husband, no matter when he came or in what condition, she gave welcome and care.

It was not only through a sense of duty that she now ministered to his needs. It was through a new grace that lifted up her soul and gave her strength. Now she understood that "unless the grain of wheat falling into the ground die, itself remaineth alone."

When her fifth child, Charles Madeleine, was born on July 18, 1729, it was with purer love that she took him into her arms and pressed him to her heart, to that heart which would in years to come be the warm comfort of the most abandoned little ones. François d'Youville, again at home, was probably glad that the baptism the next day would be an occasion for the customary celebration.

Another year passed, a year of even deeper embarrassment and pain for Marguerite, of wilder excesses for her husband. It was a year also of sustaining grace, of stronger trust in the Eternal Father, "Who has revealed to the lowly the mystery of the cross."

Now the chalice of suffering was filled to the brim. François d'Youville, after a week of agony from acute inflammation of the lungs, died on July 4, 1730. The next day his funeral was held in the Church of Notre Dame, and his wife asked the Récollet Fathers to offer three hundred and sixty Masses for the eternal happiness of his soul.

Marguerite d'Youville did not look upon the death of her husband as a release from suffering and shame. "So great was the goodness of her heart," wrote her son many years later, "that all his indifference and harshness toward her could not keep her from extreme grief at his death. She mourned him most sincerely, and for a long time she wept for him."

And to crown her sorrow, already the poor mother knew that

another child of this husband was growing beneath her heart. There were bitter tears, such tears as her own mother had shed, when little Ignace was born the following February. No wonder that five months after his birth this baby too was laid to eternal rest.

Now, with her son François, nearly six years old, and baby Charles, just one, Marguerite d'Youville faced the future. Her husband, for whom she sincerely grieved, had not only left her penniless; he had bequeathed debts to the amount of almost eleven thousand pounds, and a name held in dishonor by the people of Montreal.

Yet this valiant woman, serene and trustful, only turned to God. "O Father of all consolation," she pleaded, "sustain us in our trials. . . . Be the sole object of our love. . . . Accomplish in us the designs of Thy mercy."

II

THE TRUTH

Sanctify them in truth . . . *That they all may be one* . . .
JOHN XVII:17, 21

CHAPTER SIX

IN THE SCHOOL OF CHARITY

MADAME D'YOUVILLE, in the bewildering interval between the death of her husband and the birth of her sixth child, Ignace, quietly studied the problems that would have to be solved sooner or later—her livelihood, her husband's debts, the education of her children. Through the kindness and generosity of her own family, who sympathized tenderly with their beloved Marguerite, she was able to pass these difficult months in comparative peace and comfort. With their help, too, she made her plans for the years to come.

However, her decision not to return to the world of fashion and gay festivity in which they moved, and to which she would have been welcomed as lavishly as before her marriage, did not please them. Already, under the guidance of Father Dulescoat, she had seen that the Lord is sweet. Already she had met Him in the poor and suffering, and now she could not find it in her heart to turn away from Him in them. Nor could she compromise, sharing the pleasures of the worldly while serving the poor in their needs. There were no half measures for her!

It was indeed painful, especially at this time of dependence on the kindness of her relatives, whom she loved deeply, to offend family spirit by withdrawing from the way of life in which they were happily interested. It was not that she had grown accustomed to solitude in the company of her mother-in-law. It was not her late husband's shameful conduct that now fostered her reserve. It was not her poverty, for she still possessed the riches of fine family ties. She was far too healthy in mind, too balanced in spirit, to yield to influences as transitory as these. On the contrary, it was an interior and irresistible attraction to works of charity that inclined her now to direct her life along lines that would lead eventually to a complete dedication to Christ in His suffering members. Whether her family approved or not, this was the way wherein she must walk.

It was not until the early spring of 1731 that Madame d'Youville began to untangle legal formalities subsequent to her husband's death. On the fourth of April she requested the guardianship of her children. The next day the court named her guardian and appointed Jean François Malhiot as official deputy.

Madame d'Youville, by the terms of her marriage contract, was free to accept or to renounce the property and possessions which she and her late husband had held in common. She chose to renounce them. At first sight this decision may seem strange; but in view of the fact that a renunciation automatically freed her from responsibility for any debts or mortgages resulting from her legal union with François d'Youville, it was a wise move. For his personal debts, however, she loyally assumed obligation. To these were added the expenses of his funeral, amounting to 123 pounds, and the generous stipend of 273 pounds for the requiem Masses which the Récollet Fathers offered for the repose of his soul.

At Madame d'Youville's request, Philippe de la Découverte, Jean Malhiot, Timothy Silvain, and two lawyers met at her home at eight o'clock in the morning of April 24, 1731, to make a complete inventory of all the joint possessions of François d'Youville and herself. Under oath she personally estimated the value of each and every article of furniture, utensils, dishes, silver, clothing, jewels, papers, books, pictures. Beginning in the large, front bedroom on the second floor, she listed first her beautiful dower bed at a value of ninety pounds. Then came her upholstered chairs and her pretty folding table, the rare tapestries, and the little trundle bed where her babies had slept, some of them for so short a time. The little mirror with a gold frame was listed, too, and valued at twelve pounds.

In between the lines of the long inventory of more than 120 different items, one can read the record of a home once proudly maintained, and now honestly surrendered.

A lovely, carefully kept set of table silver, valued at 414 pounds, was the most expensive item. The big iron stove, next in value, had pipes that warmed the rooms above. There were three heavy irons for pressing linen, an old warming pan, and a big pudding dish, a knife case holding six good knives with real porcelain handles, a large copper kettle weighing nine pounds, a small saucepan, a little footstool, a handmade quilt, beautiful table linen, pillows and thick bolsters, a book containing lives of the saints, and four volumes of Roman history. There was a large bundle of baby clothes—little shirts, old shoes, seven tiny bonnets for a little girl, and three for a little boy. In a large chest valued at eight pounds were the personal effects of the late Francois d'Youville: his brass sword with gold-and-silver handle, a pair of old boots, embroidered silk stockings, brocaded vests, gold and silver lace, a fine blue velvet suit. Could it have been the elegant costume of his marriage contract day?

Not a single detail was omitted; not a penny was added to the estimated value. As for the articles in the little first floor store, which by this time Madame d'Youville had opened, she declared, again under oath, that they did not belong to her but had only been loaned by two merchants, to be sold for them on commission.

After three days of painstaking work the inventory was formally closed, signed, and sealed. The long, detailed document, preserved in the judiciary archives of Montreal, bears in ten different places the firm and decisive signature, *marguerite*

Lajemmerais veuve youville. Only her maiden surname was honored with a capital letter.

What a deep humiliation it must have been for the young widow to lay before the cold, unsympathetic eyes of the law each and every item belonging to her home and her dear ones! How it must have hurt her to express in pounds and pennies values that only the tender sentiments of her heart could rightly estimate!

After the completion of the inventory the process of law was very slow. Nearly a year later, on March 10, 1732, all the independent property of Madame You de la Découverte, which she had left to her son François, was sold at auction. On the fourth of the following July, the second anniversary of her husband's death, Madame d'Youville received a formal court order to accept or to renounce her possessions. On the eleventh, she legally renounced all claims to her inheritance.

A month later the law seized the property of the late François d'Youville, and on the fifth of September the bailiff announced a general sale. Piece by piece the furnishings of the home on the Market Place fell under the hammer of the auctioneer.

Among the few personal articles which Madame d'Youville was able to retrieve was a beautiful Parisian clock with a fine walnut case and a copper dial inlaid with dark blue enamel numbers on a white enamel field. This treasure was her husband's wedding gift. It may still be seen in her room at the Motherhouse of the Grey Nuns of Montreal.

For several years Madame d'Youville continued to live in the house on the Market Place by a lease for which she paid 181 pounds a year. She was summoned to court unexpectedly on November 17, 1733, for not having paid her first year's rent; but the case was dismissed in her favor when she claimed that she did not believe that she had to pay it until she had been legally notified to do so, especially since the security of Ignace Gamelin, her brother-in-law and a rich merchant, was in the meantime sufficient guarantee of payment. She would abide by the fine points of the law!

During the legal proceedings demanded by her inheritance, Madame d'Youville had settled the pressing problem of gaining a livelihood for herself and her children. For some time before the death of her husband she had been obliged to sell her own handwork in order to provide the necessities of life for the little ones dependent on her, their father having failed to do so. Now she would open a store.

Some years before, Madame You de la Découverte had turned two rooms on the first floor of her home into shops equipped with display shelves and counters for the sale of simple household articles. In spite of a favorable location on the Market Place, her store did not prosper. Perhaps her neighbors knew that she was already a wealthy woman in no need of their pennies. Perhaps her cold, unfriendly manner, or her high prices had discouraged their approach. Undoubtedly her son's invasion of the commercial rights of the people had kept them from giving any support to her venture. After her death dust and cobwebs had gathered in the store, windowpanes had been broken, iron hinges and bolts had rusted. Here and there narrow wall boards had become loose, revealing rough, grey stone.

One day in midsummer of 1730 Madame d'Youville pushed open the creaking wooden door of one of the shop rooms and surveyed the bare possibilities that lay before her. First of all, the place could be cleaned from ceiling to floor. The broken windowpanes could be replaced. The counters and all the shelves could be scrubbed and covered. The whole interior could be whitewashed. From friendly merchants commodities could be procured and sold on a commission basis. She could easily dispose of her own handwork. Already she could visualize neat rolls of colored cloth on the shelves, and fine linen, and boxes of pins, tape, thread, needles, buttons both plain and fancy. She could display delicate lace and satin ribbons, buckles, brooches, and feather fans. For the children—there were so many children in the neighborhood—she would provide candies and little sweet cakes. Yes, there were great possibilities here, thought the young mother. Somewhat encouraged now, she closed the heavy door and hurried up the stairs to her children.

Long accustomed to seeking advice, Madame d'Youville talked over her plans with her mother and sisters. Under the circumstances they had little choice but to approve, for certainly they could offer no substitute project. They were able, however, to give her assistance more substantial than counsel. Through their influence merchants were found who were willing to loan her attractive wares. Madame Anne Soumande, a widow like herself, supplied merchandise valued at 2750 pounds. Jacques Maugé furnished goods amounting to 350 pounds. Friends and relatives made generous contributions, helping at the same time in the many details of preparation.

Came the day, finally, when the little store was ready, the clean, white fulfillment of Madame d'Youville's vision. What visitor could resist the fresh and attractive appearance of her display, the excellent commodities, the reasonable prices? Above all, who could resist the kindly, gracious lady who welcomed all, young and old, rich and poor, with the same simple courtesy? There were some who came first in curiosity and then through satisfaction. Clients who once had turned away from these counters in bitter discontent now came back in smiling confidence to find exactly what they sought.

No wonder that her business prospered. No wonder that her stock soon had to be replenished and enlarged. Her merchants, promptly reimbursed for the goods that they supplied, found it to their own advantage to co-operate even more completely. Madame d'Youville, they learned, was a competent business woman, honest, straightforward, just. Her natural integrity and unerring sense of truth combined with the supernatural virtue of charity to forbid overcharging and every other device of making money beyond the sanctions of equity.

74

Within a few years the extraordinary success of the little store made it possible for Madame d'Youville to assure her living, to pay her husband's debts, to provide for the education of her sons, and bounteously to help the poor. This was the reward of her faith in the divine promise: "Seek first the kingdom of God and His justice, and all these things shall be added unto you."

In the meantime, each day in the store brought new experiences and new friends. Gradually Madame d'Youville's sympathetic eagerness to please won the hearts of her clients; and many, sensing her understanding of pain and anxiety, confided their own. Often a few steel pins, a bit of trimming, or a yard of cloth served as an excuse to talk to the kindly listener who knew how to comfort the sorrowful and counsel the doubtful, to encourage the weak and lift up the fallen. Personal suffering had enlarged her own heart and had filled it with compassion for the sorrows of others.

It was during this period, on July 17, 1731, that baby Ignace, truly a child of sorrow, closed his tiny eyes for the last time. How ardently his mother had longed to keep this little one, so frail and so dear! Nevertheless, bowing to the Divine Will in a spirit of faith, hope, and love, she quietly laid his delicate little body in the arms of her Eternal Father.

It was one of the remarkable traits of Madame d'Youville's character that she did not permit herself to dwell inordinately on the misfortunes of her life. Her sense of values kept sorrow in its place. Therefore, it could do its work of refining, unhindered by useless anxiety or vain complaint. Yet she was neither phlegmatic nor stoical. "The slings and arrows of outrageous fortune" could and did pierce her to the heart. Her trust in Divine Providence, however; her faithful submission to the will of God; her childlike dependence on the Eternal Father formed in her soul a constant attitude of docility toward suffering. She was truly patient. In the blessed school of Christian endurance, she became eminently fitted to guide other sufferers.

From her place behind the counter of the little store Madame d'Youville could look upon humanity in the Market Place. Tuesdays and Fridays were days of special activity there, for habitants from nearby towns would display their handmade or home-grown products in the open markets. Because there were no public clocks, the great bells of Notre Dame would ring at eight o'clock in the morning to signal the opening of sales and again at eleven to sound the closing. Sometimes, if her own business was slack, as it was likely to be on these days, Madame d'Youville herself would go among the vendors, passing encouragingly from stall to stall, buying from those who needed most to sell. Often she opened her slender purse to the poor who could not buy.

During all the years that Marguerite d'Youville lived in the Market Place, her tender heart was touched most of all by the unhappy culprits in public punishment. Fastened in stark humiliation to the pillory or iron collar, they seemed most pitiable, most afflicted. These she would encourage to patient endurance and to repentance. Many a time she would beg from door to door for the means to bury decently the poor criminals hanged on the high gallows and left there with no one to claim them. This charity she would perform also for those who died alone in the city prison on Notre Dame Street, which she visited frequently.

While Madame d'Youville's business ability was being exercised in the affairs of her store, her heart was being gradually fashioned for the eventual performance of all the corporal and spiritual works of mercy. It was through full and fruitful participation in parish activities, under the personal guidance of Father Dulescoat, that her charity found definite direction. Enlightened by God, he soon perceived that she was specially fitted, both by nature and by grace, to be an apostle of charity among the suffering poor of Montreal. The followers of Jeanne Mance were caring for the sick at Hôtel-Dieu; the daughters of Marguerite Bourgeoys were educating the young; the Charon Brothers, dedicated to the care of old men and orphans, were striving to fulfill their end, but obstacles to their success were becoming alarmingly hard to surmount. In time their General Hospital might have to be put into the hands of more capable managers. But the suffering poor of the city—women and children particularly—were still without security and care.

Madame d'Youville, thought Father Dulescoat, had the heart and the mind, the love and the will, the tenderness and the courage to answer the social needs of the time. She had, moreover, the simplicity to be guided by her spiritual director.

As a member of the Confraternity of the Holy Family since 1727, she had won not only the appreciation of Father Dulescoat but also the warm admiration and confidence of her associates. She was outstanding for her zealous interest in the works of the society as well as for her personal virtue. The unhappy circumstances of her domestic life were generally known, but no one could fail to respect the patient, humble, and very beautiful young woman who attended the meetings in the large sacristy of Notre Dame as regularly as those circumstances would permit.

Not until the spring of 1731, however, did Madame d'Youville's attendance in the Confraternity become regular. Concerned with the care of her children, with the business of her store, and with the demands of legal entanglements, she still had time for charitable work among the poor. Parish records testify that she was elected counselor on June 5 of that year, and reelected a year later. Though she was a young newcomer, she must have been considered suitable for a position that required tact, prudence, balanced judgment, and exemplary charity. Her serenely serious and thoughtful manner gave the impression— and rightly—of trustworthy capability.

This spring of 1731 was memorable for the people of Montreal for a special reason. It was at this time that Pierre de la Vérendrye, Madame d'Youville's uncle, left his home on St. Joseph Street with his sons and about fifty adventurous followers to explore the vast Canadian West. Mothers, sisters, and wives of the gay adventurers tried to share the brave enthusiasm of their men, forming *"Pour la patrie!"* with their lips until their hearts could take up the refrain; but tears mingled with their smiles as the large expedition set forth for the great unknown.

In the party was young Christophe Lajemmerais, realizing his great ambition at last. Madame d'Youville, waving farewell with the rest, was glad for him and proud of his achievements. Like his father, he had already distinguished himself in his dealings with the Indians; he understood perfectly the country and customs of the Miamis, the Foxes, and the Sioux. Brave La Vérendrye, knowing the caliber of this nephew born for exploration and leadership in danger, sent him ahead of his own men to Lake La Pluie, where he built Fort St. Pierre, naming it in honor of his heroic uncle. This was the first of a series of forts that were opened up to protect western Canada.

Two years later La Vérendrye sent Christophe back on a mission to Governor General Beauharnois. He brought with him a fine supply of furs, a thrilling account of their discoveries, and an excellent map of northern Ontario, which he had made himself. Having spent the winter in Montreal, he rejoined his uncle, but soon pushed on beyond the Lake of the Woods to the Winnipeg River, where La Vérendrye had just built Fort Maurepas. Privation and hardship now had their way, and he became desperately ill. Two of his cousins, returning to the fort, found him at the point of death. In spite of their efforts to revive his strength, gallant young Christophe died on May 10, 1736, at the age of twenty-eight.

Now, in our day, the Grey Nuns direct La Vérendrye Hospital at Fort Francis, the very place where the young brother of their foundress once bravely built his Fort St. Pierre.

In the meantime, back in Montreal, Madame d'Youville pursued adventures of an entirely different nature. Often she visited the General Hospital outside the city walls in order to help the poor old men there who no longer had adequate care. Out of her own slender resources she brought them little comforts as well as necessities. She would mend their clothes; she would try to put in order the confusion in which they lived. But her heart ached because she could not restore the broken windows and the leaking roof of their poor, cold dwelling place. It seemed such a shame that this General Hospital, once the pride and joy of philanthropy, should now be falling into ruins. No wonder Father Dulescoat was concerned about it!

The extraordinary solicitude of this holy priest for the suffering poor of Montreal and his zeal for their sanctification in the midst of their pain gradually broke down his own health. Though he obediently restricted his activities in the parish, making use, in the meantime, of every prescribed remedy, he died on February 7, 1733, in his forty-fourth year. His death was a severe loss to all, but to none more than to Madame d'Youville. For six years kindly Father Dulescoat had been her spiritual guide, advising her in problems, encouraging her in trials, manifesting the will of God in her regard. Now she must seek another guide.

It is almost amusing to read what Father Charles d'Youville Dufrost wrote about her relations with her spiritual directors. In a short biography of his mother, he insisted:

She was not one of those persons who importune their confessors from morning till night, piling up a hundred conferences without drawing any profit from them. She was not at all one of those very pious beings eager to change confessors, wanting to be directed by everyone they meet; nor was she one of those who by the length of their confessions wear out their directors and cause waiting penitents to be guilty of complaint and impatience. Those who knew Madame d'Youville particularly know that she made her confessions very briefly. She was conscientious but not scrupulous.

One rather suspects that the good Father d'Youville Dufrost had met a few penitents considerably unlike his mother!

The saintly Father Dulescoat had done his work. It was in the Divine plan that another Sulpician priest should continue the direction of Madame d'Youville's spiritual life and guide her in the work destined for her to perform. This priest was Father Normant.

Born at Châteaubriand in France in May of 1681, and trained for the priesthood at the Seminary of St. Sulpice in Paris, Father Louis Normant du Faradon came to Montreal in 1722, eventually to succeed Father Belmont, then Superior of the seminary. Not only was the young priest outstanding for his virtues; he possessed a special aptitude for administrative affairs and a thorough knowledge of canon law. His judgment was excellent; his moderation, dependable; his wisdom, profound, for it had its source in God.

During the years of his apostolic labors in Montreal, Father Normant had won the confidence and affection of the people. As Superior of the seminary since 1732, chief pastor of Notre Dame, and Vicar General of the Bishop of Quebec for the district of Montreal, he had deeply at heart the spiritual and temporal well-being of his flock. No one was more interested in the poor. Like Father Dulescoat, he was seriously concerned about the deterioration of the General Hospital. He, too, knew that the day was coming when it would have to be either discontinued altogether or turned over to more efficient administrators.

Father Normant had probably agreed with Father Dulescoat that Madame d'Youville possessed remarkable aptitude for works of charity. He had perceived with genuine admiration the silent fortitude with which she had borne her husband's cruelty and neglect; her resourcefulness in managing her store, so that she could meet her financial obligations; her maternal fidelity to the complete well-being of her sons; her wisdom in legal matters; above all, her selfless devotion to other sufferers. God evidently had a great work in store for such a soul, thought Father Normant, and there seemed to be little doubt that this work would be among the poor and afflicted. Her heart was made for them; and personal experience had given her training of rare practical value.

When, therefore, after the death of Father Dulescoat, Madame d'Youville put herself under the spiritual guidance of Father Normant, he knew just what course to take with her. She should be led along the way of fervent piety and Christian charity, particularly through the parish societies to which she already belonged.

It has been noted that when the Confraternity of the Sacred Heart was inaugurated at the Ursuline Convent in Quebec in 1731, Madame d'Youville immediately became a member. The twenty-third day of October was assigned to her for the future as her day of reparation to the Divine Heart. Never in the years to come did she forget her pious obligation on that day.

On March 16, 1733, Madame d'Youville was enrolled as the twenty-eighth member of the double Confraternity of the Blessed Sacrament and of a Happy Death. Each day she recited certain prayers; each week she passed a special half hour in adoration before the Blessed Sacrament; once a year, on an assigned day, she made a Holy Hour. These were devotions regulated by her membership; no count can be made of those inspired by her love. Whenever the Blessed Sacrament was exposed for the veneration of the faithful, all members were expected to spend at least one hour in adoration; and when Holy Viaticum was carried to the dying, they formed a guard of honor. There is no doubt that Madame d'Youville had her share in all these devout practices.

While the principal end of this Confraternity was to procure for its members the great blessing of a good death through devotion to Christ in the Eucharist, it also aimed to inspire solicitude for the suffering souls in purgatory and prayerful zeal for their eternal happiness.

It was above all as a member of the Confraternity of the Holy Family that Madame d'Youville was prepared for her ultimate dedication to a life of charity. On May 25, 1734, she was chosen mistress of postulants. In this office it was her responsible duty to direct a probation of three or four months for those who wished to become registered members. It was especially her warm mother spirit that animated her dealings with the beginners, always inspiring them, not with devotion for herself, but with zeal for God's work among the poor. How kindly she must have initiated her charges into practical methods of ministering to the needs of the sick and destitute! Out of the spiritual richness of her own experience she impressed upon them the great importance of a kind and humble heart in dealing with the unfortunate, and the supreme necessity of seeing Christ in the afflicted.

At the same time, Madame d'Youville was chosen a Lady of Charity. Under this lovely title it was her privilege not only to visit and console the sick, but also to beg for the poor and to distribute the alms collected. At the death of a member, Ladies of Charity took turns all day watching and praying beside the deceased. On the day of the funeral they followed the remains to the church, bearing lighted candles in their hands. The dignity and devotion of these ceremonial attentions to the dead must have inspired deeper reverence and charity.

In May of 1735 Madame d'Youville was elected Superior of the Confraternity for the one-year term allowed by the rules. Then, because of her unusual aptitude and devotedness as mistress of postulants and Lady of Charity, she was returned to both posts repeatedly from 1736 to 1741, in which year she became treasurer, the last office that she held. By that time she had become engaged in a far greater work, combining all the offices of the Confraternity.

These years of experience in supervised authority over others were most important to Madame d'Youville's future work. She needed a real apprenticeship in practical associations. Her leadership, however, was active, never dictatorial; it was a full, selfless participation in the work to be done. She led the way—all the way.

Madame d'Youville, in her position of authority, studied and respected the special aptitudes of her co-workers. Some were more successful than others in collecting alms; some, more tactful in handling particularly sensitive cases; some had the comfort touch. As for herself, she felt it her first duty to give an example of regularity, piety, and wholehearted charity. Every moment that she could spare from her home and children, including the management of her store, she gave to the work of the Confraternity. No wonder that she had the reverent love of her associates and the full confidence of Father Normant!

Among the suffering poor themselves Madame d'Youville was soon welcome and beloved. Searching out the most destitute, the paralyzed, the crippled, the blind, the mentally afflicted, the lonely aged—many of all these the victims of cruel Indian wars —she would gently bathe their pitiful bodies, wash and mend their clothes, or replace filthy rags with clean, whole garments begged from friends in better circumstances. She would scrub their poor living quarters, make up their cots with warm quilts, replenish fires in their small charcoal or wood braziers. She would bring them food; patiently she would feed those who could not help themselves. She would comfort their anxious, aching hearts, for she understood that "not by bread alone" is the whole man fed.

Madame d'Youville somehow saw everything to be done for the poor and she found a way to do it, a way that soothed and reassured. Gentle, sympathetic, even reverent, because she truly saw Christ in the poor, she cared for them as tenderly as she would have ministered to Him. That sense of security and confidence, which her own brothers and sisters, and her mother, too, had felt in her presence years before, flowered now in the hearts of the abandoned poor. She was strength, relief, love. She was an angel of peace and consolation in their unhappy world.

Undoubtedly the inner secret of Madame d'Youville's success in her many domestic and parochial duties, and, above all, in her care of the poor, was her fidelity to practices of solid piety. Every day she attended Holy Mass, receiving Holy Communion as often as she was allowed to do so. Not even the most severe Canadian winter could keep her from daily participation in the

Blessed Sacrifice. Often she was the first in the early morning to break through the great drifts of snow that piled up in the Market Place and along St. Francis Xavier Street. Sometimes, against the cold blue-whiteness of dawn, there was only the strong, lonely figure of this valiant woman making her way to Mass. And the way was easy because her heart was warm.

Every afternoon, too, unless duties at home prevented her, she climbed the hill again to Notre Dame for a quiet personal visit to the Blessed Sacrament. Frequently she would take her sons with her, François and little Charles, teaching them through priceless example that love of Christ in the Eucharist which later in their lives attracted both of them to become other Christs in the priesthood.

No matter how many obligations Madame d'Youville had in the parish among the poor, her duty as a mother kept first place. Little Charles was only one year old when his father died, but François was six; and very soon his mother took him herself to the parochial school conducted by the Sulpician Fathers on the corner of Notre Dame and St. Francis Xavier streets. It was only a block and a half from home.

Charles remained at his mother's side until he was old enough to go to school with François, absorbing during all these years those loving details about her that he was later to incorporate into his biography of the great foundress.

Finally the older boy was ready for Quebec. François had confided to his mother his great desire to be a priest. Happy, grateful as only a mother can be whose son is chosen by God for a consecrated life, Madame d'Youville increased her work in order to furnish all that he needed for his studies in the seminary.

When the time came, in 1737, for François to leave home, his mother accompanied him to Quebec and saw to his establishment in the Sulpician Seminary there. Warm indeed were the sentiments of her thankful heart when her son took his place in the same seminary where her two beloved brothers had been ordained. Both were now laboring for God's interests in their own parishes.

Madame d'Youville returned to Montreal. She was now alone with Charles, eight years old. Her debts were paid; her store was thriving; her work among the poor was well established.

Then Father Normant, inspired by God to believe that for this valiant woman a greater work was in store, suggested that she should prepare for it yet more completely by taking a few destitute persons to live with her in her own home—a suggestion that gave words to the desire of her own heart.

"It will be a wise experiment," he explained. "You will see what you are able to do, and the people of Montreal will become accustomed to your direction of a house for the poor."

CHAPTER SEVEN

LES SOEURS GRISES

IF MADAME D'YOUVILLE was destined by God to put new life into the old General Hospital, then Father Normant, her spiritual director, was the true instrument of the Eternal Father in making known the Divine Will. Already he had begun to prepare her gradually for the great undertaking. The building was certainly falling into ruins, but a change in administration would take time and considerable tact. The hospital had been founded by very rich men for very poor men; and a very poor woman would unquestionably have to prove herself before the people of Montreal would accept her.

For the destitute of the city to receive her devoted care in peace and gratitude was one thing; for the comfortable upper classes to recognize her authority in a house of charity established through the munificence of the wealthy was quite another. It would not matter that the Sulpician Seminary had given the land for the hospital in the first place. Philanthropists had built and maintained it.

Even though Father Normant, as Vicar General and chief shepherd of the poor in Montreal, had a right to be concerned about all his people, the Bishop himself, the Governor General and the Intendant were the actual administrators of the institution. Only they could make changes. They had not yet come close enough to the situation to realize that changes would soon have to be made. Moreover, the name of D'Youville still recalled to them certain associations suggestive of anything but works of charity.

Another obstacle of a more personal nature presented itself for Madame d'Youville's consideration. Some of her own relatives had never reconciled themselves to the fact that a member of their distinguished family should make a total sacrifice of herself for the poor. They would be among the first to oppose her taking over the hospital.

With Father Normant, Madame d'Youville faced these facts. The thought of saving the institution, of giving to the poor old men there all the care that they needed appealed to her noblest ideals; but she knew that many years would have to pass before she could undertake a responsibility so heavy and so involved.

The works of God move slowly. She would await His moment. In the meantime, she would stretch out her hands to the needy— hands eager to help. She would take some of the most abandoned into her own home.

How could she help thinking first of poor Françoise Osseau, blind for the last four years, whose husband, Pierre Le Beuffe, was already at the General Hospital? Only men were taken there; and now she was desolate, incapable of supporting herself.

The Ladies of Charity in the Confraternity had been doing their best to provide the necessities of life, but they could not guarantee her support for the rest of her days.

It was on November 21, 1737, the feast of the Presentation of the Blessed Virgin Mary in the Temple, that Madame d'Youville gently guided Françoise Osseau up the steps of her home in the Market Place. There was a clean small room for her, into which her possessions, such as they were, had already been moved. There was security now. Most of all, there was a kind, strong hand on her forehead smoothing back her hair, and a soft voice uttering welcome and love.

When Madame d'Youville went to bed that night, she felt that in the room adjoining hers Christ Himself was peacefully resting. *I was a stranger,* the words echoed unmistakably in her soul. *I was a stranger, and you took Me in.* Now she had really begun her work.

The next morning, after Mass, the care of Françoise Osseau was her first thought. Madame d'Youville, assisting her to dress, making up her bed, guiding her in the simple breakfast of bread and water and perhaps a little barley that Charles helped her to prepare, considered the possibility of receiving other dependent persons. She knew many in desperate straits whom she could take. How much she could do for them!

It was not long, however, before she realized that in this work she would need help. Alone she could not take proper care of the poor and at the same time manage her store. She had to work harder than ever now, because François in the seminary must be provided with all that he needed; and Charles was growing fast. To neglect her children would be to offend God. With several associates in her work for the poor, she could fulfill her maternal duties and also carry out her plans to receive other needy persons into her home.

It was through friendship, one of the richest sources of inspiration and achievement for a soul like hers, that Madame d'Youville found the answer to her problem.

Some time before, she had become acquainted with Louise Thaumur, the daughter of Dominique Thaumur de la Source, a surgeon who lived on St. Francis Xavier Street, not far from the Market Place.

Louise, born in Montreal on October 9, 1706, had lived quietly in her comfortable home all these years, devoting herself to practices of piety and works of charity without any definite thought for the future. Her meeting with Madame d'Youville was the turning point of her life. Never before had she seen anyone so reserved and yet so friendly, so majestic in manner and yet so simple and selfless. She marveled at the older woman's endurance, her resourcefulness, her apparently unbounded capacity for work. How Madame d'Youville had been able to bear years of pain and humiliation and at the same time grow in piety, womanly beauty, and devotion to others was a wonder to Louise Thaumur. Because her own life had been sheltered and easy, she was irresistibly drawn to one who had always followed admirably the difficult way of the cross.

The attraction was mutual. To Madame d'Youville, Louise Thaumur's lovable and peaceful nature was a happy grace. She appreciated the younger woman's solid virtue and her delicate understanding; and she recognized in her that fine spirit of trustful co-operation which is so strong a support to one who must bear the burden of leadership.

Between these two friends the love of God and a common eagerness to do great things for Him encouraged long spiritual confidences in which their aspirations for the future had frequent mention. One day, during a particularly stimulating conversation, Madame d'Youville suggested that they should make a novena together at the tomb of Father Dulescoat. Louise heartily agreed.

The novena was almost a retreat in its holy concentration. Every morning the two women attended Mass in silent recollection. Afterward, side by side, they knelt at the tomb, begging the saintly priest who had once directed them both to obtain for them from the Eternal Father the knowledge of His will.

On the ninth day of their prayer they paid a visit to Father Normant at the seminary, hoping that through him who was now their guide a message might be given. Besides, it was an opportunity to tell him that Françoise Osseau was now safely settled in Madame d'Youville's home and that perhaps other dependent persons could be received in the future.

Touched to the heart by the charity shown to this poor forsaken woman, Father Normant turned to his visitors with more animation than they had ever before seen him manifest.

"How wonderful in heaven!" he exclaimed. "How wonderful in heaven will be the joy of those who serve God in the poor!

To shelter them, to feed them, to clothe and comfort them, to visit them in prison, and to care for them in sickness is to do all these things to Christ Himself. We have His word for it. What glory such mercy gives to God! What glory in heaven will be the reward of the merciful! And yet, my dear friends, do not be deceived. A life devoted to the care of the poor is a life of suffering, a life filled with sacrifices of every kind. Only those should undertake it who can detect, under the rags of the wretched poor, the seamless garment of the beautiful Christ!"

Madame d'Youville needed no more. Her soul enlightened by the graces of her fervent prayer, her heart inflamed by the promise and the challenge of Father Normant's words, she resolved then and there to spend the rest of her life in the service of the poor. Would her companion join her in this consecrated work?

But Louise Thaumur hesitated. Deeply touched, not only by Father Normant's appeal, but also by Madame d'Youville's immediate response, she still could not make up her mind to follow her example. Though she was accustomed to voluntary self-denial, she was completely unacquainted with personal hardship. Carefully nurtured and beloved in a comfortable home, esteemed everywhere as the daughter of a prosperous physician, she honestly found it hard to decide at once what to do. To spend the rest of her life with the poor, sharing their poverty at every moment, would be very different from playing the part of a lovely Lady Bountiful on occasion. She would need more time to ponder and to pray.

Wisely, Madame d'Youville did not urge her. But while she waited, sure that Louise Thaumur would not long hold back, she looked around for other companions. Naturally, she considered first her associates in the work of the Confraternity.

Of these, Catherine Cusson, somewhat delicate but zealous and eager, was the first to respond. This young woman, aged twenty-eight, had lost both her parents many years before, and had since been living with two older sisters in Notre Dame parish, not far from Madame d'Youville's home. A skilled dressmaker like her sisters, she was highly respected not only for her industry but also for her piety and charity. There was no reason why she could not now leave her sisters and work entirely for the poor. As soon as she had decided to do so, a great peace and confidence filled her soul, making her understand that for this very purpose God had destined her.

At the same time another Catherine offered her services, the pious daughter of Robert Demers, a tailor of Montreal. Though three years older than Madame d'Youville, she too was gifted with a fine spirit of docility and faithful co-operation. Quiet, capable, always self-controlled, she would be a strong support in the work that they hoped to undertake.

By this time Louise Thaumur had resolved her doubts. Encouraged by the response of Catherine Cusson and Catherine Demers, both of whom she knew, she also made her decision once and for all to give herself to the poor.

While Madame d'Youville sincerely rejoiced to receive her close and very dear friend, she had already prepared herself to forge ahead with other companions if God so willed. Not even in the company of the most intimate associates would she ever escape that profound, interior loneliness which is the lot of all those who enter wholeheartedly into the achievement of a great and original design.

It was on December 31, 1737, that the three volunteers met at Madame d'Youville's home, where she received them with wide-open arms and warm, motherly heart. Well did she understand that they were giving to God all that they had to give. Completely they were trusting her to lead them.

United now in their heroic purpose, these four women, the first Grey Nuns, consecrated themselves simply and privately to the service of the poor. It was the real beginning of the great Congregation that now numbers close to seven thousand members engaged in every kind of work in all parts of the world. Here was another "mustard seed," planted in the rich soil of Montreal.

In the archives of the original Motherhouse, a precious document, the Register of Professed Sisters, bears evidence in the handwriting of three of these pioneers, Madame d'Youville herself, Louise Thaumur, and Catherine Demers, that December 31, 1737, was their profession day. It was therefore also the birthday of the Congregation. Catherine Cusson was professed then, too, but died many years before the Register was formally begun.

Religious profession, as we understand the term today, is an open declaration, in the presence of witnesses, of one's dedication to God by vows, in accordance with duly authorized rules. Such a profession was not, of course, made by Madame d'Youville and her companions. In humble reticence, they never made known the full nature and scope of their sacred promises in consecrating themselves to the service of the poor. Whether it was in the privacy of their own hearts or in the presence of Father Normant, we do not know. There is only the Register to testify that on the day of their union they made a definite act of consecration which they called profession.

Father Antoine Sattin, chaplain to the Motherhouse, whose material for the second biography of Madame d'Youville, written in 1829, was drawn from the reminiscences of a Grey Nun who had lived with the foundress, has this to say on the subject of their promises: "The regard that they had for poverty, obedience, and chastity was such that before God, Who was their only witness, they voluntarily made a formal promise to be faithful to these virtues."

Elsewhere in his biography Father Sattin claims: "Though they were consecrated to the poor, they lived in the practice of the evangelical counsels."

Although the love of God in the poor was the motivating force that united Madame d'Youville and her companions in simple dedication, the little group was by no means a religious community in the approved sense of the term. It was an association of secular persons bound only by their common aspirations.

In those days religious communities could not be formed on French soil without the approval of the King of France. As contemplative or charitable orders, they had to depend largely on royal subsidies, which usually amounted to an annuity of two hundred and fifty pounds for each member. Under these conditions, the King was slow to grant approval for new Congregations. Those already existing were sometimes a severe strain on the royal purse.

For sixteen years, therefore, Madame d'Youville's association, though heroically charitable in purpose and activity, was neither civilly nor canonically recognized as religious in organization. Both Father Normant and Madame d'Youville must have had in mind the ultimate formation of a duly authorized Congregation, but they knew the wisdom of proceeding slowly and prayerfully until God should make known His will.

The four associates, on December 31, agreed to spend the following year in gradually putting their plans into execution. They would continue to live in their own homes for the present, but would work together as much as possible, taking care of the poor persons whom Madame d'Youville would receive. She could not receive many, however; her rooms were too small and too few. But the lease for this house on the Market Place would not expire until the first of November. Perhaps by that time they could rent a house in a more suitable locality, a house large enough for themselves and their poor, and then they would live in common.

In the meantime, they would all contribute to the general revenue from their earnings. Catherine Cusson and Catherine Demers, skilled in sewing, already had many clients whom they would continue to serve; and Louise Thaumur could help them. Perhaps in time they could sew for the King's stores in the

Market Place. Then their income would indeed be assured for the future.

Finally these four courageous women, united more closely than ever through their eager planning, agreed to keep secret as much as possible the great work to which they had consecrated themselves.

Before many weeks, however, their close and unusual association began to excite comment. It was now known that blind Françoise Osseau was being cared for in Madame d'Youville's home; her husband in the General Hospital had spoken gratefully of her relief and contentment. Would more destitute persons be taken? Who was going to take care of them? It was impossible now to deny or to hide the truth.

Some relatives and friends were surprised and even shocked. This was a new thing indeed! Were not the poor sufficiently cared for in their own homes by the good members of the Confraternity? Who was the widow of François d'Youville to collect the destitute persons of Montreal in her house and then get other people to take care of them? Was it true that they were aiming to take over the General Hospital in time? And how did they propose to support themselves and their poor?

Some questioners with particularly long memories subtly wondered if the liquor traffic would provide revenue, as once it had, in this very house too.

Already the sinuous stirrings of curiosity were beginning to arouse suspicion and blind antagonism—not among the poor who would profit by the heroic self-sacrifice of a few good women, but among excellent people not quite virtuous enough to resist envy of a good work which they were not themselves inspired to perform.

Mere words, however, could not deter brave women dedicated to deeds. In the noise about them they kept silent and continued their work.

As spring passed into early summer they realized even more sharply that the house in the Market Place would soon have to

94

be abandoned. It stood in the very center of all the agitation that was ever aroused in Montreal. Drunken Indians from the woods often stumbled into the store or lounged on the steps outside, as they had done in summers past; for even to the red men Madame d'Youville was a friend. But lately loud and ominous remarks from passers-by had reached her ears as she attended to to her affairs at the counter.

"Look at those Indians! Where did they get their firewater this time?"

"Maybe the widow d'Youville sold it to them in secret, just as old You and his son——"

A coarse laugh covered up the words as the men passed on.

The ugly comments grew. Madame d'Youville's associates, passing in and out of her home, frequently met a barrage of jeers. Already the suspicious questionings of relatives and friends had degenerated into the gibes and insults of the common mob that thronged the Market Place in the summer time. Somehow the sight of the quiet women, plainly dressed, intent on something far removed from the noisy confusion around them, irritated the careless idlers into malicious mockery.

"Voilà! Les soeurs!"

"Les soeurs grises!"

The rabble took up the taunt. *Les soeurs grises!* The tipsy nuns!

Without a word, but with burning cheeks and swiftly beating hearts, the brave women went on. Sensitive, kindhearted, they could not be totally indifferent to the cruel experience which they had suffered. And yet, were they not called *nuns?* For the infinite honor of this term, could they not endure the adjective?

Weeds also grow from beginnings as small as mustard seeds. From a few idle, mocking words grave accusations came. Madame d'Youville and her companions were seriously blamed for much of the intoxication of the Indians who lounged in the Market Place; they were even accused of being intoxicated themselves, or at least befuddled and foolish. And where did they get their liquor? Was not Father Normant helping them with something? Perhaps the Sulpicians were providing it! Maybe they thought that they could get the allegiance of the red men that way!

Another rumor grew, however, that had its root in truth. It was true that Father Normant was helping Madame d'Youville and her associates with something. Curious but more intelligent observers surmised that he was preparing them to take over the General Hospital. There must be some kind of connection, they concluded, between his interested support of these women and the fact that he, as Vicar General, acting in Montreal for the Bishop, would not permit the Brothers at the hospital to take any more subjects. Was he allowing them to die out so that he could have Madame d'Youville and her companions installed? Madame d'Youville and her companions—*les soeurs grises*, the people called them!

There was no doubt now that the time had come for the four women to find a more secluded place for their work. It would be very difficult to do so, for Montreal was growing fast, crowding up to the city walls.

Fortunately, however, the widow Anne Soumande, one of the merchants who supplied goods for Madame d'Youville's store, announced that her mother, Madame Le Verrier, had just the place for them, a big stone house on the corner of Notre Dame and St. Peter streets, almost directly across from the church of the Récollet Fathers. Only one story high, with a large attic that could be made into rooms with dormer windows, it would serve very well indeed. In the northwestern corner of the city, it would be far enough from the noise and disturbance of the old Market Place.

In giving up the home where she had lived for so many years, Madame d'Youville had to surrender also the store which was her main source of income. Yet the experiments of the past few months had proved that through needlework she and her associates could earn enough to support themselves and their poor.

They had already begun to get commissions from the King's stores. Eventually Catherine Demers, experienced in tailoring, would undertake the elaborate military uniforms so much in demand. Working diligently together, they would manage very well.

Secretly the four women began to settle their possessions in the big Le Verrier house. They agreed that each one would keep her personal property, clothing, furniture, a few religious or familiar treasures. Only their earnings would be contributed to a common fund. Altogether now they had a treasury of about four hundred dollars to be used for their work. As servants of the poor, they too would be poor.

Finally the new home was ready. All the floors had been scrubbed; the walls and ceilings had been freshly whitewashed; the windowpanes were sparkling through clean curtains; beds were ready; chairs and tables had been placed. There were a few religious pictures on the walls; and, standing on a plain wooden cabinet in the little parlor, was a small brass statue of the Blessed Virgin Mary, the gift of a kindly priest who wished them well.

It was on Thursday, October 30, 1738, that Madame d'Youville and her three companions crossed the threshold of this house which would henceforth be called the cradle of the community. Within it, for the first time, they would live together, dedicated to a common way of life. Within it would be generated those traditions and customs which through more than two hundred years have been cherished as the heritage of every Grey Nun.

Turning at once into the little parlor at the right, the four humble pioneers knelt reverently before the statue of the Blessed Virgin Mary, shining there before them in the bright morning sunlight. Each one, in the sacred silence of her own heart, begged the Queen of Heaven to be her mother and her guide. Then, in the name of all, Madame d'Youville, serene and self-controlled, besought the Mother of God to bless their little society and to accept the consecration which they now made of themselves, for the rest of their lives, to the service of the poor, the most abandoned members of Christ, her Son. During this simple but deeply affecting ceremony, Catherine Demers, like Madame d'Youville, revealed no sign of emotion; but Louise Thaumur and Catherine Cusson could not restrain their tears.

That evening Father Normant called to assure himself of their safe settlement and to bring them little gifts, scissors, writing paper, needles and pins, rosaries and other small articles of devotion. These were very precious things! A paper of good steel pins cost three pounds in those days and excellent writing paper was a luxury.

Kindly Father Normant would have been glad to leave these brave women lighthearted and delighted over their little presents; but, as he gave them his blessing, he thought it best to strengthen them for impending trials.

"Dear Sisters," he began, unconsciously using the term, "this is a happy hour, but you must remember, even while joy is in your hearts, that the cross is the foundation of all God's works. You must expect to be contradicted and actually persecuted by worldly people, as all the saints have been. Arm yourselves, therefore, with patience, charity, and gentleness. Many good citizens here are disturbed over your union and the opening of this house. They fear that you will soon move into the General Hospital; and they have other plans for that poor house. Be patient; keep silence; and, above all, trust in God."

Father Normant's fears were by no means unfounded; nor was his warning vain. Even as he left the house that evening, he noticed groups of men and women loitering about, apparently trying to find out what was going on.

Two days later, on the feast of All Saints, the four women, leaving together to attend Mass at Notre Dame, were openly assailed in the street. Angry citizens, persuaded now that Father Normant intended to get these women into their General Hospital, blocked their way, hissing, mocking, reviling them.

"Les soeurs grises!" they shouted. *"Grises! Grises!"*

Madame d'Youville, imperious in her spiritual strength, made her way in silence through the crowd, followed by her companions, equally silent, equally courageous. Several men, infuriated by their unassailable peace, picked up stones and savagely hurled them, striking the gentle women as they passed on. Only Christ, Whose experience they were now sharing, could understand their strange joy.

Here, in cruel detail, was the reaction of the mob. The next morning, in the office of the royal notary, twenty-eight distinguished gentlemen of Montreal signed a solemn petition addressed to Count de Maurepas, Secretary of State. The document ran:

The officers, merchants, residents of the city and government of Montreal in New France, very humbly represent to Your Grace that in the month of August, 1692, the Bishop of Quebec, Count Frontenac, the Governor General, and the Intendant Champigny permitted the establishment of a House of Charity in Montreal for poor orphans and for crippled, aged, infirm, and otherwise needy men. To build this house, the late Father Dollier, Superior of the seminary in Montreal, granted a suitable piece of land to François Charon, Pierre Le Ber, and Jean Fredin, for themselves as well as for those who would join them, and their successors; that for the establishment, the late François Charon spent about two hundred thousand pounds, and the late Pierre Le Ber, most of his very considerable inheritance; that after the death of the late François Charon, Brother Chrétien Turc, being Superior, went to France and borrowed large sums of money which he squandered on unworthy conduct and rash undertakings without the knowledge of the community of Brothers Hospitallers in Montreal, which debts made the Brothers of the Christian Schools withdraw from them, although they had until then been inclined to unite; that, moreover, the priests of the Seminary of St. Sulpice were opposed to the union. Since the Superior, who is the Vicar General, is not willing to allow them to receive subjects, the number of Brothers is at present reduced to five, of whom three are very old; and the two young ones are not enough to attend to the schools and the care of the poor old men, residents as well as pensioned soldiers, and also to the administration of the goods and affairs of the entire house.

That this action on the part of the priests of Montreal, who have in all probability influenced Bishop Dosquet of Quebec, formerly a member of their Community, forbidding the reception of new Brothers, and dispensing from their vows of stability several who were frightened by what was suggested to them, namely, that when they were old, they would be out on the street, gives the impression that the priests of the seminary would take possession of the house as soon as the work stopped, by virtue of a certain clause in the contract by which the land was given to the hospital, and that the Superiors would then have *les Soeurs Grises* put in charge of it.

This scheme, Your Grace, is utterly contrary to the intention of the founder, to the pious purpose and wish of His Majesty, and to the public good, since this house is a refuge for poor orphaned children, old men, residents as well as pensioned soldiers, and a school for the children of all their families from Montreal and from all the parishes in the land.

This it is, sir, which obliges petitioners to beg Your Grace to grant your protection to the hospital, to urge the Brothers of the Christian Schools to join the Brothers Hospitallers in Montreal, and to obtain from His Majesty the subsidy of three thousand pounds which had been granted to them in the reign of His Majesty, to help in the support of Brothers for the schools, and of which subsidy they have been deprived for a number of years; and the petitioners and their children will be under an obligation to redouble their good wishes and to pray for the health and prosperity of Your Grace.

This rambling, somewhat incoherent expression of helpless but proud authority was signed by Governor de Beaucours of Montreal, the King's procurator, Lieutenant General Raimbault, six military officers, and a number of prominent residents of the city.

Even worse, it was signed by Ignace Gamelin and Pierre Maugras, the brothers-in-law of Madame d'Youville herself. This public rejection on the part of her relatives would have been painful to her, for her family feeling was tender and deep, had she not by this time become accustomed to rebuffs. "Not even His brethren believed in Him," she said to herself, remembering the example of Christ.

The petition addressed to the Secretary of State by the leading citizens of Montreal is revealing in an important detail. The term, *les Soeurs Grises,* even capitalized in the original manuscript, is used readily, without any explanation whatever of its meaning, as though not only the writers of the petition but also the intended readers were already familiar, on this date, November 2, 1738, with the group of women whom it designates. They must have been known for some time, therefore, under this humiliating title.

Not until seventeen years later was "grey," the alternate meaning of *"gris,"* substituted for the first and unfortunate "tipsy." Then, in 1755, Madame d'Youville, grounded in humility and wishing her Sisters to be always reminded of that fundamental virtue, deliberately chose grey material for their religious habit, thus perpetuating the original name in a new meaning.

During the early years, however, the associates adopted no definite religious costume, in obedience to the royal prohibition on this point. Without consciously aiming at uniformity, they wore simple black dresses, unrelieved by trimming or jewelry. Needless to say, they gave no attention to the elaborate coiffures popular in those days, but arranged their hair in a practical style, plain but not unattractive.

Among the common people of Montreal the petition of 1738 was highly inflammatory. Aroused by the example of their leaders, they magnified the implications of the title, *les Soeurs Grises,* into fantastic but none the less malicious proportions. Out of the dead past they dug the misdemeanors of François d'Youville and his father; they interpreted Madame d'Youville's patient endurance of wrongs as connivance in her husband's wrongdoing; they charged her and her companions with deliberate drunkenness. Several calumniators, more unscrupulous than the rest, said that the Sulpicians, in league with *les Soeurs Grises* to destroy the General Hospital, were supplying them with liquor. Malice reached its proper depth when a few particularly evil-minded slanderers whispered accusations of immorality against the poor and humble women.

All these shocking charges finally reached the ears of Governor General Beauharnois. Scandal seethed in the land.

In the midst of the storm Madame d'Youville and her companions remained calm, remembering Father Normant's prediction. All storms must pass, they told themselves patiently. Taunted, insulted morning after morning as they crossed the street to Mass, they continued, nevertheless, to seek in the Holy Sacrifice their only support.

One cold morning as they knelt at the altar rail to receive Holy Communion, the priest, passing along from one person to another, stopped before Madame d'Youville, the Sacred Host uplifted in his hand. Reverently she waited, her eyes lowered, her lips parted.

"These are the women," he thought to himself, studying the whiteness of the Host in his hand, "these are the women whose names are clouded in scandal. Public sinners!"

And he passed them by.

Trembling, hurt to the depths of their souls' pure innocence, they remained kneeling for a few moments and then returned quietly to their places, their eyes lowered, their hands folded over their hearts.

Even the rabble stood silent as the stricken women left the church that morning, tears running down their cheeks.

CHAPTER EIGHT

TRIAL BY FIRE

NOTHING came of the strange document addressed to the Secretary of State, even though it was signed by the elite of Montreal. Perhaps the French authorities thought it wise to let the whole turbulent affair run its own course.

Although the full fury of the storm against Madame d'Youville and her companions was eventually spent, it was years before the rumblings of evil charges had completely died away. To none of them did she ever make an answer; and no one ventured to defend her, realizing perhaps that beside her spiritual strength any material defense would be futile and superfluous.

Father Normant, however, lost no time in building for the new society the strong protection of a rule of life. As a religious priest thoroughly trained in canon law, he was eminently fitted to draw up regulations suited to the state that they were now gradually entering. He prescribed a series of spiritual exercises, the pattern of which has been followed in the Congregation ever since, with only those variations required by wider activities and the laws governing religious communities. Moreover, he personally guided the four women in these exercises, teaching them methods of prayer and religious practices hitherto unknown to them.

In order to have the longest possible time for work, the Sisters—now so called—arose at five o'clock in the morning. Assembling in the little oratory of the Blessed Virgin which they had set up for themselves, they said their morning prayers together and meditated in peaceful silence for half an hour. Then, even despite inclement weather, they would make their way to the parish church of Notre Dame for Mass. Three times a week they received Holy Communion together, but on the other days each communicated in her turn, remembering the intentions and spiritual needs of the others. On this day the happy recipient would also make an extra visit to the Blessed Sacrament and perform a definite act of penance.

Personal care of the poor, household duties, needlework of all kinds filled each morning, broken only by a short period of spiritual reading. Sometimes Madame d'Youville herself read to the others while they sewed. In her strong, compelling voice the lives of the saints or the ascetical counsels of holy writers became more real, more practical, more appealing. After she had finished, they would go on with their work, sometimes in thoughtful silence, sometimes in pleasant conversation, until the time set aside for the examination of conscience, a quarter of an hour before dinner.

But dinner had to be prepared, and other meals as well! This part of the establishment Madame d'Youville managed herself, generously assisted by the others. Surely she was far more experienced than they in the purchase and preparation of foods according to a limited purse! Meals were plain, sometimes even coarse, but always wholesome. Delicacies appeared only for the sick.

Ordinarily, every moment of every afternoon was also spent in work until five o'clock, when the Sisters assembled again in the oratory for the recitation of the rosary and the Office of the Name and Crown of the Blessed Virgin.

According to a custom common to all religious communities, one day each month was set aside for a spiritual retreat. In prayer and silence the Sisters reviewed the affairs of their souls, recognizing weaknesses, forming resolutions for the days to come. Spiritually refreshed by this privilege of special union with God, they took up anew their labors for His poor.

As the number of destitute persons increased during the first year to five and then to ten, in spite of the opposition which had scarcely begun to subside, the Sisters were obliged to double their labors in order to provide subsistence for the household. Although their charges gave as much help as they could—from the very beginning Madame d'Youville wisely recognized all their capabilities as assets—it was no easy matter now to care for so many. Well into the late hours of the night they worked, completing assignments of all kinds—elaborate satin gowns for the grand ladies of Montreal, lovely embroidered christening robes, uniforms for soldiers, linens for every need. No order was ever refused. Every article was finished as perfectly as possible.

"We must do all things well," Madame d'Youville would remind her companions. "We are the servants of all for the sake of the poor, and everyone must know that we never refuse to serve."

Such extraordinary labor could never have been sustained by these gentle women, accustomed for the most part to a much easier way of life, had it not been for the constant help of God. This help took a practical form in the arrival of the first paying boarder, Thérèse Lemoyne Despins, on July 2, 1739, the feast, happily, of the Visitation of the Blessed Virgin Mary.

For this young girl, only seventeen years old, an orphan from the village of Boucherville and a distant relative of Madame d'Youville, a small room was somehow provided, which she filled with her own beautiful belongings. Cheerful, intelligent, and refined by nature; well educated and wealthy by good fortune, she was a blessing to the house in more ways than one. She was like a bright flower in a setting sometimes sober with adversity.

In Madame d'Youville, Thérèse found a loving, tactful mother who knew how to create for her a home so happy that she willingly accepted certain restrictions on her social life. It was not easy to be young and gay but alone in Montreal! Possessing neither inclination nor aptitude for personal works of charity among the unfortunate, she nevertheless honestly admired what she saw. To emulate Madame d'Youville became in time her highest aim, but for many years her natural dislike for the care of the destitute kept her from active participation in the works of the house. As a boarder quite faithfully paying her way, she was by no means obliged to render service; and Madame d'Youville, with characteristic breadth of vision, allowed full freedom for her nature and state in life, trusting the Holy Spirit to give direction to both.

But already a dark shadow was beginning to cut through the sunshine of Thérèse Despins' presence. Privation, hardship, constant exposure to extreme cold finally overcame Madame d'Youville's heroic endurance. For many months severe pain in her right knee had made walking difficult. Now overwrought tissues broke down altogether, and two angry open sores appeared, so painful that she could not move about at all.

This affliction, coming at a time when her activity seemed essential to the success of her undertaking for the poor, was a desperate test of faith both for herself and for her dismayed companions. Yet it was probably God's way of proving that the work was His and that He would sustain it in every contradiction. Not for one moment of the seven years that this trial persisted did the brave sufferer lose her patient trust in God.

Yet she prudently called to her aid all the remedies known to the medical science of her day. At once Dr. Joseph Benoit was summoned. As chief surgeon in Montreal by royal appointment, he could be expected to effect a cure. It occurred to him that if an incision were made, joining the two sores, one on each side of the knee, the infection could be more easily drained. Without benefit of an anesthetic, the incision was made. Far from being improved, the malady became much worse.

After several months of excruciating pain, Madame d'Youville called in another doctor. He prescribed a prolonged application of certain simple herbs. They had no effect whatsoever, except perhaps to increase infection.

As a last medical resort—no one seems to have even considered the services of Timothy Silvain, probably because he was having serious legal difficulties at the time—the Sisters appealed to an Austrian surgeon by the name of Ferdinand Feltz, newly arrived in Montreal. His reputation was excellent. Here, surely, was a doctor who could cure a diseased knee.

The remedy proposed by the renowned Dr. Feltz and most scrupulously followed by Madame d'Youville for four weeks was so fantastic and so repulsive that one shudders to read of it. Live toads were set upon the open wounds to suck away the poison! It was believed that from their little darting tongues some curative power flowed. Poor Madame d'Youville, patiently gripping the arms of her chair, could hear as well as feel the rasping of their rough feet on her sensitive flesh. To the amazement of her companions she suffered this horrid remedy day after day without a word of complaint. Yet she must have sighed with infinite relief when the ugly little creatures were at last taken away, leaving her to suffer in peace.

By no means did Madame d'Youville neglect the resources of prayer. Her very patience was a prayer, ascending like fragrant incense to her Eternal Father. In one novena after another she begged the kind intercession of the saints, among them, in trustful hope, her faithful Father Dulescoat. With immense difficulty and almost intolerable pain she had herself taken on a barge down the St. Lawrence to Quebec, where at the tomb of young and holy Bishop Lauberivière she made another novena. Even to this heroic effort there was no evident response. Madame d'Youville, disappointed but not at all defeated, returned home.

Now in Montreal itself another opportunity for open supplication presented itself. Antoine La Brosse, a sculptor of high talent, had offered to Notre Dame a magnificent lifesize crucifix which he had carved himself. In a colorful procession of clergy and faithful, to the singing of hymns and the chanting of psalms, this beautiful gift was to be carried to the church and solemnly erected.

Madame d'Youville, full of confidence that Christ, in honor of this triumphant occasion, would bless her with a cure, had herself carried to a favorable spot on Notre Dame Street near the entrance to the church. Here she and her companions, not less eager than she, awaited the great procession and the happy moment of the hoped-for miracle. Along came the joyful crowd; there passed the beautiful crucifix, its beams supported by strong, proud men. The head of the Crucified was inclined in Madame d'Youville's direction.

Leaning forward as her companions knelt, she whispered her pleading prayer over and over again. But nothing happened— nothing at all. The glad procession passed into the church, and the poor sufferer was carried home.

"It is the will of God," she kept repeating. Her eyes shone and a quiet smile settled on her beautiful countenance. "It is the will of God."

Her three companions, their spirit now in unison with hers, remained tranquil in their disappointment. But Thérèse Despins gave way to tears, and Charles, still with his mother, must have trudged sadly along with heavy feet and a very much heavier heart.

Now from Madame d'Youville's room, as from a living heart, there flowed to every part of the house, in an unfailing stream, the sustaining influence of her personality. Her door was always open. For everyone she had a ready smile and a warm, gracious welcome. From her chair she maintained perfect order in the house, advising, encouraging, admonishing, as needs required. Yet during this time of her trial, as throughout her life, she never imposed her way upon the other Sisters. Sometimes distrusting her own judgment, she consulted theirs. Thus she developed in each of her companions that sense of responsibility without which their burdens could not have been borne nor their achievements assured.

Sometimes parochial or legal duties or the urgent needs of the poor demanded her presence in the city. In these cases she would have herself carried in her chair, an embarrassing procedure for an otherwise strong and independent woman.

Gradually, as the seven years of her purification burned themselves out, the strange malady disappeared. Perhaps enforced rest during these years made it possible for her naturally strong constitution to repair exhausted physical forces. Although she was able to do an extraordinary amount of work while confined to her chair, she was spared the excessive bodily activity that had in previous years brought her resistance down to the vanishing point.

But physical affliction was by no means the only trial that poor Madame d'Youville endured from the very beginning of her foundation. God was pleased to send her others of far greater weight, some that touched her tender heart most poignantly.

Catherine Cusson, the youngest of the Sisters, and certainly the least robust, also fell victim to extreme hardship, bitter cold, and exhausting hours of work. During the last months of 1740 her decline was so marked that no one could doubt the dreaded presence of tuberculosis.

There was no limit to the tender care that was lavished on her. For hours at a time Madame d'Youville sat beside her bed, watching over her, keeping up her cheerful spirits, encouraging her to eat all the nourishing dainties that the Sisters lovingly prepared, often at the sacrifice of their own needs. But the disease was inexorable, and on February 20, 1741, she died, at the age of thirty-two.

The annals of the Congregation tell us that Catherine Cusson, during the three short years of her religious life, was distinguished by her charity to the poor and by her exact observance of the rule. Remarkably patient in her last illness, she was not only resigned to death but joyfully eager to meet it. In her dying hours, however, God tested her faith by allowing intense fears of the last judgment to afflict her soul. These fears she expressed to the Sisters and to her director, kindly Father Favard, who succeeded in restoring her childlike confidence in the Eternal Father before she died.

To Madame d'Youville the loss of this spiritual daughter was as painful as that of her natural children had been. Catherine Cusson had been the very first to offer her life to the foundress for her work among the poor. No one could have been more devoted. How acutely now they would all miss her diligent work, but much more her kind heart and her gracious, religious spirit! As a pioneer, she had been very close to them.

Even while the mortal illness of this dear Sister weighed on the hearts of her associates, another threatened loss of far greater weight sent them to their knees in urgent supplication. Father Normant became ill, so dangerously ill in fact that hope of his recovery was almost abandoned.

It was frantically now that Madame d'Youville and the Sisters prayed. What would ever become of their work without him? Who else was standing between them and the hostile forces that would destroy that work?

Pounding on the very doors of heaven with her fervent prayers, Madame d'Youville solemnly promised that if Father Normant were restored to health, she would have a votive light burned before the Blessed Sacrament every year on the feast of the Presentation of the Blessed Virgin Mary, a feast of deep significance to the Sulpicians. Moreover, she promised to have a special painting of the Eternal Father made in France. This was a promise that would involve considerable cost to the struggling society, but no sacrifice was too great for the life of their beloved director.

If God had seemed deaf to Madame d'Youville's pleadings for her own cure, He hastened now to hear her prayers for Father Normant. This priest, so essential to their work, was speedily restored to health.

On November 21, the feast of the Presentation, one can still see a very special votive light burning before the Blessed Sacra-

110

ment in Notre Dame Church; and in the vast community room of the Motherhouse in Montreal hangs a beautiful painting of the Eternal Father, the fulfillment of the generous promise that Madame d'Youville earnestly made. Not always is thankfulness for divine favors so enduring!

In the grateful jubilation occasioned by Father Normant's recovery, the foundress could not forget that the number of workers in her little society was now reduced to three. But Catherine Cusson, lately arrived in the courts of heaven, could hardly have lost interest in *les Soeurs Grises* who had just afforded her Godspeed.

At any rate, the Eternal Father seemed pleased to make good the loss of this dear and valuable Sister by sending two more to replace her, another Catherine, of the Rainville family, and Thérèse Laforme. Indeed, for "good measure, pressed down and running over," still another Catherine, surnamed Menard, presented herself, but finding the new life too difficult, she regretfully withdrew.

Catherine Rainville, noble of birth, well-to-do, and exuberantly healthy, was thirty years old when, on July 23, 1741, she asked to be associated with Madame d'Youville in her work for the poor. From the very beginning she proved the solidity of her virtues and her excellent qualities of mind and heart. Sound in judgment, ingenious and resourceful, she was also remarkably mild in temperament. To the immense relief of the foundress, it was delightfully easy to train this young woman in the spirit and ideals of the society. She assimilated both with rare and astonishing speed.

It was on October 22 of the same year that Thérèse Laforme, the daughter of a Montreal surgeon, joined the little group. She brought with her not only the stability of her twenty-seven years but also the special characteristics of foresight and prudent charity, combined with an unusual aptitude for creating and maintaining good order. Her spirit was so accurately attuned to Madame d'Youville's that she could fulfill the foundress's wishes almost before she had expressed them. Especially important in these early years was her initiative, her faculty of making quick and fearless adjustments to emergencies with the good-humored assurance that comes of sound training in a secure and happy home.

It is interesting to note that Madame d'Youville's new society, still assailed on one side by the dignified protests of the aristocracy and on the other by the vulgar attacks of the mob, as well as from above, so to speak, by the well-meant disapproval of certain clerics, could yet attract the love and lifelong service of sterling, thoroughbred young women like Thérèse Laforme and Catherine Rainville. Such is the power of integrity rooted in God.

The little house on the corner of Notre Dame and St. Peter streets, now recognized as a refuge for the needy, attracted two other young women in the summer of 1741, not as religious aspirants but as free boarders willing to render service in return for the security of a home.

Marie Bénard-Bourjoli, only sixteen years old, was a native of old Boucherville, like Thérèse Despins. Antoinette Arelle, in her twentieth year, came from Longueuil, a neighboring village with its share of Boucher descendants. Both girls, as happy and helpful members of the household, became so strongly attached to Madame d'Youville and so absorbed in works of charity that they joined the society in 1747. In the same year, Agathe Véronneau, the pious daughter of a prosperous merchant near Three Rivers, also gave herself to the work of caring for the poor.

On December 31, 1744, the anniversary of the founding of the society, Madame d'Youville, Louise Thaumur, and Catherine Demers looked back over the seven years that had passed. Of famine had they been, or of plenty? Of both, they thought gratefully, and blessed by the Eternal Father with the incomprehensible bounty of His Providence. There had been trials of overwhelming magnitude, yes; but in spite of these—perhaps because of them—the society had grown, the work had prospered.

"And best of all," laughed Madame d'Youville's companions, "our dear Mother is completely cured!"

Now, with ten of God's poor comfortable and happy, with three fine young boarders to spread good cheer, with one of Madame d'Youville's sons praying for them in the seminary at Quebec, with two healthy novices already sharing the work and loving it, with Father Normant well and strong again and busy in their behalf, what more could they ask?

Their thankful hearts indeed rang out the old year and rang in the new. God was smiling on them.

One month later, at midnight of January 31, 1745, Madame d'Youville suddenly awoke from heavy sleep. Wild screams pierced her ears. Fire! Fire! Thick smoke blinded her eyes and smothered her breathing. Leaping out of bed, fumbling for clothing as she slid her feet into one old shoe and one old slipper, she ran from her room to find that half of the first floor was already in flames. An old stove banked for the night had failed its charge.

There was no time to lose. Fortunately the most helpless of the poor, among them blind Françoise Osseau, were on the ground floor. While Madame d'Youville and Thérèse Despins forced these out of doors, half clad, barefooted, terrified, the rest of the household tumbled down the stairs, catching up as they fled whatever they could save. Someone thought of the statue of the Blessed Virgin that graced their oratory.

Again and again, until angry flames leaped from the doorway, Madame d'Youville fought her way back into the house, making sure that everyone was saved.

Outside, in the deep snow and piercing cold, she gathered the poor victims close around her, as if her arms could keep them warm. Shivering, stunned, almost unbelieving, they watched the great, gripping, hungry flames consume their home.

Suddenly, with a sharp cry, "My shoes! My shoes!" a poor demented woman broke away from the group. In spite of Madame d'Youville's swift and frantic efforts to hold her back, she darted across the street, straight into the burning house. For one terrible moment before she perished, her screams rose high above the roaring of the flames.

Almost overcome with horror and grief, Madame d'Youville nevertheless went about, trying to comfort and sustain the others, even while she gave her attention to the grave danger that now threatened nearby homes because of falling sparks.

By this time a crowd had gathered. Many sympathetic persons covered with their own coats the half-clothed victims of the terrible fire. Some offered refuge and other aid. Clemence Lajemmerais and her husband, who lived only a block away on Notre Dame Street, were among the first to arrive, appalled at this latest affliction to their sorely tried sister.

But a few malicious stragglers had also run to the scene. Interpreting this disaster as a punishment from God on what they in their blindness considered Madame d'Youville's evil ways, they flung their ugly judgments into the very faces of the sufferers.

"See those violet flames!" they jeered. "Now all that brandy is burning that you hid away for the Indians!"

Madame d'Youville had no ears for words like these. Other voices were reaching into her heart.

"Mother! Mother!" pleaded her abandoned poor, pitifully pressing against her, catching her hands, touching her cheeks with their frozen fingers. "What can we do without you now? Do not leave us! Keep us with you anywhere!"

"Nothing can take me from you," she comforted them, "nothing in this world! We shall find another house, never fear, for God is our Father, and He will provide."

She began at once to make provision for the dispossessed. Those who had relatives in the city would go to them until further plans could be made. Quickly, for the flames were dying down now and the piercing cold of this January night could no longer be endured, they hurried to whatever refuge they could find.

The next morning, in the cold, blue, winter light, Madame

d'Youville, Louise Thaumur, and Catherine Demers returned to the ruins. Within the jagged, smoke-blackened walls smoldered the ashes of all their possessions. Nothing else remained.

"My dear Sisters," said Madame d'Youville quietly, "we have had too much comfort, perhaps too much attachment to worldly things. Hereafter we shall live more in common and in greater poverty."

Her two companions understood perfectly this language of heroic renouncement. Up to this time each one had retained complete ownership of her personal possessions, including whatever money she had. Only the revenue from their work for the poor had been put into a common fund. Now there should be a change. They agreed to go with her at once to tell Father Normant their resolution.

The good priest listened carefully to the outline of their plans for the future, and he thoroughly approved the changes that they suggested.

"This very day," he told them, "I shall put into writing what you have proposed. Come back tomorrow, and I shall have a statement for you to sign."

The next day, February 2, they returned to Father Normant, who read to them the precious document which has since been looked upon as the foundation stone of the Congregation. Carefully inscribed on good strong paper in folio, it read as follows:

We, the undersigned, for the greater glory of God, the salvation of our souls, and the relief of the poor, wishing sincerely to leave the world and to renounce everything that we possess in order to consecrate ourselves to the service of the destitute, united only by the bonds of charity (without any intention on our part of forming a new Community), in order to live and die together, so that this union may be firm and lasting, have unanimously agreed and of our own free will have promised the following:

First: Henceforth to live together for the rest of our lives in perfect union and charity under the direction of those who will be given to us; in the practice and faithful observance of the rule which will be prescribed for us; in complete submission and obedience to the one among us who will be charged with the government of the house; and in entire poverty and renunciation, putting in common from now on everything that we possess and everything that we shall possess in the future, without keeping for ourselves the ownership of it nor the right to dispose of it, making by this act a pure, simple, and irrevocable gift to the poor, which no one among us nor among our relatives may claim after our death for any reason whatsoever, except landed property, however, if there be any of it, which we can dispose of freely.

Second: Unreservedly to consecrate our time, our days, our work, even our lives, to labor, the product thereof to be put in common to provide subsistence for the poor and for ourselves.

Third: To receive, feed, and shelter as many poor as we can take care of by ourselves or by the alms of the faithful.

Fourth: All persons who will be received in the association will bring with them everything that they have: linen, clothes, furniture, and money, all to be put in common, nothing excepted or retained, renouncing every right of ownership or withdrawal by a voluntary and irrevocable gift which they make to the members of Jesus Christ. And if they have any income or annuities, they will be included and put into the common fund. All landed property will be excepted, as said above, which they can dispose of at death.

Fifth: If anyone of those who will have been received in the society is obliged to leave it for good reasons, she will not claim anything that she may have brought to it, having freely surrendered it and made a gift of it to the poor; but she will be satisfied with what others may have the charity to give her.

Sixth: If, in the course of time, there are no persons capable of maintaining this good work, or if, for some other reason, it is not wise to continue it, the undersigned wish and intend that all property, movable and immovable, will be put into the hands of the Superior of the seminary at Montreal, to be used according to his discretion in good works, and especially for the relief of the poor, transferring to him every right of ownership, making to him a gift of it, in their name as well as in that of the poor, to whom everything belongs, declaring anew that such is their intention.

This act of union having now been read and reread, we do approve it and with the help of God's grace we oblige ourselves with all our hearts to fulfill its terms. Made at Montreal in the presence of the undersigned, February 2, 1745.

Madame d'Youville signed the document without hesitation, and then gave it to Catherine Demers and Louise Thaumur. Both wrote their names at once.

The original copy of these first solemn promises is still carefully guarded in the archives of the Congregation. With two other sheets in Father Normant's handwriting, one outlining daily religious exercises, the other prescribing the spirit that should animate the Sisters, this document forms the basis of the first Constitution, drawn up in 1781.

Thus it would seem that the more God took away from Madame d'Youville, the more she gave to Him.

CHAPTER NINE

THE CHARON BROTHERS

FOR almost three years after the disastrous fire the Sisters and their poor had reason to remember One Who had not whereon to lay His head. Yet in this period of moving from place to place they proved the strength of the spiritual bonds that united them, and convinced even their worst calumniators that God was their support.

Several days after the tragedy a rich and generous merchant by the name of Fonblanche offered them the free use of a small house on St. Paul Street, one block west of the old Market Place. In joyful gratitude and humility Madame d'Youville accepted this refuge and hastened to assemble her poor. So thankful were they all to be reunited to their mother that they scarcely noticed the cramped quarters in which they now found themselves.

One of their first acts was to set up the little statue of the Blessed Virgin Mary, which someone had saved from the flames and pressed into Madame d'Youville's hands during the anguish of that night.

Their plight had touched the sympathy of many kind souls in the city, who now gave them beds and other indispensable articles of furniture as well as clothing and fuel. The greatest charity came from the Sulpician Fathers at the seminary, who supplied almost all their food during the fifteen months that they

118

occupied the Fonblanche house. This assistance enabled them to provide for other urgent needs and to resume their sewing, the most important source of their income. To assemble materials and equipment under the circumstances must have been a task of heroic proportions.

Order was soon established in the new home and spiritual exercises were resumed. Emergencies often bring out of hiding certain qualities and powers unsuspected in reticent or diffident individuals. Not only the two novices but also the three boarders, Thérèse, Marie, and Antoinette, devoted their capabilities magnanimously to the many problems that grew out of the late disaster. Young and strong, they were able to do a great deal of work impossible now to Madame d'Youville and her two Sisters on account of their endless sewing.

Yet the refugees could not remain indefinitely in this house on St. Paul Street. Too small to accommodate in reasonable comfort the nine poor persons who remained, it could not receive more. And more were now asking to be received.

As the months passed, Madame d'Youville continued to look for a more suitable place. At last she learned that on Notre Dame Street, exactly opposite the Récollet Fathers' church, and only a block from the ruins of their old home, a certain Dominique Lapalme had a fine, large house for rent. Delighted with this news, she hastened to secure the building with a lease for three years. This was in the early summer of 1746.

There was no secrecy this time in moving from the region of the old Market Place to Notre Dame Street, as there had been in 1738, when Mother d'Youville and her associates took possession of the ill-fated Le Verrier house. It was a joyful caravan that passed along the streets to the new home, and there were many good neighbors who called down the blessing of God on them as they went.

To settle their possessions took only a few days, for many hands and happy hearts make light work. This house was all that they had hoped for—spacious, comfortable, strongly built, close to the church. Now their work could really grow.

119

Yet it seemed destined to grow, not in sunshine, but in the shadow of the cross. Scarcely had they made themselves at home when there fell across their lives a very dark shadow indeed.

Early in the morning of July 16, 1746, Dominique Lapalme knocked at the door and asked to see Madame d'Youville. Hurrying into the little parlor, she found him standing in the middle of the floor, evidently ill at ease.

"Madame," he began uncomfortably, "it is my unhappy duty to tell you that you must leave this house."

"Leave this house!" she echoed in astonishment. "Why, we have just come! I have leased it for three years!"

"This is a very special case, madame. It is Governor de Beaucours who wishes to have it for his wife. He insists that it is much more suitable for a governor than for such women as you. It is a compliment to me, madame, and you see, I——"

"But it is impossible for us to leave now, sir! We must have at least three months to look for another place. It is not easy to find a place in Montreal at this time."

"Very well, madame. I am very sorry. I must report your answer."

And Dominique Lapalme departed.

So Governor de Beaucours wanted this house! Governor de Beaucours had been the first to sign the document of protest against *les Soeurs Grises* in 1738. Governor de Beaucours had approved the disgrace of her uncle and godfather, Captain Jacques-René Gaultier—brother of the great La Vérendrye—because he had deliberately failed to arrest his own brother-in-law, Timothy Silvain, for assaulting a friend of the Governor; and he had even publicly stripped the unfortunate Captain of military rank and uniform! More than that, it was Governor de Beaucours who had just lately stopped the explorations of La Vérendrye himself and was even now ignoring his appeals for justice and the opportunity to continue his great work for France.

This was plainly a family affair, perhaps a question of reprisals. She could expect little consideration from offended authority.

Kneeling in the little oratory, she raised her trustful heart to the Eternal Father. If He wanted them to stay in this house, they would stay. If not, Divine Providence would find them another house. Then quietly she sought her companions and told them what had happened.

One week later Madame d'Youville received a summons to court. There presiding was Guiton de Monrepos, the King's councilor and lieutenant general, the Governor's friend whom hotheaded Timothy Silvain had assaulted!

In a few moments the decision was rendered in no uncertain terms. Poor Madame d'Youville's plea for three months' grace was rejected. If she had not completely vacated the Lapalme house by the fifteenth of August, she and her companions and all their belongings would be put into the street by a detachment of soldiers. Moreover, she must leave the place clean and well repaired.

There could be no answer to a decision like this. Madame d'Youville, never doubting for a moment that God was permitting this colossal injustice for a good reason, hurried home to prepare her Sisters for their retreat.

They might indeed have had to suffer the shame of forcible eviction had Madame La Corne, the daughter of former Governor de Ramezay, not been touched to the heart by their misfortunes. Indignant because of the action of the court, she personally took the trouble to call upon the foundress and offer her home on the corner of St. Paul and St. Claude streets. So that Madame d'Youville and her poor could have full freedom, she planned to withdraw to her summer home. This generous woman was indeed the instrument of Divine Providence. As a member of one of the oldest and most respected families in New France, she could afford to brave the chagrin of Governor de Beaucours and his friends.

It was anything but a joyful caravan that now moved through

121

the length of the city. This was a particularly rough part of the way of the cross. It was a costly part, too, for the aged and infirm could not walk so great a distance, and all their possessions as well had to be taken in carts. Yet, inspired by their mother, who begged them to be cheerful, the others tried to bear bravely the burden of the journey until they could lay it down at last in the little oratory of their beautiful new home. Now began again the work of adjustment.

As another bitter Canadian winter settled down over Montreal, Madame d'Youville's innate delicacy and consideration for others could not abide the prospect of Madame La Corne's remaining in her summer home. As soon as possible, therefore, she began a long and difficult search for another house. She had to be cautious this time. She could not expose her destitute people to any further disruption.

At last, through the influence of Father Normant, she was able to rent a large stone house on Notre Dame Place, very near the church. The owner, a rich trader-merchant named Paul d'Argenteuil, Lord de Cuisy, was really independent enough to keep the terms of the lease.

The household now numbered eighteen persons, including the five professed Sisters of the society, for Catherine Rainville and Thérèse Laforme were now full-fledged. Agathe Véronneau had joined Marie Bénard and Antoinette Arelle in the novitiate, so called. Thérèse Despins still shared the fortunes of the society but not its dedication.

Before the end of 1746 *les Soeurs Grises* and their charges were settled in the new home in accordance with the two fundamental qualities of Madame d'Youville's power of administration—order and the spirit of prayer. Everyone shared in the thorough foundation cleaning, and no one worked harder than the foundress herself as she supervised the work and at the same time spared the strength of weaker members.

Father Normant's special contribution to their peace and joy at this time was the appointment of their first regular confessor. Responsibility for this office fell to Father Michel Paigné.

Scarcely had the De Cuisy house been put in order when Madame d'Youville, experiencing relief and relaxation for the first time since the fire, became dangerously ill. Too strong in soul to yield to the weaknesses of the body, she had at last exhausted all her physical forces. She had borne too much. Now she succumbed. Utterly unable even to struggle against her illness, she lay for months in danger even of death.

To Catherine Demers and Louise Thaumur fell the responsibility of the house. Having shared with the foundress from the beginning all duties and trials, they were ready to meet daily demands and even this emergency.

Who can describe the grief—almost the despair—of the anxious household for whose sake their mother was now in the depths of pain and exhaustion? Never was the little oratory without suppliants, a Sister, some of the poor, relatives even, begging the Eternal Father to restore to health her who was so precious to them all. Day and night they importuned the Good Physician until at last they had the ineffable joy of seeing their beloved mother gradually return to health. Priceless was the first soft smile that she could give them, priceless the pressure of her frail white hands. Light again in her clear, dark eyes was a joy that filled the house.

To Father Normant particularly, Madame d'Youville's critical illness was a matter of serious concern, for affairs at the General Hospital had also reached a crisis. Two broken-down old Brothers, one seventy-nine years old and the other in his late sixties, were now trying to take care of four decrepit men ranging in age from eighty-eight to seventy-three years. The least aged of this pitiful group was, incidentally, Pierre Le Beuffe, the husband of Françoise Osseau. The building itself, once the pride of Montreal, was now an eyesore on the island.

What a tragic termination of what had been, from a worldly

and financial point of view, one of the most promising projects ever begun in New France!

When, in 1680, the wealthy Jeanne Le Ber, mystical and lovely, had turned away from a glamorous world to become a recluse, a wave of pious philanthropy had swept over the city. Eight years later, her two brothers, Jean and Pierre, and a friend of theirs named Jean Fredin, had leaped to the proposal of François Charon, a rich and zealous merchant, to found a general hospital, or house of hospitality, for needy men and for orphans. Every kind of worldly fortune smiled upon the project.

Father Tronson, Superior of the seminary, entered heartily into the plan, to the extent of donating eight or more acres of land at Pointe-à-Callières, on October 28, 1688. This section, outside the city walls, was separated from Montreal proper by the St. Pierre River.

Building could not proceed at once, for these were the years of Indian wars. In fact, it was in 1691 that an Iroquois arrow took the life of young Jean Le Ber, one of the associates. On the day of his funeral his father donated thirty-two acres of fine land at Point St. Charles, with all the buildings thereon, to be used for the charitable project in which his son had been engaged. It was stipulated in the contract that all revenue and produce of this farm should be used in perpetuity for the relief of the poor in Montreal, subject to the management of the Sulpician Fathers.

Such a foundation as Francois Charon proposed was an urgent need in Montreal and indeed in all New France. As a result of many years of Indian wars, the land had more than a just share of widows, orphans, and crippled, blind, or otherwise incapacitated men. The mentally ill created a problem of dire proportions. A Bureau of the Poor was set up in 1688 by the Superior Council to relieve the sick poor and to place orphans in homes or apprenticeships; but it functioned as such departments always function when they have no money in the treasury.

Bishop Saint-Vallier took a long step ahead in 1692 when he

opened a general hospital in Quebec. The letters patent that he received from the King for this establishment authorized him to make similar foundations whenever and wherever the need arose. Of all such institutions the Bishop, the Governor General, and the Intendant should be the chief administrators.

Young François Charon and his associates had only to take advantage of the letters patent of 1692 in order to proceed with their foundation. They had all the money they needed—even the secluded Jeanne Le Ber had donated ten thousand pounds, and other generous souls had followed her good example. They had almost nine acres of fine land at Pointe-à-Callières, adjoining the gardens of Pierre You de la Découverte—an ideal location on the banks of the St. Lawrence River.

Within two years a magnificent building was constructed, thirty feet wide and ninety feet long. It was by far the largest and finest institution in Montreal. Built entirely of stone, with a good slate roof, it had three high stories besides a spacious attic lighted and ventilated by many dormer windows. Valued at one hundred thousand pounds, it was the pride and joy of the city. Wealth and charity had met in this hospice for the poor, of whom many were soon received.

The special letters patent of this General Hospital, dated April 15, 1694, authorized the Charon Brothers, as they called themselves, to live in community. Bishop Saint-Vallier, profoundly impressed by the lively spirit of charity and zeal which had so far animated the founders, allowed them to have a little chapel in which the Blessed Sacrament was reserved and where Mass was daily offered. Even a belfry was added to the building, so that to the solemn call of a bell the Brothers could regulate their exercises. Without royal sanction they could not yet call themselves a religious community, but they hoped in time to win from the King even this concession. It was certainly not in the shadow of the cross that the General Hospital was founded.

Francois Charon, unquestionably pious and charitable, indefatigably zealous in the interests of the poor, lacked, nevertheless, that essential sense of complete dependence upon God without which even the most auspicious project must eventually fail. He believed infallibly in his own powers. He was above all else a businessman, confident that on his labors alone all the success of the hospital depended. It seems not to have occurred to him that in a spiritual matter, such as the founding of a religious brotherhood, God alone, in His own way and in His own time, is the Master of all plans and of all preparations.

According to his own light, François Charon multiplied his activities. Whatever occurred to him as good to be done he immediately proceeded to accomplish. For the orphans in the hospital he opened a school of arts and crafts, for which he had to pay teachers. To support this venture he began a wholesale brewery business, for which he had to build a huge windmill. All other operations were suspended until the windmill was finished.

Home affairs were not sufficient to engage the energies of this man. To the Royal Court he dispatched a plan for regulating the fur trade on the Mississippi and Niagara rivers. He sent one of his Brothers to take care of the Tamaroa Indians in the West. Then he became seriously concerned about the sick in the mission post of Detroit.

Meanwhile the success of Marguerite Bourgeoys in teaching little girls inflamed him with the idea of teaching little boys. He thought of sending all his poor old men to Quebec in order to devote himself entirely to the training of school teachers. He might indeed have attempted to carry out this notion had he not remembered his plan to form a religious institute.

For a long time he sought a priest who would be willing to undertake the religious formation of Brothers, but no one would assume so grave a responsibility. Then he tried to have his society joined to one already established. He applied without success to the seminary at Quebec, then to the seminary in Montreal, and finally to an institute of teaching Brothers in France. Here was a problem that seemed to have no solution.

In 1700 Jean Fredin, one of his associates, discouraged by the breathless activities of his Superior, went to France, never to return. Many other members had by this time given up their attempts to serve in the General Hospital and had returned to the world.

In August of the following year, François Charon, rashly anticipating royal approval, adopted a religious costume for himself and his remaining co-workers. It was black, made like a clerical soutane, with collar and cuffs of cheap white batiste. Professed Brothers would be distinguished from novices by a cross of white wool worn on the front of the habit. But Pierre Le Ber, the one other remaining associate, refused to wear this new costume, nor would he pronounce any vows, although he continued to live at the hospital until his death in 1707. To the establishment he bequeathed ten thousand pounds.

François Charon had presumed too much. When the news reached France that the Charon Brothers had adopted a religious habit and had made vows, the Secretary of State, on June 30, 1707, wrote peremptorily to the founder:

His Majesty has commanded me to tell you that he absolutely does not wish that those with whom you have made this establishment should pronounce vows, nor that they should have rules, or uniform habits, nor that they should be called Brothers. In a word, he orders that they be disbanded rather than be formed into a monastery or community. I ask you to conform in this matter to the will of His Majesty.

A copy of this plain and unmistakable order was sent to the Governor General and to the Intendant.

Instead of obeying the King's command without further ado, François Charon went to France in the fall of 1707 in the hope of having the orders modified, if not completely revoked. Far from succeeding in his hopes, he seems to have provoked the King to such an extent that the prohibition of the year 1707 was amplified and openly proclaimed in the Market Place.

There was no incentive now for volunteers to give their lives and labors to the General Hospital. Some who were already there lost interest and took up more permanent and more profitable employment elsewhere.

Even while regretting François Charon's independence, one has to admire his courage and perseverance. For ten years he continued to manage the poor hospital. Then, finding it impossible to get recruits in Montreal, he went again to France. While returning in 1719 with six teachers and an annual grant of three thousand pounds from the King for their support, he died on board ship on the ninth of July.

François Charon was succeeded in office by Brother Chrétien Turc. The new Superior, ignoring the royal prohibition entirely, pronounced his vows on October 2, 1722. The community was now composed of eleven members.

Brother Chrétien, strangely, was more fortunate than his predecessor in that he succeeded in having rules approved for the government of the Brothers on October 8, 1723. Bishop Dosquet named Father Nicholas Boucher, granduncle of Marguerite d'Youville, and Father Francois Chèze, from the seminary, to put the institute into canonical form and preside at the elections. Henceforth the association would be known as the Brothers of the Cross and of St. Joseph. Though approved by the Bishop, they still lacked royal sanction.

In order to strengthen the society, to put it somehow on a religious foundation, Brother Chrétien went to France and begged the Superior of the Sulpician Seminary in Paris to train in their novitiate those who would work in the General Hospital in Montreal. This request the Superior was obliged to refuse, since the seminary had neither the grace nor the facilities to form teachers or hospital Brothers.

Now Brother Chrétien proceeded to get into extraordinary trouble. Having stocked the hospital with supplies acquired in France on credit, he borrowed a considerable amount of money without the consent or even the knowledge of the Community.

This money he squandered on reckless and extravagant projects. He even hoped that the Bishop would liberally make good his losses. Pursued by his creditors, he fled to the Spanish Antilles, but was ordered back to Quebec to take the consequences of his mistakes. He was summarily deprived of office, but the poor Brothers of the General Hospital were held responsible not only for his debts in Canada but also for those which he had contracted in France.

As for Brother Chrétien, he returned to the Spanish Antilles after his trial, and there he founded a hospice for the poor; but he was wise enough to leave the administration of its funds to others. After many years of simple service to the poor, he died on May 21, 1755.

Two years after Brother Chrétien's departure from the General Hospital in Montreal, the King, utterly disgusted with the situation, discontinued his annual grant of three thousand pounds for the support of teachers. From this time the decline of the hospital was rapid. Discipline died out in the house. Bishop Dosquet forbade the Brothers to receive new members, because they could neither form them in the religious spirit nor provide for them. He dispensed from their vows several who wished to return to the world.

One old Brother, in a last desperate hope of saving the society from extinction, went to France to persuade the Brothers of the Christian Schools to unite with them. Two of these Brothers were actually sent to Montreal to study the situation, but when they learned that their union with the Brothers of the Cross and of St. Joseph would mean the assumption of an enormous debt, they quickly withdrew.

The next step in the story of the General Hospital was the formal document, already quoted, which was sent to the Secretary of State by the leading citizens of Montreal in 1738. We have noted that to this document there was no response. By this time the Royal Court, tired of instability and incompetence, wanted action, not words.

129

But words continued for a long, long time. On August 15, 1740, the Governor General and the Intendant, ignoring the fact that Bishop Dosquet had definitely forbidden the Charon Brothers to receive new members, wrote as follows to the Secretary of State:

Father Normant is suspected of having discouraged subjects who wanted to consecrate themselves to the service of the poor; and he claims that it would be better to substitute for the Brothers a community of women. We are waiting for the new Bishop, to plan with him some way of keeping the Brothers. It would be a good thing, however, before he leaves France, to keep him from being influenced by those who are interested in suppressing them.

As soon as Bishop Pontbriand arrived in Montreal, he saw for himself the sad state of affairs. He lost no time in telling the Brothers that they could not go on as they were, and he even made known his intention of putting *les Soeurs Grises* in charge.

Later, however, under pressure, he changed his mind. On the advice of the Secretary of State, expressed to the Governor General and the Intendant in 1743, he tried to put the hospital into the hands of the Sisters of the Congregation of Notre Dame. But these Sisters had all they could do to support their schools for girls. Then the Bishop approached the Sisters of Hôtel-Dieu. These, too, were unable to do more than care for the sick.

Thus the chief administrators, still stubbornly resisting Father Normant's proposal to put Madame d'Youville in charge, came to no conclusion at all, and matters stood as they were.

Within two years the Secretary wrote again, urging some arrangement, so that the King could make a decision with regard to the hospital, which was going from bad to worse in every respect.

One of the Brothers, in fact, had given such grave scandal that the Bishop had ordered him out; but the Superior had refused to send him away! A rebellious faction had then defied the Bishop, and he had been obliged to impose two canonical censures before the rebels would submit. With the exception of the Superior, they all resigned their administration of the hospital. This was in October of 1745, while Madame d'Youville and her few associates, in the Fonblanche house, were recovering from the fire that had destroyed their home.

As the crisis approached, Father Normant used every opportunity to draw the attention of the administrators to Madame d'Youville's devotion to the poor in her own society. She had certainly given every example of self-sacrifice and resourcefulness in the face of all kinds of trials and contradictions. Yet politics and personal feeling continued to oppose the will of God.

In November, 1746, the Bishop wrote to the Secretary of State:

We have not yet made any arrangement for the Charon Brothers. The Governor General and the Intendant are always very busy. The Brothers, except the oldest, continually write me that they cannot live, that it is beyond them to take care of the poor, that the house is falling to pieces for lack of repairs. It is absolutely necessary to make some provision for them. I would already have done this by putting Madame d'Youville in charge, with the five persons who are associated with her in Montreal, but I have been waiting all year for orders from you.

It was just at this time that the King named the Marquis de Lajonquière to replace Governor General de Beauharnois, whose personal antagonism to Madame d'Youville had persisted for many years.

On March 31, 1747, the Secretary of State wrote again, this time to Bishop Pontbriand.

In the present state of affairs at the General Hospital, it becomes more urgent every day to make some arrangement that will prevent the complete dissolution of the institute. When the Marquis de Lajonquière arrives in the colony, you must work out the problem with him and the Intendant Hocquart, so that I can get the approval of the King.

When Governor General de Beauharnois learned that his successor was on his way to New France, he showed remarkable expedition for one who had for so long dallied with an urgent matter. Admitting at last the deplorable state of the hospital, and wishing perhaps to have the honor of taking a step to improve it, he conferred seriously with the Bishop and the Intendant. The only hope on the horizon was Father Normant's suggestion to put the ruins into the hands of *les Soeurs Grises*.

"Otherwise," Father Normant had warned them, "the General Hospital must by law revert to the Sulpician Seminary. I remind you that the Charon Brothers, in receiving the land from Father Tronson in 1688, agreed that if someday the work should cease, both land and buildings should be turned over to the seminary, unless the Brothers who remained could reimburse the donors. The value is estimated at two hundred thousand pounds."

The two aged Brothers who survived certainly could not furnish this sum. The contract still stood; and if by law the General Hospital should revert to the seminary, it would immediately be turned over to Madame d'Youville. There was nothing for the administrators to do but to yield to the inevitable.

"Just provisionally," the Governor General reluctantly conceded, "for I must lay this matter before the King."

In a letter addressed to the Royal Court on August 27, 1747, Governor General de Beauharnois explained that he had provisionally named Madame d'Youville directress of the General Hospital so long in question. He added that since the institution had been neglected over a long period of years, and since repairs would have to be made before the place would be habitable, he had authorized her to make whatever repairs the King's procurator and a staff of experts would consider imperative, and to render a strict account of expenses. He concluded by saying that Madame d'Youville and her associates and the poor that she already had with her would be maintained at the hospital, along with the two aged Brothers and the four old men who remained.

On the same day a formal commission was dispatched to

Madame d'Youville, asking her to assume provisional management of the General Hospital until such time as royal approval
would confirm her administration of its affairs.

The decisive hour had come.

"The people must know that we never refuse to serve."
Madame d'Youville had said this many times—so many times,
in fact, that now she simply raised her heart to the Eternal
Father and from His hands immediately accepted the charge.
Yes, she would raise up this house falling into ruins.

CHAPTER TEN

A HOUSE IN RUINS

MADAME D'YOUVILLE lost no time. The speed with which she entered upon her new duties was a startling contrast to the deadly delay that had hung for years about the affairs of the General Hospital.

It was on September 1, 1747, that she received her commission as directress. Although she was still in the first stages of recovery from her serious illness, she immediately conferred with her associates. Not able herself to assume active management of the preparations for taking over the hospital, she put Louise Thaumur in charge.

"First of all, you must see for yourself what is to be done," she advised. "Go tomorrow, you and Catherine Demers, to get a general idea."

"We shall see only ruins," remarked Louise Thaumur. "Even the old men there are ruins."

"Yes, but be sure to comfort them. Tell them that they will be well taken care of. It might be a good thing to take food out to them—clean clothes, too, if you can find some."

Early the next morning the two Sisters set out for the hospital. It was a dismal view indeed that stretched before them after they crossed the St. Pierre River. All the outbuildings were tumbling down, they noticed; and a few acres of arable land, at one time richly productive, lay idle and untended. Weeds grew waist-high where neat flagstones once had marked the pathway to the main entrance. With difficulty they brushed through to the sagging steps.

Brother Joseph Dellerme, who had seen them coming, cautiously pushed open the old, weather-beaten door that hung on one hinge. Behind him, in the dim and musty hallway, peered Brother Jean Jeantôt, nearly eighty years old. Here was the last survivor of the fervent group that had made profession with the founder forty-five years before.

The two old men were a pathetic sight. The black tatters hanging upon their thin bodies had once been fine soutanes—forbidden and unblessed. All the despairing, homeless aged of the world looked out of their faded eyes at the two women who smiled back in sympathy and gentle assurance.

"Have you come to send us away?" asked Brother Joseph in a voice that had forgotten hope.

"Oh no!" answered Louise Thaumur quickly. "We have come to take care of you. You will not have to fear any more."

"We have brought you bread and dried meat and wine," added Catherine Demers, lifting the cover of a large basket that she carried.

But not even the sight of wholesome food could turn their attention from the soul-sustaining words that Louise Thaumur had just spoken. Come to take care of them! No need to fear any more! After years of desolation and dread, of neglect, insecurity, stalking fear, what welcome words were these!

Pitifully the poor old men groped for some response to this message of salvation. But the Sisters by this time had stepped into the room on their left. What a sight met their eyes! Four old men, the last destitute dependents of the Charon Brothers, ragged, unutterably dirty, crouched there in dull despair. One of them slowly turned his head in the direction of the visitors, but there was no other movement. For them life was no longer movement; life was just hopeless waiting for misery to end.

Four wretched cots leaned against the inner wall of this room; from their flat, blackened mattresses damp straw spilled. Plaster, fallen from the ceiling, lay scattered on the floor. On a badly stained square table in the middle of the room a few cups, a bowl, and some broken spoons told of the last meager meal that the poor old men had shared.

The room across the hall apparently belonged to the two Brothers. Less depressing only in that it was less crowded, it also confirmed the ruin of this house that had once been the finest in Montreal.

Only these two rooms, besides the chapel, in which the Blessed Sacrament was no longer reserved, were now in use. The Sisters, increasingly dismayed as they picked their way from floor to floor and from room to room, saw that the rest of the building had long been abandoned to dirt and destruction. Violent storms, pounding Pointe-à-Callières year after year, had broken most of the windowpanes and ripped away large pieces of the fine slate roof. Heavy rains had lashed in through the windows, rotting the frames, warping the floors. Great drifts of snow, piling up inside, winter after winter, had melted through plastered ceilings and down the plastered walls. Rank, smothering vapors of decay hung like a thick fog in the deserted quarters.

Furnishings were moldy and stained. Kitchen and table utensils were rusted and broken, most of them beyond repair. All the linen in the house, whether for personal or domestic use, was in rags.

The general idea, which Madame d'Youville had advised her Sisters to get, could be expressed in one word: ruins.

Yet for the old men the warm sunlight of hope had already pierced the gloom. No matter how ruinous the situation might appear to visitors, those who had long lived in the midst of it could now look forward to relief. And relief shone in their poor old faces as they tremulously wished the blessing of God on the two women who had brought His message.

To Madame d'Youville the condition of the hospital, vividly

detailed by her Sisters, was no surprise. For years she had been a visitor there herself. Many a time had she mended the old men's clothes, mended them until there was nothing left to mend. For a long time she had watched ruin descending upon the hospital as inevitably as night descends upon a bright day. No one knew better than she to what far depths the desolation had fallen. And no one was better prepared to lift it up, to push back the darkness, to let in the light; for God Himself had prepared her.

Events moved forward rapidly now. The next day Louise Thaumur called upon François Foucher, the King's procurator, to arrange for a staff of experts to determine urgent repairs. Then she assembled a corps of women for the vast work of cleaning the old building from attic to cellar. The very next morning they began their task, supervised by two of the Sisters; and for eighteen days, from five o'clock in the morning until the evening Angelus rang out from Notre Dame, these women scrubbed and scoured. This foundation cleaning, which Madame d'Youville considered essential, cost eight hundred and thirty-one pounds.

In the meantime, a fine staff of experts, pompously accompanied by the King's procurator, studied the situation: Nicholas Moran, a carpenter; Jean-Baptiste Le Cavalier, a joiner; René Gassien, a specialist in roofing; Antoine Durousseau, an iron forger; and Michel Neveu, a glazier.

The repairs listed by these experts as essential would have discouraged anyone but Madame d'Youville. The exterior entrance to the chapel, being completely destroyed, would have to be replaced. New steps for the main door were needed, and two hundred feet of flagstones. There would have to be a new floor and new windows for the old men's room, which also had to be plastered throughout. Since all the rooms on the second floor were badly damaged, the walls and ceilings would have to be plastered and all the woodwork replaced. The same repairs were necessary on the third floor, as well as in the attic and basement.

Seventy new large window frames would have to be made, eight smaller ones, and eight interior doors. Fifteen dormer windows needed new roofs. Finally, it would take 1226 windowpanes, seven by eight inches each, to replace all those which had been destroyed.

The financial outlook was likewise appalling. To the heavy debt of thirty-eight thousand pounds under which the hospital had been staggering since Brother Chrétien's unhappy administration, the cost of all these repairs would now be added.

Nor was this all. A survey of the two hospital farms at Chambly and Point St. Charles revealed the sad fact that these possessions had become liabilities through sheer neglect. They were now producing only nine hundred measures of grain annually, of which half was the reward of poor farmers still trying to cultivate the land. In order to increase the output of these farms, the main source of subsistence and revenue for the poor at the hospital, the buildings would have to be repaired, and such farm equipment as was known in those days would have to be bought.

Madame d'Youville, still confined to her room, studied all the aspects of the situation as relayed by her efficient helpers. The annual income of the hospital from all possible sources—pensions, alms, farm profits—had in the early days of the institution been close to 2100 pounds; now it was about 750 pounds, all of it subject to seizure by creditors.

Nevertheless, discouraging as these figures seemed to be, there were now credits to be considered as well as debits.

In the first place, Madame d'Youville was no longer under a moral obligation to provide for her sons. François would be ordained to the priesthood on September 23, and Charles had just been named one of the beneficiaries of a burse established in memory of Bishop Saint-Vallier for the support of seminarians. Now their mother could allocate to the hospital the funds which she had faithfully set aside for them.

Moreover, by the solemn promises which she and her associates had made on February 2, 1745, the little treasury of the society, existing now only for the poor, had been somewhat enriched by the possessions of new members. Just at this time another boarder, Marie Louise du Bralye, aged sixteen, was received for 120 pounds a year.

Finally, the grievous trials to which Madame d'Youville and her poor had been subjected had not only softened the hearts of many prominent people but had opened their purses as well. As soon as relatives and friends learned that the lawful administrators had really commissioned her to direct the hospital, they made generous contributions to her cause.

Yet not even the sum total of these assets was sufficient for all the repairs that had to be made. Madame d'Youville, having been authorized to make them, had to launch out into the deep. Under the circumstances, she felt justified in borrowing ten thousand pounds in order to get the two farms at Chambly and Point St. Charles on a productive basis. In no other way could she establish a steady revenue for her poor. This was a measure that had to be taken at once. Although it was now too late for planting, a great deal of other work could be done in preparation for the spring.

By the nineteenth of September all preliminaries were completed. The inventory of goods belonging to the hospital had been made and registered. Wild, overgrown weeds on the grounds had been mowed down and burned; all debris had been carted away. Already other carts, loaded with lime, stone, wood, slate, glass, were forming a daily caravan from the heart of the city out to the old ruins across the St. Pierre River. Every available workman was pressed into service, so that the building could be made habitable before winter set in again. The Sisters and their poor worked also from dawn to dusk. Never before had old Pointe-à-Callières seen such activity.

It was during these first weeks that Madame d'Youville made one of her wisest decisions: to preserve the customs and traditions that had grown into the General Hospital under the direction of the Charon Brothers. This house had been generously dedicated to works of charity. Because of its heroic purpose and the spirit in which it had been founded, it had become dear to the people of Montreal, so dear that they were willing to let it die out rather than fall into unfriendly or alien hands. Certain devotional practices had developed there, which the people loved and even shared. All these Madame d'Youville decided to retain. She had come to fulfill, not to destroy.

A significant opportunity to show her intention was almost immediately at hand—the feast of the Exaltation of the Holy Cross, celebrated then as now on the fourteenth of September. To the Brothers of the Cross and of St. Joseph this feast was of precious importance. Madame d'Youville, with her usual exquisite tact, directed that it should be celebrated with all its wonted splendor.

In spite of all the work that was then going on, the great day began with High Mass in the old chapel of the hospital and ended with solemn Vespers. From the seminary the Sisters had borrowed linens, vestments, and other necessities. Colorful autumn flowers decked the altar, lovingly placed there by the two old Brothers. To them this feast was indeed the exaltation of their own cross.

Since 1747 the two festivals of the Holy Cross and that of St. Joseph have been celebrated with special honor by the Grey Nuns in abiding memory of the Charon Brothers. In spirit, at least, the original foundation has survived.

One work of the Brothers, however, Madame d'Youville could not at this time retain—the school of arts and crafts for children that François Charon had initiated and maintained at a tragic loss. In the terrible years that had passed, the enterprise had died out, but there were still a few citizens who hoped to see it revived. To settle the matter, Madame d'Youville asked the administrators to dispense her and her Sisters from the education of youth, for none of them was equipped to reorganize the project. It was all they could do to support the works of charity to which they were dedicated.

It was not until many years later that the Grey Nuns opened vocational schools for the Indian children of northwestern Canada. Now they are engaged in every form of education, industrial and professional; and at the present General Hospital in Montreal a complete four-year course in household arts for women fufills the original plan of François Charon.

Six weeks after Madame d'Youville received her commission, repairs at the hospital were sufficiently advanced for her to take possession herself. On October 7, 1747, a strange procession advanced slowly from the Cuisy residence on Notre Dame Place, down St. Francis Xavier Street, through the old Market Place, and across the St. Pierre River to the main entrance of the old hospital. Madame d'Youville, still too weak to make the trip on foot, lay on a thin mattress in a wooden cart drawn by one horse. Beside her walked several of the Sisters, followed by their poor. Another cart carried their oldest charge, paralyzed Marie Morin, aged ninety. The youngest, little Angélique Brindamour, an orphan only six years old, scampered along, thoroughly enjoying herself.

To Madame d'Youville, sensitive as those of keen perception and delicate sympathy invariably are, this journey must have been a burning humiliation. Exposed to the crude curiosity of those who ran along the street to see who lay in the cart, and then to their surprised and raucous laughter, she was comforted only by the remembrance of Him Who had been made to walk a much more painful way.

But devoted Louise Thaumur and Catherine Demers were waiting to receive their mother, who in her weakness was nonetheless their strength. Gently they helped her down from her strange chariot and guided her into the hospital. How pleased she was to see the transformation that had already been effected, and how quick to show her pleasure!

"This is so bright and clean!" she exclaimed when she saw the old men's room completely renovated. Turning to Catherine Rainville, she added, "The old men will be your charge, dear

141

Sister. And you, Sister Bénard, you will take care of the women. You are specially fitted for that work."

"Please then, dear Mother," asked Sister Bénard, "let me be the one to show you their room on the second floor."

Everyone followed close as she carefully led the way to her new charge. It was a large, bright room that they entered, spotlessly clean, simply furnished. Already an air of permanence pervaded it, a comforting atmosphere of security and peace.

"This is exactly what I wanted," Madame d'Youville remarked, smiling in affectionate appreciation at the Sisters who had prepared this pleasant room for the poor. "You have done well!"

"Oh, thank you, Mother!" they chorused happily. "But now you must come to your own room."

On the same floor two small adjoining rooms had been fitted up for Madame d'Youville's use. One, simply equipped with a long, high desk, double cabinet, and a few plain chairs, would serve as an office. Through a square opening in the left wall the black, shining pipe of a small iron stove passed into her bedroom. Here a low wooden bed, its mattress now freshly filled with clean straw and covered with one of Madame d'Youville's own handmade quilts, invited her to the rest that her tiresome journey had earned. A small table nearby held her brass candlestick and sterling silver snuffers, two little treasures that had survived the years. Near the large double window stood a heavy, red-brown desk, its slanting cover closed for the present. To one side, beneath a grey-toned picture of the Holy Family, waited a strong wooden prie-dieu.

In 1921, fifty years after the old General Hospital was abandoned for the more spacious and modern building that now stands in the heart of the city, these rooms were transported to the basement of the new institution, and there, under the sanctuary of the chapel, they were set up again, just as they had been in Madame d'Youville's time.

"Yes," the Sister guide today patiently explains to doubting

142

visitors, "these are the very floors that our venerable foundress walked upon. The walls and ceilings are the same. The windows fastened there now are the ones that she pushed open many, many times. This furniture was hers, all hers except the bed, which is an exact reproduction. This was her own prie-dieu too. Would you like to kneel upon it?"

Kneeling reverently in the very place where Madame d'Youville herself had talked with the Eternal Father, one feels unmistakably the influence of her abiding spirit. One remembers, too, the burdens that she carried there two hundred years ago.

From the first days of Madame d'Youville's administration, extraordinary success attended the affairs of the General Hospital. Once order was assured, the spirit of prayer and of work began to permeate the house. In peace and charity, in watchfulness and strict economy, the Sisters proceeded to heal the wounds of the past and to build up a new and wholesome life for the years to come.

There were many visitors to old Pointe-à-Callières in these early days. Montreal citizens, reluctant to believe that Madame d'Youville, frail and buffeted, could really bring order out of chaos, came to see with their own eyes what she was doing.

Before many months had passed, several wealthy, independent women, impressed by the cleanliness and peace of the hospital, requested the privilege of living there as boarders. Not less were they attracted by the happy example of Thérèse Despins and by the unfailing charm and courtesy of the foundress herself. Madame d'Youville, too wise to reject a steady means of income, received them gladly. Rooms on the second floor were prepared for them.

Now Montreal saw another strange sight. Several fine carriages, followed by cartloads of magnificent furnishings, moved sedately through the streets of the city out to the General Hospital. Surprise conquered curiosity as spectators silently watched well-to-do but solitary ladies establish residence there in peace, security, and comfort. This was a development totally unexpected, a development maintained to this day.

It was also in 1748 that women of another type were received at the hospital, women described then and now as fallen.

For three years Father Antoine Déat, pastor at Notre Dame, had been trying in vain to persuade the government to provide a shelter for women who, mainly for economic reasons, were living sinful lives and consequently multiplying social problems for the whole community. There was little use in lecturing to these women; they had to have security and some practical incentive to virtue.

Father Déat, recognizing in Madame d'Youville a strong woman with an understanding heart, sought and received authorization from the Intendant Hocquart to ask her to make a place for them. From parish funds he would pay the costs. Instantly she agreed to accept this new responsibility; these fallen women also were children of God and should be led back to Him.

On the third floor of the hospital she fitted up twelve private rooms, each with a large dormer window. This new department, called Jericho, from the name of an earlier but unsuccessful establishment of the same kind, had no connection with the rest of the house, except in Madame d'Youville's maternal heart.

This latest project presented a very difficult problem. To lead young and attractive public sinners out of their evil ways and into a good life, and at the same time to make them glad to undergo the change, was an extremely delicate undertaking. They were not by any means delighted with the prospect of being isolated at Pointe-à-Callières, completely separated from their evil haunts and former associates.

But Madame d'Youville understood God's love for the Mystical Body of Christ. His Son, of Whom these women were weak and erring members. Looking beyond the frailty of the flesh to the immortality of the spirit, she made herself a channel of His love for them. Patient and kind in making known to them the regulations essential to their reform, but firm in exacting obedience to these regulations, she succeeded in teaching the inmates of

Jericho to love and fear her as children love and fear a good mother.

Like a good mother, too, she was practical in her dealings with them. For example, believing that through vanity they might again fall, she made them cut their hair short—a measure not unknown under similar circumstances today.

Occasionally, but less frequently as time went on, the women of Jericho resisted confinement; but the foundress never faltered in her discipline; and finally she had the joy of seeing four of them completely repentant. All became contented in their seclusion, even rendering valuable service to the institution; for Madame d'Youville believed in the efficacy of what modern social workers call occupational therapy, even for moral ills. Only charity, however, could have created an atmosphere as peaceful for these outcasts as for the wealthy ladies comfortably residing on the second floor.

Madame Elizabeth Bégon, whose delightful letters picture in Pepysian vein some aspects of early French Canadian social life, wrote to her son-in-law, the lord of Villebois, on January 8, 1749:

Today we saw Madame Bouat, who, as I told you, has been at the Charon Hospital with Madame d'Youville since St. Martin's Day. It it funny to see her: she does nothing but preach and talk about the joy of living retired from the world. She assured us of the conversion of four of the women who were taken to the Jericho. She visits them from time to time. All Madame Bouat fears is that the soldiers may want to get these women out of captivity, but I do not believe that for that purpose they would want to do anything out of order.

Madame Bégon was quite mistaken. One evening a soldier, intoxicated and angered beyond control because the unhappy object of his passion was being kept in seclusion, kicked his way into the hospital and demanded his mistress, threatening to shoot Madame d'Youville if she refused to give her up. The Sister portress, terrified by his appearance and especially by the pistol that he waved in her face, fled to warn the foundress of her danger. But Madame d'Youville, having heard the uproar, suddenly appeared in the doorway, calm, majestic, utterly fearless.

"Leave this house at once!" she commanded.

The poor fellow needed only one glance into her steady eyes, one quick intuition of her spiritual strength. Instantly crest-fallen, he turned and stumbled out into the night.

But other libertines of Montreal, less open in their attempts to do away with Jericho, and therefore more to be feared, soon had on their side an ally of prime importance, the new Intendant, François Bigot, who arrived on August 28, 1748.

This Intendant, whom historians generally agree in qualifying as the most unscrupulous official who ever dishonored the administration of New France, had but one consuming interest—to live in luxurious pleasure at all costs. He proceeded at once to develop that interest.

There was no method of cheating with which he was not familiar, no dishonorable practice unknown to him. He altered official accounts in his own favor; he charged the royal treasury for supplies which he kept for himself, or sold at a profit, instead of sending them to their destination; he forced the farmers to sell their grain to him on his own terms and then in their need to buy it back from the King's storehouse at exorbitant rates.

The intendancy, which should have been the center of justice, became the breeding place of outrageous perfidy. Revelry reigned in the Intendant's residential palace, degenerating into debauchery at Beaumanoir, his country home, built for the glamorous Angélique des Meloises, wife of Mayor Péan, of the city of Quebec.

Endowed, however, with sufficient political cleverness to keep himself in office in spite of these excesses, Bigot soon drew into his orbit those who could profit by his patronage and at the same time serve his purposes.

Among these followers were the licentious pleasure seekers of

Montreal who thought Madame d'Youville altogether too zealous in her works of charity. With regard to Jericho, for example, did not the new Intendant think that she was too severe in cutting the hair of the women there, restricting their liberty in such a cruel—but effective—way? Would he not look into the matter?

François Bigot perfectly understood their complaints, and he thoroughly agreed with them. Moreover, this was a situation that he knew how to handle quite satisfactorily. Therefore, on August 17, 1750, he wrote an ominous letter to Madame d'Youville.

I have been informed that Jericho is beginning to cause abuses which might be of considerable consequence in the future if I do not establish order there.

And what has most surprised me is that you have taken it on yourself to cut the hair of the women who have been sent there, even of one among them who was confined by surprise. If I had not as much consideration for you as I have, I would have you prosecuted for having acted so indiscreetly. I am glad to teach you, if you do not know it, that it is the business of a superior court to impose such a shameful penalty.

To prevent similar abuses, I expressly forbid you to take any girl or woman at this Jericho except by my order, which I shall send you in writing when I consider it expedient to confine any of them; and maintenance will be furnished at the King's expense. I trust that you will not fall again into the fault that you have committed; otherwise I shall effectively remedy the situation. . . .

I think, madame, that I have written enough on this matter, and I hope that no other complaint about this establishment will be brought to me in the future.

The tone of this letter, charged with antagonism, was undoubtedly the keynote of François Bigot's attitude toward Madame d'Youville and the whole General Hospital. Evidently he had something more on his mind than her so-called fault in cutting the hair of a few fallen women.

147

It is true that he had made a formal, even courtly, visit to the hospital shortly after his arrival in Canada, but his expression of satisfaction in the improvement being made there was plainly lukewarm. In a man of his type, hard, grasping, profligate, there could be no deep feeling for the poor, much less an understanding of the divine urge to assist them. It was not what Madame d'Youville had raised up out of ruins that interested him; it was what he could get out of it. Now, on a pretext to which he gave far more emphasis than was necessary, Bigot showed his hand. It remained to be seen how he would play it.

Unfortunately it was Bishop Pontbriand who in good faith gave the wily Intendant an opportunity for further action.

It will be remembered that Madame d'Youville's commission to direct the General Hospital was only temporary, pending the approval of the King. The Secretary of State had ratified the provisional nomination in a letter dated February 12, 1748, but he had added:

Whatever may be the success of this arrangement, I must warn you that His Majesty is in no way disposed to consent to anything that might lead to the formation of a new community of women in the colony. There are already too many of them.

Nevertheless, as the condition of the hospital continued to improve under Madame d'Youville's capable management, the administrators were more inclined to believe that they had done the right thing in putting the institution under her care. Bishop Pontbriand, in a letter of September 8 to the Abbé de l'Isle-Dieu, Vicar General of the colonies, wrote, in reference to the foundress, "She is a person of extraordinary merit, and I think that the hospital will be very well off in her hands. As earnestly as possible I recommend this good work to you."

The Abbé de l'Isle-Dieu, in making his report to the Secretary of State on February 22 of the following year, developed at length the high praise that Bishop Pontbriand had expressed. He stressed the Bishop's opinion that the hospital should remain in her hands, not only because of her piety, zeal, capability, and intelligence, but also for a more eloquent reason—her proposal to liquidate the enormous debt left to the institution by the Charon Brothers.

The Vicar General explained that Madame d'Youville in her letters to him had said that if the Royal Court would grant letters patent to the small community of pious women that she had formed for the service of the poor and the care of the sick, she would raise eight thousand pounds to discharge the debts of the hospital.

It is evident that Madame d'Youville had lost no time in trying to secure for her association the protection of letters patent. As early as October in 1747, she had communicated with the Abbé de l'Isle-Dieu. She had even presented to him the argument that a new community would not be formed in the case of *les Soeurs Grises,* since they were only replacing one that had been suppressed.

But no argument whatever could break down the King's opposition to the establishment of a new community of women. Already he was supporting two of them, one at Quebec and the other at Three Rivers, which the late Bishop Saint-Vallier, in his zeal, had founded without sufficient security. Now the royal treasury was nearly empty, and France was on the verge of another war with England. Instead of increasing the number of communities, it was necessary to reduce them.

To this end, the Secretary of State, in a letter to Bishop Pontbriand on the first of March, suggested the union of the General Hospital of Quebec with Hôtel-Dieu of that city, and also the union of Madame d'Youville's General Hospital with Hôtel-Dieu of Montreal.

Bishop Pontbriand could not bring himself to agree to this plan. The Hôtel-Dieu was solidly established in both cities and should not be disturbed. The General Hospital of Quebec was especially dear to his heart, and, besides, it was very poor. The good Bishop thought that the General Hospital of Montreal, being of latest and least secure foundation, should be sacrificed to the good of all; and he suggested the union of this hospital with that of Quebec.

Governor General Lajonquière, not familiar with the whole situation, readily agreed to the proposal. The Intendant Bigot was delighted. The end of the Montreal establishment would mean the end of Jericho. For political reasons he had already shown such marked preference for the General Hospital at Quebec that other communities were offended, a result that nourished his perversity. He did not fail to consider that funds derived from the sale of the property and possessions of the Montreal Hospital would relieve the poverty of the Quebec house, and perhaps he might be able to claim a share for himself.

Therefore, in a letter of October 1, 1749, to the Secretary of State, the Governor General and the Intendant Bigot suggested the union of the two institutions.

Replying on June 14 of the following year—communications were slow in those days—the Secretary approved the proposal on the condition that a small refuge for the poor would be left in Montreal, in charge of two religious from the General Hospital of Quebec. Unfortunately he supplemented this condition with another, "if the General Hospital of Quebec is not large enough for all the needy of the colony."

Preferring to consider the Quebec Hospital large enough, the chief administrators felt themselves justified in suppressing the Montreal house entirely, without leaving even a small refuge in case of need.

In a private conference on October 15, 1750, they carefully drew up an ordinance abolishing the provisional contract made with Madame d'Youville in 1747. This act also transferred the ownership of all property, movable and immovable, from the General Hospital of Montreal to that of Quebec, and authorized the religious of the Quebec house to negotiate the sale of all the buildings belonging to the Montreal Hospital, even furnishings of too little value to be moved. All the dependent poor of

Montreal would be transported to Quebec, whether they liked it or not.

To this devastating document a quiet codicil was added: if any particular persons had remarks to make about this sale, they should present themselves to the Intendant within three months. In other words, the administrators decreed the sale of the General Hospital and then permitted protests against it. Some months later, the Abbé de l'Isle-Dieu, commenting on this illogical procedure, remarked ironically, "In your country they hang a man first, and then they try him."

In order to render even retroactive protests completely ineffective, the crafty Bigot planned to withhold the public proclamation of the ordinance until the last boat of the fall season had left for France. Particular persons of Montreal could now protest all they liked; their words could not reach the King in time to prevent the sale of the hospital. The negotiations once concluded, the Royal Court was not likely to take the trouble to cancel them. Did Bigot forget, or did he ever know, that time and tide wait for no man? Did he think that his duplicity could always succeed?

In the meantime, Madame d'Youville devoted all her energies to the restoration and development of the hospital, totally unaware of the secret transactions vitally affecting her work.

Brother Joseph Dellerme had claimed some of her attention during the first weeks of her administration. Having received a consoling invitation from his relatives in France to spend the rest of his life with them, he made his plans to leave the General Hospital. Since he had generously given the best years of his life to the care of the poor, Madame d'Youville considered it only just to provide him with a pension for the years that were left. Therefore she granted him an annuity of three hundred pounds, which he received until his death on March 19, 1772.

Seeking first of all the spiritual well-being of the hospital, Madame d'Youville sought from Pope Benedict XIV permission to establish there a branch of the Confraternity of the Sacred

Heart. Within a few months she received a bull dated May 5, 1749. Father Normant and Father Déat were the first to sign the register as members.

Three years from the date of Madame d'Youville's accession as directress, a remarkable transformation had taken place in the General Hospital. Order and the spirit of prayer had again done their work. The repairs had been completed. The constant industry of the Sisters had sufficed to provide the necessities of life for the poor, now thirty in number. With contributions made by friends from time to time, other current expenses had been met; and even the two farms were beginning to show a profitable return. The Sulpician Fathers, always their faithful friends, had taken up special collections for the hospital in Montreal and surrounding towns, with such success that debts had been somewhat reduced.

Thus, by the grace of God and with the devoted help of the Sisters, Madame d'Youville now had all the affairs of the hospital well under control. Once more the future looked bright.

It was at this time, on November 16, 1750, that Madame Silvain, Marguerite d'Youville's mother, took up her residence at the hospital as a paying boarder. Her eldest son, Father Charles Lajemmerais, had died at Verchères a few months before. After many years of hardship, humiliation, and grief, how consoling it must have been for this mother to spend her last years in the company of a daughter whose very presence had always spelled peace and security! She remained at the hospital until 1758, but died at Varennes on October 24 of that year, at the age of seventy-six.

Madame d'Youville, in order to keep strict supervision over the food expenses of the house, had made herself personally responsible for the purchase of supplies. Still too poor to lay up large quantities in advance, she would go to the Market Place two or three times a week, accompanied by several of her poor. From store to store, from stall to stall, she would carefully stretch her resources to meet the needs of the hospital.

152

Early in the morning of November 23, 1750, she set out as usual with her big market basket. It was a cold day, and a sharp wind was whistling down from old Mount Royal.

Madame d'Youville led the way briskly across the bridge and through the port gate of the city wall. Just then the wind brought to their ears the ruffle of drums in the Market Place.

"That means the public proclamation of an ordinance," she observed. "We shall hear it."

In a few moments they were among the groups that had assembled to hear the crier's message. One never knew what law would be next decreed. Another ruffle of drums; again the official voice rang out, "Hear ye! Hear ye!"

Silence settled over the people. Even the wind was listening. Solemnly the crier announced the usual formal beginning. This was a proclamation of the chief administrators of the hospitals of Canada.

Then suddenly in the cold stillness the startled foundress heard her own name. Stunned, almost deafened by the violent beating of her own heart, she caught the awful words as wave after wave of shock broke against her consciousness.

". . . Madame d'Youville . . . provisionally charged . . . General Hospital of Montreal . . . orders of the King . . . no longer holds . . . All property . . . to General Hospital of Quebec . . ."

On and on the words crashed into the air, beating like blows on her whole being.

But at last the long proclamation came to an end. By this time Madame d'Youville had regained her outward composure, although undoubtedly her inner peace must have struggled a little longer with the colossal injustice that had just been perpetrated. To think that they made this matter known to all Montreal without first telling her! There surely had been time for the administrators to warn her, since the act had been drawn up on the fifteenth of October.

Then her kind heart, accustomed to consideration for others, was glad that now she could gently let her Sisters know before the unexpected official announcement reached them.

If Madame d'Youville could be serene, could make no comment whatever to her companions, could, indeed, smile quietly into the eyes of the Eternal Father Who had providentially permitted this shocking event, the people who had also just listened to the proclamation were by no means so controlled. Murmurs of indignation grew rapidly into loud recriminations against the administrators. Even as she hurried away from this scene of her public humiliation, she could hear angry protests and excited threats.

Only the maternal heart of this valiant, unselfish woman knew how to soften the blow for her Sisters and all their charges. How she longed to bear for each one of them the grief that this cross must bring! Yet she did know how to strengthen them, and they all understood her way, the glad, strong way of a Christian.

"It is the will of God," she told them quietly. "Blessed be His will! Our Eternal Father has us all in His keeping. If He wishes this house to endure, it will endure. Let us now prepare to render our accounts."

When the bailiff came to present the ordinance, Madame d'Youville received him with quiet courtesy. Already she knew what she would do. She and her companions listened in silence to the solemn orders that meant the destruction of the hospital.

"The administrators have agreed that since the season is now so far advanced, you may remain here until next July," the bailiff remarked in conclusion. "You will have plenty of time to settle your affairs and to make an inventory of all the property with which you are charged."

"Thank you, sir," Madame d'Youville answered simply.

CHAPTER ELEVEN

THE TRIUMPH OF TRUTH

A S MIGHT be expected, it was Father Normant who directed the formal protests that now began to assail all those responsible for the arbitrary proclamation of November 23. Informing Bishop Pontbriand of the course of events since that unhappy day, the Vicar General wrote:

The ordinance has created great disorder here, not only because of the beating of drums which announced it, but still more by the criticism, slander, and calumny that it has caused. Everyone has been so shocked by it that without restraint and against the rules of charity they have expressed bitter resentment against Your Excellency and Monsieur Bigot, who they presume are responsible for it, not, however, blaming the Governor General for a measure which they believe to be contrary to his sentiments. I have been and I am deeply grieved to see disorders so unworthy, God so offended, and the confidence and respect so diminished which the faithful owe to Your Excellency. It is, in my opinion, a very poor way of defending a good cause.

Father Normant then proceeded to explain objectively the reasons why the people of Montreal were reacting so violently to the recent decree. They believed that it arose out of political preference for the General Hospital of Quebec; that it was depriving the poor in Montreal of their legitimate rights in favor of strangers and contrary to the expressed intentions of the founders; that the ordinance was null and void, since it had been drawn up without the knowledge and consent of all the parties concerned, and proclaimed after all opportunities for protest to the King had passed; that, contrary to law, the Intendant Bigot had made himself both magistrate and contracting party.

However reasonable these objections were, they could have no effect unless they were presented in conventional form to the proper authorities. Father Normant therefore prepared a formal supplication, addressed to the Secretary of State and sent in copy to the chief administrators. It read:

The Governor, the King's lieutenant, the commander, officers, clergy, lords, magistrates, businessmen, townsmen, and habitants of the city and government of Montreal have the honor to represent to you the numberless advantages which the General Hospital, established here by legitimate authority and invested with all requisite formalities, is procuring for this community, and the imperative need of maintaining it.

In the letters patent which His Majesty granted in 1692 for the foundation of the General Hospital in Quebec, he recognized the fact, as in Article 28, that the said hospital would not be sufficient for the needs of the colony. He foresaw that the number of indigent would increase as the colony grew. His Majesty realized also that because of the distant location, the poor who lived far away could not be taken there nor be helped by it; wherefore he considered it necessary to establish a second hospital in this city.

This was easy to do because charitable persons offered to found it. The letters patent contained the explicit statement that *the establishment should be perpetual, without being changed either in location or for any other good work . . . for the relief and care of the poor of this city. . . .*

Divine Providence inspired a number of charitable persons to donate a part of their wealth to establish the hospital for the needy of this community. The intention of the founders was to provide for the poor of this area, and not to send their money elsewhere, which they would never have given if they had thought that their intention would not be fulfilled. . . .

One can neither add nor take away anything from legitimate authority expressed in positive terms. To do so would be to reject the King's word; to render the letters patent null and void; to act contrary to the will and intention of the founders and benefactors; to close one's eyes to the most urgent need of a great many poor people in this community; to be exposed to the mortal shame of seeing an endless number of needy of both sexes and of every age dying of want, for the relief of whom many charitable persons have provided by contributing freely to the support of the General Hospital. . . .

No one can deny the usefulness and even the necessity of the institution for retired soldiers and sick and aged men, as well as for orphans and abandoned children. It is a refuge for fallen women and for the mentally ill. In epidemics it is a very useful asylum for convalescents and incurables; and there is even a ward for the treatment of social diseases, the results of licentiousness in the city. . . .

It is true that there are many debts to be discharged and further repairs to be made, but we trust in Divine Providence, and we expect a great deal from the charity of good souls. We can hope that in the course of time the affairs of the hospital will be settled by the wisdom and capability of those women who are now in charge and who still offer their industry and devotion if they may be considered worthy to continue to care for the poor. . . .

It is impossible now because of the distance between the two cities and because of the feebleness of so many of the poor, to transport them to the Quebec Hospital, already too small for its own people.

The undersigned suppliants know too well the goodness of your hearts and your solicitude for the poor to believe that you will be unmoved by their unhappy state, or that you will deprive them of the relief which the charity of good citizens has procured for them in the establishment of the General Hospital, founded only for that intention and on the assurance of the King that it would be perpetual.

Concluding, the suppliants asked that Madame d'Youville and her companions would be granted the legal administration of the hospital and all the rights and privileges of the letters patent of 1694.

This remarkably straightforward supplication, a striking contrast to the petition of 1738, was signed first by Governor de Longueuil of Montreal, successor to Governor de Beaucours, and then by seventy-six prominent citizens. Among them were many who had put their names to the earlier document repudiating *les Soeurs Grises*. Integrity had conquered.

With the help of Father Normant, Madame d'Youville and her companions also prepared a petition to the administrators, similar in substance but more deeply personal in expression. Beginning with a reminder of the Superior Council's promise to have their provisional commission ratified by the King, they declared that having dedicated themselves to the work, they had made every possible effort to restore the house which they had found in ruins. Diminished in no way was their zeal for the care of the poor, whose servants it was their glory to be. Indeed, more ardent than ever was their eagerness to consecrate their time, their work, and their lives to the support of the institution!

The conclusion of Madame d'Youville's appeal is a masterpiece of supernatural faith and sound prudence. She wrote:

If your knowledge of the debts which overburden the house and of the repairs which must be made is causing you to fear that it cannot be supported without extraordinary help from the Court, which cannot afford it, then the suppliants have the honor to tell you that their confidence is entirely in Divine Providence; that they will always receive with utmost gratitude the favors and benefits which the Court may be pleased to grant, but that they will never importune it for anything at all; that they pledge themselves within three years to liquidate the debts of Brother Chrétien in France, to come to terms with his creditors, and to pay as soon as possible the debts that he contracted in Canada.

To which end they ask to replace the Charon Brothers, to enjoy all the rights, favors, and privileges expressed in their letters patent . . . in consequence of which they promise to render an annual account of the revenue of the hospital and of the alms which may be given to the poor; and if in the future His Majesty may for unforeseen reasons consider it expedient to withdraw the administration of the hospital from the suppliants, he will be held accountable to them for the improvements, repairs, and all reimbursements which they will have made from their funds, so that they may be repaid in place of the creditors whom they will have satisfied.

Early in January of 1751 Madame d'Youville personally carried to Quebec her own petition and that of the citizens of Montreal. The trip would have been a hardship at any time, but in the depth of a Canadian winter it was a positive danger. Yet no danger was too great for this apostle to the poor.

What was her humiliation and disappointment to find herself coldly received by Bishop Pontbriand! From him at least she had hoped for aid. Unwilling to commit himself to a definite stand in the matter, he refused even to accept the petitions.

"This is a civil matter," he protested. "I am concerned about the formation of a religious community."

The Intendant Bigot also rejected quite bluntly the supplications that Madame d'Youville presented to him. Why should he waste his time on these, he thought to himself, handing them back to the humble woman before him. By the time they reached France his plans would have been fulfilled, and the King would hardly take the trouble to undo what had already been done.

From Governor General Lajonquière Madame d'Youville received a gentleman's courteous attention to her mission. Only then did it occur to him that he, the highest official of New France, had permitted action in a serious matter without a study of facts. Slowly it dawned on him that a wrong had been done. Be it to his credit that he promised mediation.

It was not until October 19, however, after a great deal of muddy water had passed under the bridge, that he wrote to the Secretary of State:

Although I had the honor of writing to you conjointly with the Bishop and the Intendant regarding the union of the General Hospital of Montreal with that of Quebec, I cannot, nevertheless, dispense myself from forwarding to you the representations made by all classes of Montreal to the Bishop, to Monsieur Bigot, and to me on the imperative necessity of allowing this hospital to remain. . . . Monsieur Bigot persists in his original opinion, to which I had subscribed without first having foreseen the harm that this union would bring to the poor of Montreal.

In the meantime, Bigot had done more than reject Madame d'Youville's petitions; he had also refused to approve her accounts. With one pretext after another he delayed his examination until she was obliged to return to Montreal. Then, between her and the unscrupulous Intendant there followed an interchange of revealing letters: simple, courteous, clearly unequivocal on Madame d'Youville's side; specious, distorted, crudely false on Bigot's.

On February 5 the Intendant wrote:

I have examined the accounts that you sent me of the receipts and expenditures for the years 1749 and 1750 and that of 1748, which you had previously forwarded, by which it appears that the expenses exceed the receipts by more than 10,486 pounds. I have remarked that the receipts of the house, not counting revenue from the farms, almost balance the expenditures for food and maintenance for the poor, but that the upkeep of the farms at Point St. Charles and Chambly have cost twice their income, a fact which greatly surprises me.

Let me remind you, madame, that the ordinance of 1747 appointed you directress of this hospital only, to care for the needy sheltered there, and of the grounds belonging to it; and that it authorized you to receive the income of the said property, to be used for the food and maintenance of the poor and for the essential repairs to the house; but it did not permit you to make any expenditures whatsoever beyond this income.

When you noticed, madame, that this income could not suffice for the subsistence of the number of poor persons whom you had received, and that the farms were causing more expense than the profits warranted, you should have informed the administrators, asking them to settle this deficit for which you were responsible, either by diminishing the number of poor or by allowing you to sell some property in order to provide for them. Since you have not taken these precautions, and since I cannot dispose of the property of the hospital except for debts authorized and approved by the directors, I cannot be responsible for the debts that you claim; and the General Hospital of Quebec, for the same reason, will not be bound to discharge them.

Moreover, according to the rules of the hospital, not more than twelve poor persons may be received there, except in proportion to an increase in revenue. When you took over, there were only fourteen or fifteen, of whom several were on half pay. Women until then had not been admitted; and you should not have increased the number of men, much less have admitted fifteen or sixteen women for whom you opened a new department without having been formally authorized to do so. . . .

You asked me to tell the religious of the General Hospital of Quebec to have the fields planted at Point St. Charles and Chambly. This hospital will not take possession of these farms until next July. It seems just to me that you should have them planted in the spring; and I know your zeal and charity too well to think that you will refuse your attention to this matter, particularly since the seeds are ready, according to your report, and there would be no further expenditure for them.

Besides, let me observe, when you took possession of the hospital, you enjoyed the year's harvest, which had been planted by the Charon Brothers, and since you will depart at almost the same time of the year at which you came, it is fitting that you should leave the farms, with regard to cultivation, in the same state in which you received them.

I expect you also, madame, and I emphatically request you, to hire another farmer for Point St. Charles, if the one who is there does not wish to remain.

Brother Joseph Dellerme, the only survivor of the Charon Brothers, being supported by the Community, is entitled to a pension of five hundred pounds, reduced to three hundred by his own consent, if he should leave. You paid him for the first year, which ended in September of 1749. You ought to begin to attend to this pension in preference to the food and maintenance of the poor. Since his support is assured by the original endowment of the hospital, I ask you to have him paid for the year ending last September.

To this letter, breathing officious antagonism in every line, Madame d'Youville made careful and courteous reply on February 16:

I have received the letter with which you have just honored me. It surprises me very much because it seems to be entirely contrary both to the ordinance which provisionally appointed me directress of this hospital and to what you told me yourself when I represented to you the wretched state of the institution, whose property, building, and barns were in ruins demanding immense and immediate repairs.

Remember, I beg of you, sir, that you have always told me to keep everything in order and to repair what needed repairs. The Bishop and the Governor General have given me the same order. It is therefore with your consent and with theirs that I have labored for the welfare of the poor. It is true that I have not had your orders in writing; but your word is just as good. I trust it because of the respect that I owe you and because of the knowledge that I have of your integrity. I have acted accordingly. It seems to me that I am in the right, and that you cannot, before God or man, forbid me to claim the said expenses, or refuse to reimburse me for the amount that I have spent. I have borrowed this money and I owe it.

Moreover, sir, I had the honor to render my accounts at the end of the first year of my administration. At that time the expenses exceeded the receipts by more than 3377 pounds. You did not seem to disapprove of this fact nor to be dissatisfied in the least. If I went beyond my powers and acted contrary to your wish and the good of the poor, it was easy to tell me so and to forbid me to continue to make repairs. But, on the contrary, sir, you urged me to continue them because of course you knew the need of them. It is therefore not at all of myself that I have acted, sir; it is under your eyes, with your knowledge, and with your approval.

I say more, sir: it is even by your order, for in naming me directress of the hospital, you told me to keep a register of receipts and expenditures so that I could render my accounts, and by the same order you told me to make the repairs considered most urgent by a staff of experts in the presence of the King's procurator. That has been done . . . in conformity with your orders. You cannot then in conscience refuse me payment for them. . . .

When it was necessary to restore the ruined farms and to buy the essential equipment, plows, plowshares, carts, harness, and everything needed for the cultivation of the land, fencing, piping, saddlecloth, lumber, and a thousand other indispensable things, the cost had to be considerable. If I had let the old houses and barns fall down and had given up the cultivation of the land, you would have blamed me. I have acted for the best, sir, without any particular interest except the welfare of the poor; and if I have not the consolation of having pleased you, it is not through bad will but through lack of ability.

You seem to blame me, sir, for having received more poor than the foundation warranted and fixed at twelve. I never knew that the number of poor was limited to twelve, and I do not think that there is any rule which says so; but even if there were, I should not be more culpable, because I have been fully authorized to open a department for women and to receive, house, and provide for those of whom I already had charge. You have had the kindness to visit them. You seemed satisfied with this good work and you approved of it.

You have also learned, sir, through your scrutiny of my accounts, as you did me the honor to remark, that the excess in expenditures has not been due to food and maintenance for the poor. You notice that the receipts of the house, not counting income from the farms, almost balance the expenses. The excess has been incurred precisely and only for the restoration and upkeep of the farms, which by this means have become better or at least restored to their original value, and without which they would have fallen into ruins both unproductive and unprofitable. It seems just, sir, that these farms should in themselves be sufficient security for expenditures made for their improvement and preservation. You are too equitable not to recognize an argument so apt.

You have done me the honor to remark, sir, that there were fourteen or fifteen poor at the hospital when I took over, of whom several were on half-pay. I can assure you, sir, that there were only four, of whom one had half-pay. It was all they could do to live; and since I have been there, the number has passed thirty, and they have all the necessities of life, not through the income from the farms, but through the care of Divine Providence, and our industry.

163

When I came here, I did not find the fields planted nor a single furrow of land cultivated. It is I who had them prepared and planted. Therefore, sir, I am obliged only to leave things as I found them. The farmer, moreover, now wishes to leave, and I have no one to replace him; and were I to find someone, I do not consider myself sufficiently authorized to hire him.

I trust, sir, that in your goodness you will accept my accounts and sign them. They are rendered with all the equity of which I am capable.

In the meantime Madame d'Youville received from Bishop Pontbriand another sharp confirmation of his unwillingness to face the issues involved. Thus wrote His Excellency:

Madame, I had the honor to tell you that I would not concern myself with the accounts that you submitted, and that I left to other authorities the responsibility of examining them.

I doubt that by the regulations made in Monsieur Hocquart's time you were authorized to make repairs without orders, much less to make loans. Never has anyone claimed that you could put the institution into debt. Transfer of property is absolutely forbidden.

You have received many poor persons; your charity is commendable; but I am afraid one can only say that you really were not obliged to it.

You received the farms already planted; I doubt if anyone would approve your surrendering them in any other condition.

I think that the whole affair will be brought to the notice of His Majesty, who ordered the union of the General Hospital to that of Quebec. I wish he could see the difficulties that it has created!

Evidently His Excellency had already adopted the views of the Intendant, views that not even Madame d'Youville's straightforward representation could alter in the least. Too arrogant to revise his opinions or to acknowledge an error in judgment, the self-important Bigot responded to her letter with no more than a repetition of his charges.

Again she wrote, emphasizing her position. "I have always acted, sir," she insisted, "with all the integrity and uprightness possible, without any political consideration or interest, of which fault I know that some have wrongfully accused me."

Farther on in this letter Madame d'Youville cleverly observed:

I have just read, sir, in your recent ordinance, that you are permitting the sale of the building, grounds, and gardens of this hospital; and in the letter which I received from you a few days ago you stated formally that you have not the right to dispose of the property of the hospital. I can hardly reconcile the one with the other; and I think that it is only a pretext which you wish to use in order to delay reimbursement for the debts which I have contracted; the buildings and gardens are not less property than the lands on which they depend. That is what makes me hope that you will have the goodness to procure for me the means of paying my debts.

Wise as a serpent and simple as a dove! The wily Bigot must have known chagrin as the disarming candor of this charming and thoroughly competent woman continued to oppose his guile. It was not in his nature to meet her on her own ground. He would ignore her representations; he would temporize. The spring dispatches from France would soon bring the King's approval of his plans, and then this widow d'Youville would have nothing more to say. As for her debts, the Intendant shrugged. He had his suspicion about those, a suspicion based on his own shady practices.

Therefore, to make matters worse, the Bishop wrote again to Madame d'Youville on March 16, in the blurred tone habitual to him.

It seems to me that I told you last fall that someone might perhaps question what you claim is due to you and might even object to the great number of your associates and of the poor that you have with you.

You have cited the decree which made you directress in the year 1747, but it seems to me from my reading of it that there is question of repairs only for the house that you are actually occupying. However that may be, I think that some are convinced that you have not really borrowed the money, and that these expenditures have been made with alms given to you. If you produced evidence of these loans which you have contracted as directress, perhaps they would create less difficulty. I say perhaps because I am not mixed up in this business. But I have been obliged for different reasons to consent to a decreed union.

Madame d'Youville could have borne in silence an insult only personal in nature; she had done so many times in the past. Here was an insult, however, that struck at the very heart of equity. Tempering her pen in the white-hot flame of truth, she answered His Excellency.

I am sincere, upright, and incapable of any subterfuge or reservation which could disguise the truth or give a double meaning. I have really borrowed 9550 pounds for the benefit and restoration of the farms of this hospital. I owe this money and there remains to me no other way of paying it back except through the reimbursement which I am awaiting from Your Excellency and the other administrators. What I have the honor to tell you is the absolute truth, and I would not tell the least lie for all the riches in the world.

I have sought only the restoration of this hospital, and I never dreamed, in making these expenditures, of creating some kind of necessity of leaving me here to take care of it through the impossibility of reimbursing me, as some people think and say. That is not at all my character. I can assure Your Excellency that I have never thought of it.

But what has concerned me, in spite of myself and even against my intention, is the great number of urgent repairs which, piling up on one another and demanding prompt attention, have forced me as a matter of conscience to have them made, fearing, being charged with this work, lest I should answer to God if I permitted these things to be destroyed.

That is the only reason for all the expenses which I believed necessary, and which indeed were so. It is neither my companions nor the number of the poor that have caused these debts—Monsieur Bigot agrees to that. Alms and our labor have provided for them.

I beg you, Your Excellency, to have me reimbursed for these loans.

Bishop Pontbriand quickly and carefully stepped back from the warmth of this letter. On April 26 he wrote:

I credit all that you have done me the honor to tell me; and you will therefore take all juridical measures to obtain what is due to you. Assuredly the religious of the General Hospital [of Quebec] will not litigate. The King will decide all these difficulties, and then you will be in a position to have all your rights granted, to make your claims again. I hope that everything will succeed.

Small comfort to be assured that the religious of Quebec would not contest a lawsuit! Madame d'Youville had neither the desire nor the means to take her claims to court. She had done her utmost to represent the truth; now in complete submission and perfect trust she confided the outcome to the Eternal Father.

Nevertheless she suffered as any true woman would suffer when the dismantling of the General Hospital began. At the first signs of spring Bigot's men were at the doors to take away the furnishings that could be spared from the present needs of the poor.

The bishop's throne from the chapel was the first treasure to go. It was an exquisitely handcarved chair, one of the most beautiful of its kind in the whole country and the most precious possession of the hospital. Madame d'Youville, watching the men hoist it into the wagon backed up to the west door, learned once more the cauterizing lesson of renunciation.

But this valiant woman had no time to feel sorry for herself; nor had she any tendency to do so. It was doubly imperative for her these trying days to be a support to her Sisters and above all to the poor, threatened once more with eviction. The work had to go on to the very last moment of her responsibility. Moreover, it had to go on cheerfully, trustfully, just as if an angel with a flaming sword seemed not to be waiting at their door.

In any case, Madame d'Youville had no intention of abandoning the poor who would still look to her for aid; nor had her associates any intention of leaving her. Even though they could not see their way in the sudden darkness that surrounded them, they still hoped for light.

As if to encourage them, the grace of a very special vocation began to shine in the soul of Thérèse Despins. For twelve years she had lived as a boarder with *les Soeurs Grises,* sharing their joys and sorrows and yet remaining apart. Now at last she fully appreciated the enduring reality of their good example. Their virtues called to her own quiet questing: the self-denial that bought the well-being of others, the spirit of prayer that vitalized their constant industry, the love for God that blessed all other love.

To Father Normant Thérèse confided the state of her soul. Faithfully she described her empty, fruitless days; her natural dislike for personal works of charity; and her sincere desire, nevertheless, to overcome this dislike because of the example of the Sisters whose lives she now felt impelled to share. The wise priest advised her to become more familiar with the work of the house. He assured her that once she approached the poor with the belief that in them she would see Christ, she would find this contact with Him irresistibly appealing. He was right.

Yet another difficulty remained: there was no novitiate and no mistress of novices! This thoughtful and very wise young woman believed in the importance of a thorough training in the fundamental principles of the spiritual life. It was entirely in keeping with her deeply pious nature to do so. Thus it would seem that God entrusted to her the special mission of emphasizing this importance in order to strengthen the whole foundation of His work through the society just at the moment when dissolution threatened it.

Madame d'Youville herself still had too much general responsibility to give her time completely to the spiritual formation of aspirants. No one knew better than Thérèse how effectively the devoted foundress had inspired her associates to heroic service, how ardently she had fired them with her own love of God in His poor, how impelling her lifelong example had been. Yet what of the future? It was time now to establish a definite system of training for this service under the personal guidance of her who had so far shown the way.

Father Normant perfectly understood the wisdom of Thérèse's objection, and he agreed with her.

"My child," he said, "I promise you that on the day of your entry we shall have a mistress of novices."

This assurance was enough for Thérèse. Trustfully she made her final preparations to give the rest of her life to the service of the poor. On July 2, the feast of the Visitation of the Blessed Virgin Mary, she presented herself to Madame d'Youville, expecting to be turned over at once to the mistress of novices.

"My dear Thérèse," said the foundress gently, looking deep into the eyes of the young woman whom she knew so well, "God has sent you to us for a very special work. You are to be mistress of novices yourself."

Thérèse Despins was more than astonished; she was almost frightened. But already the grace of her dedication had started to take effect. Bowing her head in gracious submission to this first obedience, she began, under Madame d'Youville's personal direction, the practice of those virtues which she would later teach to others, and which she herself would always in the future exemplify: humility, regularity, devotion to work, delicate consideration for others. Kindness was her outstanding characteristic. Many years later, on being chided for her extraordinary fidelity to this virtue, even when she was imposed upon by the importunate, she quietly replied, "I would rather stay in purgatory for too much kindness than for too much severity."

Who could know in 1751 that twenty years later Thérèse Despins would be unanimously elected by *les Soeurs Grises* to succeed their beloved Mother d'Youville as Superior General?

Fortunately the young woman was not called upon immediately to exercise the grave responsibility of her office as mistress of novices. It was fifteen months later, in 1752, that her first postulant, Marie Gosselin, entered the novitiate; and her next, Thérèse Beaufrère, came the following year. What a remarkable training they must have had!

While the young mistress was finding her place in Madame d'Youville's world, other important events were happening.

The spring dispatches arrived from France. Eagerly, a trifle too anxiously, the Intendant Bigot ran through the official papers in search of a message from the King approving his procedure with the union of the two hospitals. There was no message. No, the Governor General had no word, either—nor the Bishop.

The Intendant was more than disappointed; he was worried, and he was annoyed. Now the petitions of the people and Madame d'Youville's supplication would reach the King before the union was complete. Not even the officious Bigot dared to proceed with the plan already begun until the King had spoken.

Unfortunately the Intendant had notified Madame d'Youville that she would be expected to leave the General Hospital in July. Now, without compromising himself, without seeming in the least to have made a mistake, he must keep her from leaving! Therefore, on June 19, he had recourse to a diplomatic letter.

Madame, I expected that by the first boat we should receive from the Court a ratification of the union that we have made of the General Hospital of Montreal with that of Quebec. Since we have no news yet, you may remain in the house where you are until we do have. I make this suggestion only in so far as it may be agreeable to you. Kindly let me know, so that in case you do not accept it, the General Hospital of Quebec may be able to make arrangements for the time that you should leave.

To be kept waiting was unquestionably a trial for a woman of Madame d'Youville's active, progressive nature; but this daughter of the Eternal Father understood the value of time for the perfection of the strong virtue of patience. Time, she remembered, is a means used by God for the unfolding of His plans.

In France, meanwhile, the Intendant's plans were being

brought out into the light. Father Cousturier, Superior of the Sulpician Seminary in Paris, and one of the successors of the saintly Father Olier in spiritual and material sovereignty over Montreal, received from Father Normant an account of proceedings against the General Hospital. This was a matter that would bear investigation; the administrators were trespassing on private property.

Armed with a copy of the contract made in 1688 between François Charon and Father Tronson, then Superior of the seminary in Montreal, Father Cousturier appealed to the Royal Court.

The contract definitely stated that if in the future the General Hospital should cease to exist, the land and all the buildings thereon would revert to the seminary, unless the remaining Brothers could pay its value. In view of recent events, therefore, the General Hospital had belonged to the seminary by law since 1747, and the Intendant Bigot had no right whatsoever to sell it.

Moreover, since the appalling indebtedness of the hospital was one of the reasons why the Court might be inclined to favor its dissolution, Father Cousturier was happy to present Madame d'Youville's offer to liquidate the debts of Brother Chrétien within three years. He was even happier to add that the debts could be considerably reduced without her aid. He himself had a nice little sum set aside which could be used to appease creditors; the late Father Bouffandeau, one of the Sulpicians, had left a legacy of six thousand pounds; generous friends had promised to make contributions just as soon as Madame d'Youville should be named permanent directress of the hospital.

Coincidences can be tiresome, but it is interesting to note that on July 2, 1751, the very day of Thérèse Despins' entry into Madame d'Youville's society, the Secretary of State wrote to Governor General Lajonquière and the Intendant Bigot.

I received the letter that you took the trouble to write to me on the eighteenth of last October, with the ordinance that you and the Bishop of Quebec had issued for the union of the General Hospital of Montreal with that of Quebec. When I suggested this union to you as a measure to be taken because of the affairs of the hospital, I always intended that there should remain in Montreal some kind of refuge for the poor, administered by religious from the General Hospital of Quebec. It was only on this condition that the union could take place at all. . . . You will please postpone your ordinance for the sale of the institution until further orders from His Majesty. I ought to point out to you that your orders would not be sufficient for a transaction of this kind, which can be made only by the expressed authorization of the King, and even then with certain formalities which I shall explain to you should the need arise.

There was nothing for the administrators to do but to retract their ordinance with as much dignity as their blunder had spared to them. On December 14 another proclamation was made which gracefully laid the blame for the blunder at the feet of the Secretary of State.

Whereas, by our ordinance of October 15, 1750, in consequence of letters from Monsieur de Rouillé, Minister and Secretary of State, we would have united to the General Hospital of Quebec all the property of the General Hospital of Montreal, of which Madame d'Youville and her companions had then the administration by virtue of a commission of August 27, 1747; on the representations which the said Madame d'Youville has since made to the Court, the Court has notified us that its intention is that we should suspend the said union until further orders; in consequence of which witness the resignation of the General Hospital of Quebec from this affair.

We order that the said Madame d'Youville with her companions, now and until further orders, will resume possession of all the goods of the General Hospital, of which she will continue to have the direction and administration in accordance with the commission of August 27, 1747.

We likewise order that Monsieur Foucher, procurator of the King in the jurisdiction of Montreal, whom we charged with the inventory of the said property, will have restored to Madame d'Youville the farms, animals, implements, et cetera, which were contained in the

172

said inventory and of which the General Hospital of Quebec had been put in possession by virtue of the said union; and the present ordinance will be read and proclaimed in all places where there is need of it.

As early as April 17 of the following year the Abbé de l'Isle-Dieu had the satisfaction of writing to his bishop:

Father Cousturier has informed me, Your Excellency, that the instigators and promoters of the union have already begun to have it consummated by force, by having some of the furniture carried off which it is now a question of returning to the hospital of Montreal. Consequently, and immediately, I had the honor of writing to Monsieur Rouillé to ask him to order the restoration of the furniture which had been taken away. I have no doubt that his orders will be carried out. I am warning you, Your Excellency, lest they keep you in the dark about it, for ordinarily it is easier to take away a thing than to restore it.

Under orders from the Secretary of State, Bigot had no choice but to return to the hospital in Montreal the furnishings which had all too prematurely been transported to Quebec. Was the bishop's carved throne the first treasure to be brought back?

On May 12 the King in council solemnly revoked the Intendant's arbitrary ordinance of October 1750, and ordered the chief administrators to draw up a contract with Madame d'Youville to determine her powers in the General Hospital. But before they felt satisfied to do this, they asked her to explain to them exactly by what means she proposed to liquidate the debts of the house, so that they in turn could make a clear report to the Secretary of State.

Madame d'Youville, having fully described her assets and her plans for using them, prudently concluded her long letter of June 19 in the following words:

Thus, there will remain only six thousand pounds to be paid, with some arrears. Divine Providence, our industry, and the good will of several persons who await what His Majesty may decide, are the other resources on which we depend for the full payment of the debts, for repairs, and even for appropriate improvements.

In all our affairs, sirs, we have no intention but to maintain an institution so useful to the government of Montreal. But in order to fulfill this intention, it seems necessary to us that His Majesty should be pleased to declare that this hospital, formerly administered by the Charon Brothers, may henceforth be managed by secular persons who will be dispensed from the education of youth; who will receive the infirm and aged of both sexes; who will succeed to all the rights and privileges granted to the said Brothers, so that this change, which is basically most advantageous, may not influence former donors and benefactors to withdraw their gifts, on the pretext that the direction of the house has passed into other hands; in a word, that the letters patent of 1694 and of 1697 will hold good in favor of the secular persons who will have charge of this hospital.

But if in the future, for reasons which cannot now be foreseen, it should please the King to make other arrangements, either by destroying the establishment entirely or by substituting religious, we request that in this case we may be reimbursed for the amount of 18,000 pounds which we are giving to build up this house, so that the last one among us may be able to claim the said reimbursement, to dispose of it according to her will or according to the agreements which we may be able to make together. . . .

There are still many regulations to be made on the number of young women to be associated with us; on the conditions and the reasons for which they could be dismissed; whether those who leave the service of the poor of their own volition would have the right to demand a pension. It will be necessary to regulate a thousand details in both temporal and spiritual matters. We shall conform as closely as possible to what has already been decreed for the Charon Brothers; and you, sirs, as chief administrators of the hospital, will be able to make the most suitable regulations for circumstances which may arise.

This letter, remarkable for its prudence and foresightedness, was signed by Madame d'Youville and her seven associates. Little did they dream that it would bring far greater results than they, humbly styling themselves "secular persons," would have dared to expect. It must have given both encouragement and direction even to the administrators.

In the midst of all the entanglements, legal, financial, domestic, that obstructed her days, Madame d'Youville had one great, invigorating joy—the ordination of her son Charles on August 26, 1752.

Father Charles Dufrost, as he was called, to distinguish him from his older brother, Father François d'Youville, seemed even at the time of his elevation to the priesthood to be blessed with the fine moral qualities that characterized his mother. He too loved the poor with that special love which includes a sympathetic understanding of their own peculiar suffering. It was his joy to give alms and to spread happiness about him.

Perhaps it was the fervent benediction of this priestly son that soon brought to Madame d'Youville, his mother, the most blessed confirmation of all her hopes.

When a final ordinance of September 28 limited to twelve the number of associates in Madame d'Youville's society and passed over in silence her request for a reimbursement of 18,000 pounds in case the General Hospital should someday be dissolved, she had recourse at once to the Abbé de l'Isle-Dieu. She reminded him not only of the two points at issue but also remarked that temporal authorities were having a little too much to do with the details of her little society.

There is no doubt that the good Abbé devoted himself most faithfully to Madame d'Youville's interests, for on the first of April and at the end of May he sent assurances to Bishop Pontbriand that her appeal for letters patent was being favorably heard. How gladly the Bishop must have relayed these hopeful messages we may infer from a note that he had sent her himself a few months earlier; in all simplicity he had written:

You are too equitable to doubt the sentiments of affection and respect that it is my glory to feel for you. How consoling it will be for me if our project for the establishment of the General Hospital is confirmed! As soon as there is something definite, we shall think seriously of settling details.

At last, three years after the thunder of drums in the Market Place had announced the storm of opposition which would beat upon the General Hospital, the skies cleared and the sun shone in full glory. The long-awaited letters patent were signed by Louis XV and by Rouillé, Secretary of State, on June 3, 1753, and registered in Quebec on the first day of October.

The first part of the precious document proved the careful investigation which the Royal Court had given to all the details of the case. The second part, divided into thirteen concise articles, defined the privileges and obligations confided specifically to Madame d'Youville and her companions: they should enjoy all the rights and prerogatives granted in 1694 to the Charon Brothers; they should be responsible for the debts of the hospital in accordance with their own offer to liquidate them, and they should be reimbursed for expenses made out of their own money, but not out of the income or alms belonging to the hospital; they should be supported in health and in sickness at the expense of the hospital, and the products of their own labor should turn to their profit; they should render an account annually of the income and alms enjoyed by the hospital as well as of the revenue derived from their own industry; they could not make any extraordinary transactions, loans, or expenses without the approval of the administrators; they should pay Brother Joseph Dellerme a pension of two hundred and fifty pounds a year for the rest of his life; their number should be limited to twelve, not to be increased without the express permission of the Court on the recommendation of the Superior Council; they should distribute the responsibilities of the house according to the advice of the Bishop, and they should admit to their number in place of those dead or otherwise departed only those persons approved by the Bishop; they could, with his permission, dismiss any associate whose conduct was unworthy, and any associate could withdraw of her own free will; they could retain the ownership of inheritances, like persons in the world, but no one could succeed to them.

The last article of the letters patent was, to Madame d'Youville and her associates, the most important: it authorized them to present themselves to the Bishop for the rules necessary for their spiritual life. In other words, they were granted royal sanction for the foundation of a religious community. Legitimate authority had expressed the will of God.

Guided always on the way of the cross by the white light of truth, Madame d'Youville had come at last to the portals of life in God.

III

THE LIFE

This is eternal life: that they may know Thee, the only true God, and Jesus Christ, whom Thou has sent.

JOHN XVII:3

CHAPTER TWELVE

GREY NUNS

TO THE mind of the Royal Court, harassed by financial problems, Madame d'Youville's offer to pay the debts of the General Hospital within three years was the strongest argument in favor of leaving the institution in her hands with every guarantee—and more—that she had asked. The Secretary of State, in his letter to the Intendant Bigot and Governor General Duquesne, successor to the Marquis de Lajonquière, remarked pointedly:

The most important and most urgent matter now is the liquidation of the debts of this hospital. I trust that the Abbé de l'Isle-Dieu, by means of the funds which are now in the hands of Father Cousturier, will be able to make an agreement with the creditors in France that will end the affair.

Fortunately these creditors, having been threatened for so many years with the total loss of their money, were only too glad to agree to terms offered by the Sulpician Fathers. In fact, they voluntarily settled for half the amount due to them, canceling entirely not only the other half but also the accumulated interest. Concerning those creditors who could not be located, the Abbé dryly observed to Madame d'Youville, "It was not your intention that I should look for them in this world and in the next."

In Montreal, meanwhile, Madame d'Youville had begun to do her share. Her obligation, heavy enough at best, was greatly complicated by the fact that during the past three years of political intrigue she had had to suspend all improvements at the hospital and at Chambly and Point St. Charles. Now in all places she was obliged not only to regain lost ground but also to advance at double speed.

It was the pleasure of the Intendant just at this time to put another obstacle in her path. Since the religious of the General Hospital of Quebec had begun to plant the farms, he ordered Madame d'Youville to reimburse them for seeds to the amount of eight hundred pounds. Thus the crafty Bigot was not entirely without his satisfaction in spite of the turn that events had taken against his plans.

No obstacle, however great, could keep dauntless Madame d'Youville from accomplishing the work that God evidently willed her to do. While she and her Sisters waited for Bishop Pontbriand to attend to the rules governing their religious life, they demonstrated that union in God which had sprung from pain and humiliation borne for His cause.

A common adversity had strengthened their mutual union, leveling all personal differences, minimizing the inevitable irritations of close and constant intercourse with one another. Not only frequent visitors but also those in daily contact with the Sisters—the boarders, the sick, the poor—remarked their courteous and affectionate attitude toward one another, their unfailing attention to little points of politeness, their easy deference and graceful consideration. Modestly, simply, but always cheerfully, they went about their Eternal Father's business, gathering in personal self-sacrifice the fruits of their common oblation.

Unquestionably it was Madame d'Youville who sustained the spirit that animated the Sisters. Above and beyond the fact that she was capable, efficient, enterprising, she depended so utterly on Divine Providence that her personality radiated confidence, stimulated initiative, generated joy of heart. To the inspiring picture of the Eternal Father, which the foundress had had painted in France as a prayer for the recovery of Father Normant, the Sisters often raised their eyes devoutly. The kindly, paternal face represented there, the strong right arm upraised in protective assurance, the whole attitude of providential love must have nourished their trust and their zeal; but it was the living, actual picture of their mother's complete abandonment to the fatherhood of God that made real for them an ideal so beautifully portrayed.

As trustful love enlarged the hearts of the Sisters, a new sense of security and a definite purpose loosened their spirits and liberated their zeal. To an almost unbelievable extent they increased their labors for the poor. Physical hardship melted away in the ardor of their charity. Daily, from the first flush of dawn until the last flickerings of candlelight, they worked to increase the number and the well-being of their charges.

What time did they have for their own personal needs? Only the minimum. Unable to take precious moments from their work in order to knit stockings for themselves—there was no mass production by the factory system in those days—they devised hose from strips of material left over from their orders. Handkerchiefs, too, they made from colored cotton cloth, for the Sisters were too poor to afford fine linen.

Although paying boarders at the hospital still assured considerable revenue, the Sisters' needlework continued to be their main industry for income. The range of their undertakings in this field was astonishing—from the most delicately embroidered lingerie to military uniforms and large tents. Nothing would they reject as long as it was honest and profitable. "Go to *les Soeurs Grises*," the people would say. "They never refuse anything."

For more than twenty years the King's shopkeepers were their most constant clients. From them the Sisters received commissions not only for the soldiers' uniforms but also for all the trappings and trimmings of military rank and splendor—officers' braid, decorative fringes, impressive epaulets. They made elaborate gowns for the officers' ladies and dainty dresses for their children, tents for the troops and sails for the fishing boats.

For traders who came to Montreal from the outposts of northwestern Canada, they fashioned the thousand and one attractively embroidered gifts intended to please the Indian chiefs and win their support. For days and nights before the return of these merchant-traders to their distant posts, the work rooms of the hospital were scenes of unending industry as the Sisters, the boarders, the poor—everyone who could handle a needle at all—labored to complete the assignments heaped upon them. Always it was Madame d'Youville who worked the longest; always it was she who chose the most difficult and the least rewarding task.

It was in 1754 that the Sisters began to maintain a special department for the making of ecclesiastical vestments and linens. The Church of the Assumption, built that year, gave them their first order. So delicate was the care and workmanship expended that orders multiplied.

At this time Father Claude Poncin, one of the priests of the seminary, taught the Sisters how to make altar breads and candles, as well as adaptable candle burners with copper springs, a device of great value, since fine, tall tapers for the altar were a luxury in those days. He also brought from France and gave to the hospital all the equipment needed for these home manufactures, a gift that provided another source of steadily increasing income for many years.

In July of the same year Madame d'Youville inaugurated closed retreats for women. There were many ladies in Montreal who longed to share, at least for a time, the spiritual blessings of peace and prayer enjoyed always by permanent residents.

Other methods of gaining revenue, employed by Madame d'Youville and her Sisters, were so diversified as to provoke, if not unbelief, at least breathless amazement. They bought tobacco in the leaf, had it prepared by their old men, and then sold it at a profit. Having restored an old windmill and brewery constructed by the Charon Brothers, they further increased their funds from the sale of beer. They leased their attic to the King's shopkeepers for storage—alas, the whole building is to-day a warehouse, but one cannot help concluding that the foundress herself would have had it so.

Moreover, the Sisters rented an icehouse and two small out-buildings on their property; they rented carts for hauling goods; they let their fields as pasture land for cattle; they prepared lime for cement; and they sold sand and stone for building purposes. Tradition has it that they bought and maintained a ferryboat between Montreal and Longueuil, but the most pains-taking search for proofs of this venture has revealed only one reference, Madame d'Youville's notation, *"pour notre batteau,"* in her account book.

In the old Market Place of the city they vended the products of their farms at Chambly and Point St. Charles—chickens, ducks, cattle, eggs, hides, feathers, grain, and everything else that had a market value.

Another source of income, small but steady, was derived from the rental of Madame d'Youville's pew in Notre Dame Church, inherited from her husband.

It was possible for the foundress to manage all these methods of making money for the poor—there certainly was no other reason for such extraordinary labor—only because she had the complete co-operation of all those who worked with her. Indeed, it was one of the secrets of success and happiness in the house that everyone shared in its activities.

This sharing was an inevitable effect of Madame d'Youville's quality of leadership. She herself worked with so much en-thusiasm and self-sacrifice that unconsciously but invariably she drew forth from all those around her whatever they were capable of doing. At the same time, she made a real and purposeful effort to learn the abilities of her associates and of her poor, firmly believing that God had bestowed them for constructive use.

One of her patients in the hospital had for years been a skilled tailor; to his delight and satisfaction she put him to work at his trade. He was able, incidentally, to pass many fine points on to others. A poor old man who had formerly been a shoemaker spent his last years rendering glad service to the hospital that sheltered him.

Also among the poor were an old father and mother whose son, a carpenter, had offered to live at the hospital and work exclusively there on condition that his parents would be taken care of for the rest of their lives. One smiles to read that Madame d'Youville had the charity to employ another carpenter at that time whom no one else would hire with the customary maintenance because he ate too much! Concerning one of the boarders, Madame d'Youville wrote, in the fine spirit of appreciation that always characterized her attitude toward others:

We have here a lady, the widow Robineau of Pontneuf, past eighty-one years old, who fasts and abstains on all the days of obligation and works like us for the good of the poor, although she pays her board. She is charming because of her great piety and her beautiful spirit.

One of the greatest improvements undertaken by Madame d'Youville in 1754 was the construction of a wall around the hospital, so that the property would no longer be exposed to petty depredations. This was a project suggested by the staff of experts in 1747, but repairs were so urgent at that time that it could not then be included.

To surround eight and a half acres of property with a stone wall about 3600 feet long and seven feet high was an enterprise of such magnitude that one wonders today how the foundress could have accomplished it. Yet so profound was her trust in

Divine Providence for the completion of a good work that she simply set difficulties aside and went forward with irresistible enthusiasm.

First of all she sought and obtained permission from the chief administrators. Governor General Duquesne, convinced of the real need of such an enclosure as the foundress proposed, made a personal appeal to the generosity of the public for necessary funds. Bishop Pontbriand and Father Normant each contributed five hundred pounds. Many good people followed their example.

Madame d'Youville's handwritten account of receipts and expenditures—each page a model of order, accuracy, and beauty of form—testifies that at this time, as well as in the years to come, there were many generous friends who made frequent contributions for the needs of the hospital.

Other citizens, having no money to spare for the new wall, just as generously gave the work of their hands or supplied necessary materials. There were no legal hours then to limit labor, nor were there bounds of any kind, except those of charitable consideration, set upon the eagerness of the people to share in this great undertaking. In order to save expenses the Sisters themselves joined in the work and helped the masons to no small extent by preparing lime for cement, carrying mortar in heavy buckets, and transporting stones in their aprons. Their good spirits turned the work into a profitable recreation.

While everyone was in the mood for outside activity, Madame d'Youville made the best of the opportunity to have a small house built for servants not far from the little dwellings that she had had constructed in 1750 for several persons mentally afflicted. Now within a solid wall, all her charges, in their own departments, were secure and safe.

Throughout the development of all these material interests there ran, like a golden thread in a strong and substantial fabric, the religious organization of the community. The novitiate was now a reality, for Thérèse Despins, professed on

June 30, 1753, had begun to preside over novices, one at a time, in a small but delightful room on the third floor, directly over Madame d'Youville's own quarters.

To this novitiate the foundress herself often went, for she dearly loved the young Sisters, looking upon them as her own spiritual children. Because she counted on them to continue in the future the work that God had trusted her to begin, she spared no effort to develop in them the virtues fundamental and essential to their state—charity, simplicity, generous self-sacrifice. Theirs would be a life of prayer and silence, of privation and constant work; and their training had to be adequate. Through her kindness and example, most of all, they learned what it meant to be a daughter of Mother d'Youville, devoted for the rest of their lives to the service of the poor. It was their responsibility to assimilate her spirit, to cherish it faithfully all their days, in order to bequeath it intact to the Grey Nuns of the future.

This wise mother, endowed with an extraordinary appreciation of the diversity of gifts provided by the Eternal Father for the happiness and perfection of His children, now made a place for music in her busy world. Nothing would be wasted if she could help it! Sister Bénard, gifted with a true and beautiful voice, already trained, now began to teach singing to the Sisters and to the poor. Henceforth in their chapel ceremonies how joyfully they would praise God! Fervent and French, they needed singing to liberate their love.

Now, in the twentieth century, as one listens in amazement to the old men's Gregorian choir alternating with the Sisters' younger voices in a High Mass of jubilation, one praises God for Madame d'Youville's foresight and gives thanks for a beautiful tradition so faithfully preserved.

As soon as possible after the letters patent of 1753 had given royal sanction to the Community, Madame d'Youville, in prompt obedience to the thirteenth article thereof, had sought ecclesiastical approval from Bishop Pontbriand. The time had now come to determine the costume that the Sisters would henceforth wear, the rules to which they and generations of Grey Nuns would bind themselves, the customs and traditions that would become a living part of their institute.

For nearly eighteen years Madame d'Youville and her associates had been called *les Soeurs Grises*, a name sprung from malice and mockery in the early days of the society, but retained in growing respect and affection with the passage of time. The title had become a familiar habit among the people of Montreal. Now, in a spirit of humility and self-effacement, the foundress chose grey—*gris* in French—as the color of the religious costume that the Sisters would wear, thus giving to the old title, *les Soeurs Grises*, a new and beautiful meaning, the Grey Nuns.

Grey is a practical color, and Madame d'Youville had a practical mind. She considered the fact that the Sisters could never afford very much time for their clothes. They had work to do—plenty of it—from morning till night, every day of their lives. For the same reason they agreed with her that *camelot*, a durable, closely woven cloth, much in use at the time, would be the most suitable material for their habits.

No other religious costume served as a model for the dress designed by Madame d'Youville. It was entirely original, adapted in every detail to the needs of the Sisters and to the work that had to be done. The skirt with its large double box pleats for longer wear followed the old Norman style; the heavy black cincture, with front pendant of the same material, suggested their dedication to a life of chastity. The sleeves were long and wide, but folded back halfway between the wrist and the elbow so that they would not interfere with the Sisters' work. It was not until 1781 that short, detachable, inner sleeves of the same material were added to the costume at the suggestion of Bishop Briand. He thought that the Sisters should have their religious wrists covered, work or no work!

Madame d'Youville's last word in practicality was the full,

dark blue-and-white striped cotton apron ordained to cover the habit at all times except for chapel exercises and formal occasions. Not only did it serve as a protection for the religious dress; it was also modestly becoming as well as quietly suggestive of the Lady of Nazareth, who once gave to household tasks a new kind of glory.

It was probably a sacrifice for the Sisters not to have the conventional veil as part of their religious habit. But it was a sacrifice freely and promptly made, for Madame d'Youville thought that the nature of their work among the poor and sick, in their homes and in hospitals, forbade this graceful but sometimes inconvenient distinction. Instead they adopted a kind of waist-length cape of black material, with a full pleated bonnet attached to the collar. For the headdress Madame d'Youville devised a plain, tight band of white muslin, close to the face, over which hung loosely a strip of black gauze, in the style of a widow's cap.

Another short cape and bonnet, also black, were designed for wear in the chapel and for outdoors in the summer time, and a full cloak of heavy grey material for use in winter.

To emphasize the religious nature of the costume thus appropriately planned, Madame d'Youville decided that the Sisters should wear upon their breast a small silver crucifix, also significantly designed. On each extremity of the cross a fleur-de-lis was engraved in grateful remembrance of Louis XV, King of France, by whom had been granted the letters patent that sanctioned the Community. Above the Crucified was a representation of the Sacred Heart, symbol of the ultimate in love and sacrifice. These crosses had to be made in France because of the lack of skilled silversmiths in Canada at the time.

Finally, a silver ring, engraved on the inside with the names of Jesus, Mary, and Joseph, in memory of the Holy Family, and worn on the third finger of the right hand, completed the religious costume planned by the foundress.

When Bishop Pontbriand made his first canonical visit to the

General Hospital early in June of 1755, in response to Madame d'Youville's request for ecclesiastical approbation, the Sisters were ready to show him a model of the costume that they had made under their Mother's supervision. It was a significant moment. What a surprise it must have been to His Excellency when one of the Sisters appeared before him, dressed in the new habit! How her own heart must have quickened in feminine pride and ardent hope!

Delighted with the simple, modest costume so gracefully displayed, the Bishop expressed his personal satisfaction then and there; but he reserved his formal approbation to an official letter addressed to the Community on June 15, 1755. Because this document is treasured by the Sisters as the first canonical mandate of a prelate whose good will and support had been won by Madame d'Youville's steadfast integrity, it may be of value quoted here in full:

We have observed with pleasure, very dear Sisters, all the improvements that you have made in the house whose care has been entrusted to you; and our satisfaction was greatly increased when we learned the sentiments with which you are continuing to work with a new courage and the same economy. We hope that the Lord will continue to shower His blessings upon your work, and for this end we beseech Him most earnestly.

You have asked me for rules for the interior government of your house in order to prevent abuses which imperceptibly creep in everywhere. However persuaded we might be that rules would be unnecessary for you as long as you keep the sentiments of piety and fervor with which we see you penetrated, and that charity alone is enough to keep you in the order, we believe it a duty, however, to enter into your views, if only to give you an opportunity to practice obedience, which is the soul of all communities. We have promised them to you. In the meantime, here is what we believe we ought to propose:

1. Until we make other arrangements, we approve of your following to the letter what is contained in the three loose sheets of paper written by Father Normant, which you have practiced for a long time; which three sheets we have signed, and which we wish to be faithfully

copied in a special book used to record our orders and regulations. The first sheet bears the title, "Rule"; the second is a kind of promise signed by you; the third has for title, "The dispositions with which one should conduct one's self."

2. Although you were meant to receive only old and infirm persons, we have been pleased to observe that your zeal has extended even to women looked upon as dangerous, who were sent to you by persons in authority; but we believe it a duty to warn you not to receive any of them except by written order of the Governor General or the Governor or the Intendant or the Commissioner or the Judge, and we hope that these gentlemen will pay to the hospital the board that the Intendant will determine, since it is not just that they should be supported by the resources of the poor. We wish indeed that you should be charged with this work only as long as the first purpose of your institute does not suffer. And, persuaded that one can gain the hearts of these women only by gentleness, we beg you to follow your custom and not to subject them to any corporal penance for their past life, leaving it, however, to your prudence to punish them for faults which they may commit in the house.

3. Since you think it fitting that all who comprise your Community should be dressed uniformly, we approve the costume that you have designed and in which one among you has appeared before us, that is, a grey dress with two or three pleats, an apron of some striped cotton, a black neckerchief, a kind of band of batiste or muslin, and over it a kind of headdress of black gauze. We agree that according to the custom of several religious ladies, you should wear a small silver crucifix.

4. We desire that secular persons should not enter the room in which you assemble for recreations and for work. You will see where you can arrange a room to receive them when they come to you.

5. Although you are permitted to address yourselves to all confessors who are authorized to hear confessions in the city, we ask you to go usually to the one whom our Vicar General will assign for you; he will be careful every three months to send you another. You may choose one for yourself by consulting the Superior.

6. You will continue to recognize Madame d'Youville as Superior. When there will be question of a change—which I think will not be to your taste and which ought not to be, except in the last extremity— you will follow the rules which we will shortly prescribe for you; but

since accidents may happen when we believe them least likely, we think that it is prudent for Madame d'Youville to select from her companions the three oldest whom she will instruct in the temporal affairs of the house, informing them of her plans and her resources, having them read the accounts and sign them, although they must be approved by the chief administrators, so that the three oldest will be looked upon as the three discreet counselors of the house, whom we may choose ourselves or have elected by ballot. And since the Superior is often obliged to be absent on business and for a thousand needs, we have asked Father Normant to confer with each of you in particular and to name one among you to take the place of the Superior in those cases when she cannot act. We wish that you will then make it a duty to recognize her and to obey her, and that she may have the right to command you in what seems just to her.

7. Since by the letters patent your number is fixed at twelve, we believe that you should fill it with new subjects only after they have lived in the house for two years; and when the number of twelve is complete, not more than three postulants should be received, who will probably not take the habit which you have chosen until they have lived a year in the house, received your votes and then obtained your consent.

8. Above all, my very dear Sisters, you will conform yourselves to the letters patent. You may make your representation to us on what we have just observed to you and ask us for any enlightenment that you may consider necessary. That is why we have expressly reserved to ourselves the right to change, to augment, and to decrease; and in order that we may be able to reflect more at ease, we ask you to send us at once a copy of the letters patent, and of the three written sheets that we have urged you to follow, as the rule from this time and to the letter, signed voluntarily by you.

In a spirit of prompt obedience to the expressed wishes of legitimate authority, Madame d'Youville began to put into practice the recommendations made by His Excellency. Unanimously the Sisters chose Louise Thaumur as first assistant, much to the satisfaction of the foundress herself, who had long depended on this efficient Sister for counsel and aid.

The community room, closed to secular persons, now became the setting for activity almost too sacred for description—the making of holy habits for the first Grey Nuns, Mother d'Youville and her ten companions. Their regular work for the poor could not be neglected, but somehow they managed to find time for this sewing that no one else could do. It was not only a question of fine stitches and careful handling this time; it was also a question of setting patterns and customs for countless years to come. As these pioneers sewed quietly together far into the warm nights of that summer of 1755, did there pass before their spiritual vision thousands of Grey Nuns clad in this habit that now they were fashioning?

Mother d'Youville, who always knew how to flavor events with the sweetness of personal consideration, decided that in honor of Father Normant the Sisters would be clothed in the holy habit on August 25, the feast of St. Louis and therefore the patronal feast of their faithful director.

Early in the morning of the long-awaited day, Father Normant arrived to find the community room beautifully prepared for the ceremony. He had agreed with the Sisters that the clothing, too sacred for secular eyes, should be completely private, in the presence of the novices only, who would be thus inspired and encouraged.

The eleven grey habits, neatly folded, had been placed on a table at one end of the room. Nearby, on a small stand covered with a white linen and lace cloth of exquisite workmanship, waited a shining vessel of holy water. Two tall tapers lifted up bright flames in happy immolation.

Quietly Mother d'Youville and her Sisters entered the room together and knelt before Father Normant waiting to receive them. According to a simple but very solemn ceremonial composed by himself at the request of the Bishop and used in the Congregation since that day, he blessed the habits and gave them to the Sisters, each in turn.

Retiring at once to adjoining rooms, they set aside forever the simple black dresses that for eighteen years had served their dedication to the poor. Then with profound sentiments of gratitude and joy they clothed themselves quickly in the soft grey of God and returned to the community room to kneel again before Father Normant for his paternal blessing.

It was soon over, that first ceremony of clothing, but it was memorable, all the more so because simplicity preserved intact its spiritual significance.

For Canada of the old regime, the feast of St. Louis, King of France, was a holy day of obligation, a worthy day indeed for the first public appearance of the Grey Nuns in their new religious costume. As they modestly proceeded to High Mass at Notre Dame later that morning, people bowed reverently in the streets. Others within their homes ran to the windows to see this remarkable sight.

"*Les Soeurs Grises!*" they exclaimed in softened tones of wonder and affection. "*Les chères Soeurs Grises!*"

Solemn Benediction of the Blessed Sacrament in the old chapel of the General Hospital brought to a beautiful close this twenty-fifth day of August in 1755. Up to the very gates of heaven rang the *Laudate Dominum* as the Sisters, the boarders, the poor raised their voices in grateful praise. For all of them a new era had begun!

Bishop Pontbriand, writing to the Community on September 22 of that year, addressed his letter "To Madame d'Youville, Superior of the Sisters of Charity," and he said: "I do not know how the people have received your religious costume. You have been doing the work of Sisters of Charity and I do know that they approve of this name."

The people certainly did approve of the name, under which the Sisters are now officially known, but familiar affection has kept alive the old title, the Grey Nuns.

A new era had indeed begun, an era that demanded all the fortitude that the grace of religious dedication could assure. By no means did the Sisters, clothed in their holy habit and enclosed within their new wall, retire from the world that needed more than ever their charitable ministrations. On the contrary, responding to the supernatural stimulus of their renewed consecration, they gave themselves with even greater generosity to the alleviation of human misery.

In 1755 the scourge of smallpox struck the Indian missions around Montreal. Inevitably the dread disease crept into the city, claiming so many victims that the heroic daughters of Jeanne Mance at Hôtel-Dieu could not receive them all.

Here was a need that Mother d'Youville could not ignore. Not only did she receive at the General Hospital as many women as possible who suffered from the disease; she and the Sisters, not bound by any canonical enclosure, also went to the homes of the stricken and cared for them there.

"As servants of the poor," she reminded her Sisters, "we must always be ready to undertake all the good works that Divine Providence may present to us and for which we may be authorized by our Superiors."

Authorization for this good work was not lacking, for Bishop Pontbriand had written, "In this epidemic you must be well prepared. With pleasure I approve of your receiving poor women stricken with smallpox."

Out of this emergency grew the special vocation of the Grey Nuns, as Sisters of Charity, to care for the sick. Nursing became one of their major works from that time forth, so that today many great hospitals under their management are flourishing throughout Canada and the United States.

But God's blessing on this vast work began with the sign of the cross. Sister Agathe Véronneau, struck down by a complication of smallpox and typhoid fever, recovered physically from both, but remained mentally impaired for the rest of her life. In spite of her pitiable condition, however, she was an example to the Sisters of the abiding blessedness of a personal love of God. Whatever else was taken from her, that love endured, expressing itself in the fervor and regularity which had been the poor Sister's special virtues from the first days of her religious life.

One day Mother d'Youville noticed that Sister Véronneau was not at her place in the refectory. At once she sent another Sister to look for her. It was a long search indeed, for the missing Sister was finally discovered in the gallery of the chapel, kneeling in prayer.

"And what are you doing now, Sister?" asked the pursuer, a bit out of breath from her seeking.

"I am making my meditation," quite simply replied Sister Véronneau.

"Oh. And on what subject?"

"On the love of God!"

There was nothing more to be said. This was the theme of her life; and, on the night of her death on April 20, 1764, Sister Véronneau kept repeating, "My God, I love Thee! My God, I love Thee!" Such was the spirit of the first Grey Nun to give her life for the sick.

The smallpox epidemic died out eventually, but nursing kept its place in the General Hospital. There were always the sick poor to be cared for, and those who by the nature of their diseases could not be received at Hôtel-Dieu—those, for example, who were suffering from incurable cancer. It was now well known that Mother d'Youville would find a place in her hospital and in her heart for anyone in need.

In 1756 the Intendant Bigot found himself in a peculiar position. It was his responsibility to see that wounded prisoners of war had hospitalization; but there was no more room at Hôtel-Dieu. The Sisters there had even sacrificed their chapel in order to make places for the sick. Imagine the chagrin of the proud Intendant when he found himself forced to request Madame d'Youville to open a ward for disabled English soldiers! Needless to say, she did so at once with all the good will and courtesy of her forgiving heart.

Circumstances were now such that the Intendant was obliged

to make frequent visits to the General Hospital. On one occasion he presented himself without having first sent word of his coming. But Mother d'Youville, busy making candles, was not dressed for company! One of the Sisters, who had chanced to see the Intendant's approach, hurried to warn her that he was at the door. Would she not like to take a few moments in order to make herself more presentable?

"Oh no!" Mother d'Youville answered, entirely at her ease. "I was not notified of the Intendant's coming. He will excuse me and be quite willing to take me as I am. None of all that will keep him from talking to me."

So, just as she was, Mother d'Youville proceeded to the parlor to confer with Bigot. Her direct approach, the charming simplicity of her manners, the grace that shone in her deep, dark eyes as she smiled serenely at her visitor blinded him completely to her workaday attire. She was a lady of God's Court, no matter what she wore.

CHAPTER THIRTEEN

UNDER THE BRITISH FLAG

MOTHER D'YOUVILLE'S COMMUNITY, sanctioned now by Church and State, took on a new life so abundant in activity that soon the General Hospital was too small to contain it. The ward for wounded soldiers, captured in preliminary skirmishes of increasing frequency between the French and the English, was now filled beyond capacity; and Jericho, that trouble spot of the hospital, had gradually to be abandoned. Yet the needy were growing more numerous, and Mother d'Youville's hands were still outstretched.

There was only one thing to be done: build an addition to the hospital. What did it matter that there was not a cent for this undertaking? What did it matter that materials were scarce, that the times were ominous, that all able-bodied men were on the way to war? Mother d'Youville looked upon her difficulties only as obstacles to be overstepped. If the portents were as true as they seemed, the people would need this hospital as never before.

But invincible as her spirit appeared to be in the face of staggering obligations pressing upon her one after another throughout the years, she could not always physically survive them. In the autumn of 1757, in the midst of her plans for expansion, she succumbed again to illness and exhaustion so alarming even to herself that for the first time she believed it necessary to make her last will and testament.

Life stood still in the General Hospital at four o'clock on October 8 as the Sisters silently led Danré de Blanzy, the notary, to Mother d'Youville's room for the formality of her last will. There she lay, "considering that there is nothing more certain than death, and nothing more uncertain than the hour of death."

Briefly the document drawn up that day records the pious recommendation of her soul to God, a plea for pardon of her sins, and her prayer for the intercession of all the saints in heaven. The rest is a testament of her gratitude to her companions for their "infinite attentions" to her children, for their goodness in not even requiring the payment of board during the years when the children lived with them, for their tender care of her throughout the seven years of her confinement with an infection of the knee! Therefore to her companions she bequeathed everything she had, excepting, reserving, retaining nothing at all.

Mother d'Youville's signature on this document reveals the painful degree of her weakness. Customarily firm and decisive, it wavers feebly this time up into the notary's final words. That strong right hand, itself the support of the weak, had now lost its strength.

But not for long! Her hour had not yet come, uncertain as it had seemed. The devoted care of the Sisters, their unceasing prayers, the power of her indomitable spirit over bodily infirmity—all these prevailed. On the day that she spoke again of her plans to enlarge the hospital, the Sisters knew that her recovery was sure. Life moved on with another kind of joy, although the beloved foundress, increasingly valiant in soul, never regained full physical strength.

In the meantime, Father Normant, having entered thoroughly into Mother d'Youville's ideas with regard to expansion, asked Father Montgolfier, then Superior of the seminary, to draw up plans for a new wing so located as to make the chapel the center of the establishment, and to submit these plans to Bishop Pontbriand. That His Excellency approved them we know from his letter to Mother d'Youville on January 7, 1758.

I marvel at your confidence in Divine Providence. I have observed remarkable signs of it since I have had the honor of knowing you. Father Montgolfier's plan seems to me to be in good taste. My suggestions would be more definite if I were there. In my opinion, it is only a question of increasing the number of windows. In all else, it is for you to choose what will most please you. I make this observation only to afford you a chance to see if it is possible, without adding to the expense, to give more daylight. I wish you, madame, and your charitable companions, the most abundant blessings.

At the first signs of spring, and in spite of unpropitious times, ground was broken for the new wing, and rapidly the foundations were laid. To save expenses, much of the material needed was taken from the property on which the hospital stood, and the Sisters again joined in the work, assisted by all of the poor who could render service.

It was on July 20 of this year, the feast of St. Margaret of Antioch, the great martyr who triumphed by the sign of the cross, that the Sisters celebrated for the first time the festal day of Mother d'Youville, their own Marguerite. In the midst of the great work of construction, alarmed by the echoes of war, everyone in the house was yet able to make of this day a glad and beautiful occasion. It was not often that they could assemble visible signs of grateful love for her who had given them her very life. Those who had money to offer made up a nice little purse amounting to ninety francs, a considerable sum for those straitened days. Others had gifts of their own workmanship. One can imagine the happy grace with which the good Mother received these offerings. She who knew how to give knew also how to receive, so that the joy of the giver was doubled and his heart was lifted to God.

Reinvigorated by the simple happiness of this feast day, which became an annual joy, everyone eagerly went back to work on the new wing in hopes of finishing before winter set in again. But scarcely had the good thick walls begun to appear above-ground when all work had to be suspended. The full tragedy of war with England was sweeping over the land. A great British fleet, the most formidable yet assembled in the New World, had sailed unhindered into the St. Lawrence, and Quebec itself was at stake. This was the crisis of misfortune in an era marked by decline.

One marvels at the divine balance so often struck in human affairs. History records repeatedly the loss and gain, the ebb and flow, of providential compensation. New France of the mid-eighteenth century was in the depths materially; spiritually it was on the heights. This was a time of war, of epidemics, of storms, shipwrecks, floods, and earthquakes; of famine and in-flation; of disastrous crop failures—no less than eight between 1740 and 1760—and of political graft and corruption unparal-leled in its history. And yet, in Christian homes, in hospitals, in seminaries and convents, the spirit of charity and self-sacrifice burned like a bright flame to direct the suffering souls of men to enduring spiritual realities. Out of holocaust ascended prayer; out of anguish came the essence of sanctity.

Mother d'Youville's Community, like others of the time, had grown strong in its spiritual organization while the political life of New France declined. In October of 1755, two months after the adoption of the grey habit by the Sisters, six thousand Acadi-ans, immortalized in *Evangeline*, had been deported by the British from their peaceful homes in Grand Pré, Nova Scotia, that most salient spot lost to the French by the Treaty of Utrecht in 1713. One can imagine the effect of this tragedy on the hearts of other French settlers as the news seeped into villages and towns throughout the land. Would this be the pattern of English domination, now more to them than a threat?

Anglo-French relations had indeed reached grave proportions. From the beginning of hostilities in 1744, through a ten-year truce, to the open declaration of war in 1756, the two nations had contested overlapping claims to colonial territory in the Mississippi, Ohio, and St. Lawrence valleys. They had struggled for supremacy in the fur trade, that golden key to economic prosperity in the New World, by balancing cheap English rum and expensive French brandy before the Indians who held that key; and the Indians, preferring more of the worse to less of the better, had yielded to the English. The success of British traders in Newfoundland and the Hudson Bay area had proved a northern anaconda to the fur-trading centers of the French, until the latter had been forced to surrender their claims to these areas and acknowledge the sovereignty of the English over the Iroquois.

And yet the French had long held strategic forts against British advances: Louisburg on Cape Breton Island, at the mouth of the mighty St. Lawrence; Ticonderoga on the southern Champlain approaches; Duquesne and Frontenac in the West.

Had New France not been governed during these critical years by the Marquis de Vaudreuil-Cavagnal, incompetent son of the earlier Governor General, and by François Bigot, the profligate Intendant, even these few strongholds, under the military command of Montcalm, might have stood successfully against British forces mustered by England's great statesman, William Pitt. But while De Vaudreuil complained of Montcalm to higher authorities, Bigot depleted the strength of Louisburg, and the great fortress fell to the British in 1758. Fort Frontenac and Fort Duquesne surrendered in the same year. Within a few months Ticonderoga also had to be abandoned.

Could Mother d'Youville have set one stone upon another in her new building while her native land was being threatened to its very foundations?

The great rock fortress of Quebec now became the British objective. Montcalm, constantly impeded by De Vaudreuil and Bigot, stretched his defenses thirty-five miles along the endangered shore. Every possible approach was guarded by guns and patrolled by pickets. Seventeen thousand men stood ready to repel attack, but two thirds of these, as militia or volunteers, were subject to the Governor General's arbitrary orders.

How fiercely French hearts beat for their homeland as forty British warships and one hundred transports bearing 27,000 men, regulars and sailors, anchored in the St. Lawrence to besiege the "Gibraltar of the West"!

Bishop Pontbriand, as chief shepherd of his terrified flock, strengthened with the holy chrism of Confirmation as many as he could reach. To priests he gave special faculties, so that in whatever crisis the people found themselves, they would be prepared in soul. Religious devotions throughout the land kept alive their faith, their fortitude, their hope.

As hot summer weeks slipped by, leaving the state of siege unchanged, Wolfe, the young British commander, realized that the fortress would have to be taken before winter froze his forces in the icy waters of the river. So far nothing but failure had met his attempts to scale the impregnable heights.

But every strength has its weakness, and Quebec had Le Foulon. This narrow pass, inadequately guarded, had been reinforced by Montcalm, but the improvident De Vaudreuil, belittling his precaution, had withdrawn the extra men. Here was Wolfe's opportunity.

Having learned that the French were expecting provisions at this spot on the night of September 12, the British commander detailed a picked group of scouts to intercept the supply boats, scale the upward path to Le Foulon, overpower the sentry, and open the way to the rest of the English forces.

All the world knows the story, one of the high points in the history of heroism. On the fateful morning of September 13, the red ranks of the British faced the white troops of the French on the Plains of Abraham, outside the city walls. In half an hour the battle was over, with Wolfe and Montcalm among the slain, and the standard of Great Britain waved above old French Quebec.

During the anxious weeks of this historic siege, the war had come very close to Mother d'Youville. Her youngest son, Father Charles Dufrost, pastor at Pointe-de-Lévy, now the more familiar Levis, opposite Quebec, was taken prisoner on July 24 with 287 of his parishioners as they fled into the woods to escape the enemy. All were brought on board a British frigate and kept there in captivity until the capitulation of Quebec. General Monckton, having taken Pointe-de-Lévy, turned Father Dufrost's little church into a hospital.

The news of her son's uncertain fate struck Mother d'Youville's heart just as she mourned another loss, the death of Father Normant on June 18, at the age of seventy-nine. Worn out by years of illness, this holy priest, intensely devoted to his people, had not been able to survive his grief over their sufferings and the impending conquest of his beloved country.

Though long relieved of the direction of the Sisters of Charity through Father Montgolfier's succession to that responsibility, Father Normant had continued to the end of his life to visit them at the General Hospital whenever he could, bringing them little presents according to his custom. On one occasion, having distributed a few treasures—pins, needles, beads, and the like— he noticed that Mother d'Youville, seated beside him, had nothing.

"And now, Mother, what shall I give you?" he asked regretfully. "I have nothing left!"

Not long at a loss, however, the kindly priest drew from his pocket his own silver and pearl-handled folding knife and presented it to her, quite satisfied that now everyone had been remembered.

This knife, marked with Father Normant's name, is not only treasured to this day at the General Hospital in Montreal; it is used by the Reverend Mother General on August 25 every year in commemoration of his feast day.

Mother d'Youville and her Sisters, left in 1759 with innumerable grateful memories of Father Normant, expressed their gratitude at once in the most effective manner known to them—

that is, by a High Mass of requiem. The chapel was draped with black for the solemn occasion, and illuminated with a great number of vigil lights arranged to form salutary ejaculations. It was a magnificent sight, agreed the people of Montreal; a worthy tribute to the holy Sulpician priest who, under God, had built the spiritual foundation of the Sisters of Charity, their own Grey Nuns.

But not even for Father Normant could the Sisters take time to grieve. The wartime sufferings of their people demanded all the charity of their hearts. In Montreal the fall of Quebec had multiplied disaster. Citizens facing famine themselves now had to share their poor rations with refugees from the defeated city. To extreme want and the blinding confusion of war was added that most poignant anguish—fear of losing the religion that was dearer to them than life.

Chief among the refugees who crowded into Montreal that terrible autumn of 1759 was Bishop Pontbriand. Believing that his place was with those who still survived under the French flag, he had confided to Father Jean-Olivier Briand, his Vicar General, the spiritual guidance of the victims of Quebec. In the broken city behind him he had left his cathedral in ruins, his episcopal palace destroyed.

Tradition has it that it was to Mother d'Youville and her Sisters that the afflicted Bishop first turned for shelter and care, and that with them he remained until he could take up residence with the Sulpician Fathers at the seminary. Many a prayer of gratitude must he have breathed for his eventual support of this house now open to him in his need!

And many a prayer of gratitude did the foundress also breathe when her son, Father Charles Dufrost, arrived in Montreal in the early spring of 1760 to confer with his bishop. Having been released by the British in October of the year preceding, he had found his position at Pointe-de-Lévy too dangerous and had thought it wise to betake himself to territory still French. What the reunion with his mother must have meant to both of them is easy to conjecture. Her maternal heart never lost its tender concern for her sons.

Even during this time of national crisis, Mother d'Youville kept herself on the alert for the development of her community. Realizing that the strength of her Sisters was being expended to the utmost by both labor and want, she took advantage of the Bishop's presence to ask his permission to admit some postulants and novices. These she believed could be prepared to replace the administrators, limited by the letters patent to the number of twelve. The good Bishop concurred in her opinion. Accordingly, six postulants and four novices were received. Father Montgolfier, in view of the fact that Canada was in imminent danger of passing into the hands of another nation, allowed three novices to pronounce their vows on December 12, 1759, thus bringing up to fifteen the number of professed Sisters.

Now the times grew even worse. General de Levis, the most able commander left to the depleted French forces, determined to make a desperate attempt to defeat the British and regain Quebec. Building up his army with men needed in the fields for the spring planting, he battled his way back to the Plains of Abraham. Defeat the British he did, on April 27, 1760, but only temporarily, and he failed disastrously to retake Quebec.

Driven back into Montreal at the end of May, the straggling French army only added to misery already extreme. Between stark scarcity of food on one side and exorbitant prices on the other, the people faced starvation. Maize and horse meat, and these only in meager quantities, made up the daily diet of the common people. Eggs at six francs a dozen and mutton at eighty francs a pound were only for the wealthy.

As in all times of war, the economic situation was unstable. One baker, one butcher, and a handful of storekeepers created monopolies impossible to overcome. The government issued more and more paper money; and this, converted into bills of exchange redeemable in three years only, created a state of inflation in which simple commodities were sold for seven or eight times more than they were worth.

Financially, the care of wounded British soldiers at the General Hospital involved a definite loss; for Bigot, true to himself, allotted to Mother d'Youville only three fourths of the cost of maintenance. From 1757 to 1760 he made payments in paper money scarcely more than worthless. Morally incapable of seeing her patients suffer from lack of the necessities of life, she was obliged to contract loans on interest in order to procure what they needed. These loans were a burden for many years to come.

After the fall of Quebec, provisions were so low at the General Hospital that Mother d'Youville asked the Sisters to get along on maize and water for breakfast and supper, their only meals, so that the poor and the sick could have the bread that remained. But since the farms were producing far less grain than was needed, even the bread was soon lacking altogether, and the poor shared the fare of the Sisters. The situation was indeed critical.

Then Divine Providence, in ways known only to eternal wisdom, came to the rescue. One day, as the Sisters met in their refectory for their meal of maize and water, they were startled to find in one corner of the room several barrels of fine flour. How they came to be there, no one knew—a state of affairs surprising enough at a time when every grain of wheat was scrupulously counted!

Mother d'Youville, pious but very practical, made every possible effort, with the help of the Sisters, to find out who had supplied this saving gift and how these barrels had been carried into the refectory without being seen. No one knew a thing about it. There was nothing to do but believe that the Eternal Father had supplied His daughters out of His heavenly bounty. This was certainly not the first time that He had chosen flour made of wheat!

If Mother d'Youville and her Sisters were consoled by the unexplained beneficence that somewhat relieved their physical sufferings, their hearts were made more heavy by the death of Bishop Pontbriand on June 8, at the age of only fifty-one. Months of illness and the ultimate in want and anxiety had exhausted his bodily reserve; and no longer could the soul of this afflicted shepherd support the tragedies of earth. The loss of his beloved Quebec, the misery of his flock, the sight of three British armies closing in on Montreal from east and west and south—these were sorrows too great.

Shortly before his death the stricken Bishop said to Father Montgolfier, "Tell my poor that in dying I leave them nothing, because I myself die poorer than they."

But to Mother d'Youville and her Sisters at the General Hospital poor Bishop Pontbriand left his miter, gloves, cinctures, and the few altar linens that remained to him—delicate reparation for former unbelief, paternal testament of esteem and trust!

Now the General Hospital, situated on Pointe-à-Callières, outside the city walls and close to the banks of the St. Lawrence, stood in the very path of the war coming closer to Montreal. Enemies approaching the city up or down the river, or across from the southern bank, sighted first the great grey stone building rising almost like a fortress within its solid wall.

It was indeed a fortress, a fortress of mercy for the afflicted, no matter who they were. French patriots struck down by English muskets or by Iroquois arrows, Indian victims of war or disease, British soldiers captured in battle or fallen far from their own men—all found haven here and equal care. This house was a refuge for the needy, and Mother d'Youville never qualified the term.

The plight of abandoned English soldiers particularly touched her heart. She could not turn them away from the hospital unbefriended and unemployed after they had been restored to health. To whom could they go? What could they do in a country where there was little enough work for loyal Frenchmen? Small chance had they of finding their way back to British lines through gantlets of French and Indian sentries! Never could

209

this mother of the homeless thrust outside her gate any son of God who had no home. Her love knew no nationality. Her account book records that she employed one English soldier on the farm at Chambly, twenty-one at Point St. Charles, and five at the hospital itself. Unable to pronounce hard Anglo-Saxon surnames, she designated foreign employees by their Christian names, plus the distinction *l'Anglais!*

Not only did wounded English soldiers find care and shelter at the hospital. Fugitives of war, pursued by French or Indian enemies, and facing either the walls of the hostile city or the overwhelming waters of the great river or the merciless hands of their captors, often ran desperately into the old grey building, begging for a place to hide.

"Come!" Mother d'Youville would say quickly.

Knowing that every corner of the house would be searched by pursuers hot on the heels of the poor unfortunates, she would hide them in vaults under the chapel, where neither French nor Indians would think of going. Later, when the coast was clear, she would visit them herself, bringing them food and everything else that they needed to make them comfortable. Think of this valiant Mother, treading softly the damp ground of her cellar to the vaults where these men lay fearfully waiting in the dark and silent night, her face illuminated less by the candle in her hand than by the charity that shone upon it! How calmly she strengthened these poor fugitives, planning with them their hour of escape!

When the right moment came, she would wrap them in the big grey capes and hoods that the Sisters wore in winter. Thus disguised, they would make their way to safety.

Once, however, the ruse nearly failed. As an enveloped fugitive passed through a ward where some Indians were lying, one of them, his eyes blinded by smallpox but his sense of smell not affected in the least, perceived the presence of his enemy. Leaping out of bed with a savage yell, he fell upon the escaping Englishman, cape and all, and would have killed him on the spot

210

if two strong young Sisters nearby had not succeeded in dragging him back to bed. Needless to say, the poor soldier made his escape without further regard for religious decorum!

On another occasion a young Englishman by the name of Southworth, whose descendants were still in Williamstown, Massachusetts, in 1915, found himself separated from his comrades near Pointe-à-Callières. Cautiously moving forward in hope of finding them, he glanced back just in time to see a bloodthirsty Indian stealthily creeping up on him. Preferring to give himself up to the French rather than fall into the hands of barbarians whose horrible tortures he knew too well, he dashed wildly toward the grey stone building rising up between him and the open sky. Scrambling over the wall, he ran across the yard to a small basement window, fortunately left open, and forced himself through.

Only a moment more and he had run up the stairs, along the corridor, and straight into the Sisters' community room. Mother d'Youville and a companion, working there on a great canvas tent, looked up in astonishment. Instantly sensing the desperate plight of the intruder, she rose to her feet, lifting the heavy material as she did so and giving him a quick sign to get beneath it.

Scarcely had the great folds settled over his body when the pursuing savage appeared in the doorway, brandishing his tomahawk, mouthing guttural demands that had only one terrible meaning.

But Mother d'Youville, apparently unperturbed—as if Indians and tomahawks were ordinary accidents—simply raised her arm and pointed to another door that led into an outside passage. Did she mean that the English soldier had gone that way? Or did she mean that the trespassing Indian should immediately take himself out that very door? In any case, the savage dashed through with a series of wild yells and lost himself in his search for the lucky fugitive.

Satisfied now that the danger had passed, Mother d'Youville lifted up the heavy canvas again and released her embarrassed prisoner from his strange but timely cell. Lacking the freedom of language to express his thanks, the poor fellow could only grasp her hand in both of his and write in his shining eyes the gratitude of his soul. He would repay her someday; he knew that he would! And he did!

Not only did Mother d'Youville harbor the harborless during these years of war. Dedicated to all the corporal works of mercy, she actually ransomed captives in danger of death at the hands of the Indians.

One day in 1757, not long after she had opened a ward for wounded British men, she happened to learn that a band of Indians near the hospital had captured a young soldier named John and that according to their custom they were slowly torturing him as a prelude to death by fire. Was it his cries that she had heard breaking sharply into the still night? Too horrified by his fate to think of her own safety, she hurried to the Indians' encampment. Holding up two hundred francs in ready money before the blinking eyes of the savages, she begged insistently for the prisoner's release. Since money was harder to get than English soldiers, they quickly agreed to the exchange, and Mother d'Youville hurried back to the hospital with John at her side.

In grateful return, the lucky young soldier offered his services as an orderly in the ward for his wounded countrymen; and the good Mother, remembering language difficulties, eagerly accepted him. In her humility she probably considered herself more fortunate than he. John became a valuable member of her personnel.

On the twenty-seventh of June a year later, Father Lavalinière, one of the Sulpician Fathers, traveling from the city on a lonely bypath not far from the hospital, came suddenly upon a terrible sight. Fastened to a post around which a group of naked savages were already heaping firewood was a young white woman with her little daughter, about two years old, bound in her arms. Both of them were too shocked and terrified to utter a sound.

Crying out to stop this horrible proceeding, the brave priest began to plead with the Indians to give him their pitiful victims, promising rewards and benefits especially appealing to their savage hearts. Won by his courage as much as by his promises, they finally unbound the poor mother and her child and pushed them roughly toward their rescuer.

It was immediately to the General Hospital that Father Lavalinière brought the bruised and frightened pair. With what tender womanly sympathy Mother d'Youville took them in!

Mrs. O'Flaherty—this was indeed the poor mother's name— profoundly shaken by her experience and fearing that her little daughter, Mary Louise, might again be captured by the Indians, begged her to keep the child in this safe retreat. Only too happily Mother d'Youville agreed to do so; and to Sister Bénard, in charge of the women's department, the little one was carefully entrusted.

The sequel of this incident is yet more significant. Mary Louise O'Flaherty, lovingly educated by Mother d'Youville and Sister Bénard, made profession as a Grey Nun on December 19, 1776, five years after the death of the foundress. Gifted with a beautiful voice which Sister Bénard herself knew how to train, she carried forward the tradition of chapel singing so ably begun by her teacher. Her love of silence and her gentle, kindly spirit were blessings in the religious life to which God called her. It is a bit of heavenly humor that Sister O'Flaherty, the first Irish Grey Nun, died on March 17, 1824.

In spite of Mother d'Youville's unfailing charity toward unfortunate English soldiers, the position of the hospital at Pointe-à-Callières became more and more dangerous with the passage of the summer months of 1760. The big stone building did not always impress British troops closing in on Montreal from the south as a citadel of charity.

General Amherst, for example, commanding a formidable army encamped within cannon range of the hospital, had no doubt whatsoever that this substantial structure surrounded by a seven-foot wall was a fort, bristling with guns directed at his men. Ordering his heavy artillery to be mounted, he prepared on September 7 to bombard the supposed fort.

Just as he stood ready to give the order to fire, a soldier broke his way through the lines, ran up to his commanding officer, and hastily saluted. It was young Southworth.

"Wait, sir!" he cried. "Wait! No enemies live in that house, sir. Nuns live there—good nuns!"

Urgently, vividly, he described his escape from death through Mother d'Youville's swift action, the ingenious assistance that other fugitives had received from her, the ward for wounded English soldiers so faithfully maintained by the Sisters.

Impressed by Southworth's unmistakable sincerity, General Amherst suspended preparations for bombardment and detailed five or six officers who could speak French to go to the hospital for a verification of facts.

Instant alarm showed in the face of the Sister who opened to them the heavy door of the hospital, alarm that spread like an electric charge to the hearts of the other Sisters as they caught sight of the scarlet uniforms of the men. In a few moments Mother d'Youville appeared. The flawless courtesy of her approach did not quite obscure the anxious question in her dark eyes, nor the concern of the Sisters who pressed near.

"Do not be frightened, ladies," one of the officers reassured them in easy French. "We are your prisoners."

Once Mother d'Youville understood the purpose of their visit, she took command of the uncomfortable situation with simple grace. In a few moments her irresistible charm and assurance had dispelled both the embarrassment of the officers and the alarm of the Sisters.

After a brief preliminary conversation in the community room, where the men, though undirected, did not fail to observe the poverty of its appointments and the piles of sewing from which the Sisters had evidently just been summoned, Mother d'Youville began to lead them cheerfully through all the departments of the house. She had nothing to hide. They had come to see; they would see!

Here was the old men's room, clean, orderly, permeated with peace. Several men rose slowly to their feet as the good Mother came in with her strange visitors. In her quick glance they caught the keynote of their own response.

Across the hall was the ward for wounded British soldiers. The visiting officers could hardly believe their eyes. Their own men here, clean and comfortable in the care of these Sisters! What an exchange of sentiments across the subtle barriers of military rank and reserve! And then the officers saw that, in rooms adjoining, the Sisters were attending to French and even Indian patients with equal consideration.

There on the first floor also was the men's dining room, with little evidence of abundant fare; and there, the women's, just as poor; and the Sisters' refectory, stark in its plainness, beautiful in its simplicity; and the kitchen, where big copper kettles full of steaming maize hung over the low flames of the great open fireplace.

Swift ascent up the narrow stairs at the end of the building brought Mother d'Youville and her guests to the second floor, the women's department. On one side were the resident boarders' rooms, contrasting sharply yet not inharmoniously with the rest of the house. On the other side poor old ladies rocked quietly in their large sunny room, some sewing, some praying, all contented. From another room came the pitifully small sound of infants' crying. Here were abandoned babies for whom the motherly heart of the foundress had begun to open wide. Poor little mites! Most of them were already on their way out of this life.

It was soon over, this tour of the formidable fort feared by the British commander! And what was the astonishment of the officers on returning to the little parlor, sadder and wiser men, to find refreshments of wine and biscuits waiting for them! There was not much that Mother d'Youville and her Grey Nuns could offer to guests in these times of dire want, but what they had they served with such charming politeness that the officers were completely overcome. It was with unqualified regret that they left the peaceful building to return to the noises of war.

The report that they brought back to General Amherst not only verified young Southworth's story; their glowing account surpassed it by far. The General Hospital was saved, once and for all!

Not so poor Montreal! The next day, September 8, was a day of mortal sorrow for the unhappy city. Hemmed in by three British armies, unable to make any defense, terrified by the impending destruction of their homes as well as by the prospect of torture at the hands of the Indians, the people themselves implored Governor General de Vaudreuil to negotiate surrender. Without delay he signed the articles of capitulation—prelude to the Treaty of Paris three years later, which put all Canada under the British flag.

Within a few weeks De Vaudreuil, François Bigot, and all their followers were sent back to France to give an account of the scandalous stewardship which had cost the mother country her richest colony. Although De Vaudreuil was acquitted by the Royal Court, Bigot was banished from France for the rest of his life and all his possessions, which he had bought with the blood of his people and millions of dollars stolen from the treasury, were confiscated. Justice triumphed, but New France was lost.

Officially the war was over, but for many a year every French heart was a battleground where loves and loyalties struggled for survival. Even though the terms of capitulation guaranteed the liberties, property, and religion of the Canadian people, the clause qualifying freedom of worship "as far as the laws of Great Britain permit" caused poignant misgivings in the hearts of the defeated people, so deeply French, so ardently Catholic. Many of the best families left Canada, taking advantage of the right granted by the Treaty of Paris to return to France within eighteen months.

Nevertheless, in obedience to the last expressed wishes of their shepherd, Bishop Pontbriand, Catholic priests urged loyal allegiance to the conqueror and proclaimed the *Te Deum* in all the churches of the land for the well-being of the British sovereign.

English officials, on the other hand, recognizing the essential relation between peaceful government and respect for the religious sentiments of the people, adapted their policies accordingly, with such harmonious results, on the whole, as history has been proud to record.

To Mother d'Youville, daughter of a soldier of France, the change in national allegiance was as painful as to every other French heart. She loved her country and her King as only one could love who had suffered for both. Besides, were not the name and great seal of Louis XV on the precious parchment that sanctioned her community? Would not the fleur-de-lis on her silver crucifix always remind her of this gracious Sovereign's beneficence?

It is particularly from the letters that Mother d'Youville wrote during these tragic years of transition that one learns the depth of her personal sorrow as a result of the defeat of 1760. Writing to the Abbé de l'Isle-Dieu, she pleaded:

Ask God to give us strength to bear all our crosses and to make a holy use of them. How many of them there are at once! To lose one's King, one's country, one's resources, and what is worse, to live in constant fear of seeing one's holy religion taken away!

When André Débarras, visitor on behalf of the King, had returned to his country, Mother d'Youville wrote, "Give us news of you and of your dear daughters. In the surrender that France has made of us, it is our only consolation to have news of our friends."

A year later she wrote again to this friend:

How shall we get along? How shall we live with the English? They are doing us neither good nor evil just now. We are having great difficulty in even subsisting. Money is extremely scarce, and no one can find a way to earn any. Those people do not have any work done, and their King still less. And the worst of it is that this poor country is being abandoned. All good citizens are leaving it. People are grieved to see their relatives, their friends, and their benefactors going away, never to see them again. Nothing is sadder! Every day, new sacrifices . . .

I tell you nothing about Madame de Louche and Angélique, for they are writing to you themselves. I do not know how many times they have kissed your little children's handwriting, which they bathe with their tears. They have asked me as a favor to keep your letter.

The decision of many of her relatives and friends to leave Canada pained Mother d'Youville's tender human heart. To Etienne-Guillaume de Figuiéry, her nephew by marriage, who was awaiting in France the arrival of his wife, Louise Lajemmerais' daughter, she addressed these sorrowful words:

You are seeing our dear Josephte, and we are losing her forever. I have not been to see them for several days, and I shall not go until I know that she has left. I have not courage enough to say good-by to her. I shall do my best to console her father, her mother, and her brothers and sisters when she will no longer be here. I fear that this departure will cause a great change in her father and mother. I must stop; my tears are blinding me.

The departure so dreaded evidently did not take place at once; for more than a year later Mother d'Youville wrote again to her nephew, setting her own feelings aside this time and urging the reunion of husband and wife.

I wish that I had something good to tell you, but on the contrary, poor Gamelin [his father-in-law], whose kind heart you know, is extremely disturbed on account of not having the money to send Josette to you; but I can assure you that it is beyond them to produce one hundred pounds. I am very much surprised to see how they have been able to live these last three years without any business. . . . You know that they have seven children to support. They find no place to put them; they are all big; that means more expense than when they were little. One must hope that Divine Providence, always watching over those who are faithful, will use every means on this side or on yours to give to your dear wife what she needs to go to you. I am going to ask God and have our whole community pray for help in this matter.

All our Sisters remember you very gratefully. They assure you of their regards, above all, Sisters Despins and Rainville.

Mother d'Youville's personal interest in the little family trial here revealed must have succeeded, for within the next year the beloved Josette herself had a letter.

Let us say no more about departures or farewells. Let us say that we are in good health and that you are with your dear husband. Let us now think of nothing but of striving to be reunited in heaven where we shall never again be separated. All our Sisters send thousands and thousands of affectionate regards, above all, Sister Despins, who comes with wide-open arms to tell me not to forget her. Our ladies wish to be included also, St.-Michel in the lead, and before all others, your aunt Maugras [Clemence].

We hope that you will give us news of you. They say that you had to leave on the tenth. The northeast wind was blowing and since then a delightful breeze, and the most beautiful weather in the world. We rejoice on account of it, hoping that you are now out of the river.

My regards to your husband, for whom I have as for you all possible attachment.

From the general tone of these letters, selfless, tenderly thoughtful of others, mindful even of beautiful weather, one concludes that personal grief and anxiety could not overcome Mother d'Youville's naturally optimistic spirit. Her letter to Father Villard on August 5, 1763, in the very midst of trials, shows her tendency to make the best of the situation.

We have been taken by surprise. We have always made ourselves believe that France would not abandon us; but we were mistaken in our hope. God has permitted it so; may His holy Name be blessed! If we are as free to practice our religion, and to do all the good that we find to do, as we have been since we fell under English domination, we shall not have to complain about spiritual matters, but in temporal affairs there will be more suffering. People cannot earn their living under them as they did under the French, but I hope that Divine Providence will supply their need.

Submission to the will of God! Trust in Divine Providence! Always these were the dominant themes of Mother d'Youville's life, the secrets of her serenity in the overwhelming trials that fell to her.

No matter how bitterly this brave woman felt the sorrows that seemed numberless in this era of national disaster, she did not for a moment allow personal feeling to obstruct her obligation of courteous allegiance to recognized authority. To General Thomas Gage, military governor of Montreal in the transition period, she addressed this gracious message of good will:

SIR:

Permit me to anticipate the New Year by a few days in order to assure you of my most humble regards and those of my Sisters. We are offering all our poor prayers to the Lord for the preservation of your health and the accomplishment of all your desires, as well as for Madame, your wife, and your whole family, which is very dear to us, and for which we keep an eternal remembrance.

When James Murray was named civil Governor of Canada after the Treaty of Paris in 1763, Mother d'Youville's immediate response indicated her innate and exquisite courtesy, her principles of rectitude, her strength of soul. Very simply she wrote:

SIR:

I have just learned that the King, in further recognition of your merit, has appointed you for the general government of this colony. For this honor, sir, I beg you to receive my compliments and my assurance of the most profound respect.

Permit me to request you to take under your protection the hospital which I serve. This is the favor that she asks of you who has the honor to be, sir, with deep respect,

Your very humble and very obedient servant,

M. M. LAJEMMERAIS, VEUVE YOUVILLE,
Directress of the General Hospital

This example of respectful allegiance to national authority, combined with total consecration to the welfare of the people in whatever country they serve, is but one of many traditions preserved with inviolable fidelity by Mother d'Youville's daughters.

And the British nation so devotedly served has not been ungrateful. On June 4, 1934, George V of England bestowed on Mother Marie Anne Piché, seventeenth successor of Mother d'Youville, the distinguished title of Commander of the British Empire. Never before had this extraordinary honor been given to a nun.

In recognizing the signal contributions of Mother Piché to national development, the British government necessarily acknowledged also the consecrated services of all Grey Nuns throughout the United States and Canada, and from northernmost Aklavik to Kodiak, across the Pacific to China, down to Haiti, and over Atlantic waters to far Basutoland.

But when British soldiers, marching briskly past the Motherhouse in old Montreal, respectfully saluted the humble Commander of the British Empire within those strong grey walls, could they have guessed that they saluted also the spirit of one who had signed herself in 1763 the "very humble and very obedient servant" of the first British Governor General of Canada?

CHAPTER FOURTEEN

THE VALIANT WOMAN

MOTHER D'YOUVILLE unquestionably had her share of trials in the general disorder attending the transfer of Canada from France to Great Britain. Of these one of the most serious was the financial situation. Almost overnight the Sisters' chief source of income, their sewing, was swept away; for the defeat of the French troops and their subsequent recall to France brought to an end all the business that the King's stores for years had provided. Because of the prohibitive cost of living, other clients could no longer afford to order handwork.

There was, besides, a decided decrease in every other method of making money for the poor. No one could buy building materials; no one could pay for the transportation of goods. The farms, poorly cultivated during the critical years, did not yield enough for the subsistence of the hospital personnel, much less for sale in the Market Place.

Poverty became extreme. Sacrifice was daily bread at the hospital, and there was very little of any other kind. With a bushel of wheat costing forty francs in paper money and twenty-four francs in specie, how could Mother d'Youville provide 130 bushels a month for her household, the minimum for their needs? Yet not once did she falter in her care of the poor.

Divine Providence saw to it that many good people of the city managed to share with the hospital the little that remained to them. Alms, though small, were frequent. With the gradual adjustment attending the passage of years, contributions increased. Occasional bequests were added to the assets of the hospital. From paying boarders also, many of them influential and comparatively wealthy, a reliable income was derived, far from sufficient, but at least helpful.

The most tragic feature of the financial catastrophe that followed the cession of Canada was the depreciation of money. For Mother d'Youville the ultimate loss was probably far greater than for anyone else; for in 1760 the Treasury of France owed the General Hospital 120,799 pounds, not only for a vast amount of sewing for the French troops that the King's storekeeper had commissioned the Sisters to do, but also for food and medicine supplied to wounded prisoners of war. Moreover, since the Intendant Bigot had not made sufficient appropriations for the care of English soldiers, Mother d'Youville had been forced to borrow money on interest. Now that the war was over, she waited for the Royal Court to issue a bill of exchange for the amount most justly due to her.

As the trial of François Bigot and the King's storekeeper and their scheming accomplices revealed the extraordinary frauds of which these men had made France and Canada the victims, it became evident that holders of paper money illegally acquired could not, and should not, be reimbursed. But the innocent would eventually have to suffer with the guilty. The French Treasury was impoverished; securities were unstable; relations between France and England were unsettled; and the rate of exchange continued to fluctuate.

Frequent questionings and grave concern about her bills of exchange run through many of Mother d'Youville's letters from 1760 to 1770, with the exception of courteous messages to Father Cousturier in 1763, when she wrote, "I am not at all disturbed about the bills of exchange which you have in your

223

hands belonging to the hospital; I am sure that you will take all possible care of them"; and later, "I have no anxiety whatever about the care that you will take of them, sure that it will not be your fault if they turn out badly." One cannot help feeling, however, that even these gracious assurances are polite reminders of urgent need.

Anxious months passed by and still there was no settlement nor any word of hope or explanation. "We do not yet know anything about the fate of the bills of exchange of 1759," Mother d'Youville wrote. "Perhaps we shall learn something by the last boats."

To André Débarras she wrote at the same time, "Like you, we are waiting for this decree to determine the payment of our drafts, which decree will put us a little more at ease and enable us to help a greater number of destitute."

The settlement that finally came in 1765 was little short of disaster. A decree of the King reduced to half their face value all bills of exchange that had been issued by royal officials, and all other drafts to one fourth their original worth.

To the Abbé de l'Isle-Dieu Mother d'Youville wrote in March of that year:

It is a great deal to lose . . . and not to know when all of it will be reimbursed. That is what we do not know. I hope that you will let us know where we stand in all this business. You see our great need by the bills of exchange that I have drawn on you without knowing if you would have the means to pay them. I have more debts to pay this year than any other. They say that paper money, even though registered here, will not be redeemed. . . . I leave all to Divine Providence; my confidence is in it; all that will happen which is pleasing to God.

Within the year the Abbé de l'Isle-Dieu replied:

You have been badly treated by the Court, after the way you sacrificed yourselves, you and your dear and esteemed community, for the service of the King and the relief of the poor. The communities of

Canada are not in the category of gamblers and traders who have
drained our poor colonies and caused the loss of them that we have
suffered.

The worst was yet to come, however. Another royal decree in
November of 1767 declared that bills of exchange payable by
the King would be converted into contracts paying nothing but
interest of four and a half per cent; and in January of 1770 the
interest was reduced to two and a half per cent.

When all was said and done, this drastic reduction left to the
General Hospital only 699 pounds out of the original 120,799
pounds earned through years of loyal and honorable labor.

What Mother d'Youville thought of the settlement decreed by
the King one need not surmise. Her own letters perfectly express
her reaction to the whole affair—shocked, but clear-sighted and
patient, obedient to the King, infinitely grateful to benefactors,
resigned to the will of God, completely confident in Divine
Providence. To her procurator in France she wrote:

I learn of the treatment that the Court has given our bills of exchange. It is very harsh and does an immense wrong to the wretched
poor of this country. We had acquired them with a great deal of
trouble and labor. With regard to the drafts, lists, and statements of
work for the ordinances, we had almost a third of them through
alms. . . . Blessed be God! One must carry his crosses. It is true that
He gives them to us in abundance in this sorrowful land.

To the Abbé de l'Isle-Dieu she appealed, "I cannot help begging you to redouble your efforts to draw the attention of the
Court to our sad lot. It could pay us more than the others without causing any jealousy, and give us a little ready money!"

Evidently the Abbé made every effort to reduce the losses
suffered by the General Hospital on account of the King's decrees, for Mother d'Youville wrote again:

I do not doubt in the least the trouble that you have taken to obtain
from the King some indemnity for the losses that we have incurred on
our bills of exchange. . . . We have obligations to you that we could

never discharge if we could not, as members of Jesus Christ, draw from His treasury to repay the kindnesses that are done to us, of which yours have a value to be paid only by this heavenly money. Often my Sisters and I importune Our Lord and His Divine Father, Who has been the object of my great confidence for almost forty years, to preserve you for us for many years to come, and then to reward you with eternal glory.

The burden of unbelievable loss could not keep out of Mother d'Youville's letters spontaneous expressions of gratitude, humility of heart, and greatness of soul. To the Abbé she wrote again:

I cannot adequately express my gratitude to you for all the good services that you have rendered us. I wish sometimes that I had business which would oblige me to go to France, so that I could convey my appreciation fully by word of mouth; and then, I refer that to God, Who keeps an account of all the good that is done to the poor. I pray and have others pray that He will grant you all that you can desire for time and for eternity.

Innate delicacy and consideration for Father Cousturier, who had also done his utmost to safeguard the interests of the General Hospital, drew from Mother d'Youville's grateful pen this letter of August 21, 1766:

I am sure that you have taken all precautions necessary to turn our bill of exchange to account, but for all that, the King is the ruler and there is nothing to be said about what he does. It is indeed certain that we acquired it most honorably and that it should not be confused with those that were not. I shall conform myself to all that you do. Father Montgolfier has told me that he would arrange everything; that is why I have no anxiety. He has done and he is still doing for us much more than I would have dared to ask of him.

The death of Father Savarie, procurator of the General Hospital, on January 27, 1767, complicated the final settlement of financial affairs in France. On August 25 of the following year, Mother d'Youville patiently observed to the Abbé de l'Isle-Dieu,

"We do not yet know if we have a procurator, nor who he is, but I depend on your usual kindness and await with patience what you will let us know."

On the same day, however, she expressed herself a little more firmly to Father Villard:

We have not yet had any news from France. I trust that you have had the goodness to name a procurator for us, for I seriously must know the state of our affairs in France. If we have something, we really need to use it. I dare not do anything until we have news.

It was not until 1769 that Mother d'Youville gave up hope that the Abbé de l'Isle-Dieu could win justice for the hospital from the Royal Court. Then she wrote: "I hardly believed that you could get any indemnity from the Court. They say that it is very harsh. It has done us a great wrong. May God forgive it!"

Mother d'Youville's final word on the whole unhappy subject was addressed to Father Maury, the new procurator, on September 21, 1770:

The news was spreading here when I received your letter, that the interest on Canadian paper money converted into contracts was reduced to two and a half per cent—something that no one in this country could believe. Indeed we have been classified with those who did a great wrong to the King of France, and all the communities of this land are the victims of it; and many honest people are ruined. The innocent are suffering for the guilty.

There was nothing impassioned or vindictive in Mother d'Youville's acceptance of the great wrong that had been done. She faced facts, and she did her best to have justice done to the poor hospital that she served so faithfully. No one could have done more.

The loss of hard-earned money was not the only trial sustained by Mother d'Youville and her Grey Nuns after the cession of Canada. For several years the fear of losing complete freedom of worship and even of being disbanded as a religious community hung like a black cloud over their lives. In spite of the

227

reassuring terms of the Treaty of Paris, religious communities of men and women continued to feel insecure under English domination; nor were they without reason for their fear. Monsieur d'Eon, one of the French agents to the British Court, writing from London on October 11, 1763, to the Duc de Choiseul, remarked:

We do not know the plan for religious that the English are going to adopt in Canada, but no one doubts that, while allowing the practice of the Catholic religion, they will at the same time suppress all communities of men and women, which they claim are useless in the colony.

Moreover, the refusal of Governor General James Murray to allow the election of a bishop to fill the vacancy lately caused by the death of Bishop Pontbriand caused grave fears in the hearts of the faithful. Secretly they held an election in which Father Montgolfier was named to the episcopal office. Without delay he set out for London to appeal for the preservation of religious communities in Canada.

Before he had time to leave Quebec, however, Mother d'Youville wrote to him in haste:

Forgive me if I importune you again! You did me the honor to say before your departure that you would speak to the Fathers of the Chapter and let me know if we could give the habit to our postulants who are to be lay Sisters and to receive a few others who are presenting themselves. I am sure that you will make every effort to obtain this permission and to give it to us yourself. You understand our need better than anyone else. You know, moreover, that of the number of twelve administrators, almost half of us are no longer good for anything.

Since I have had no answer at all from you, I am afraid that you have forgotten me.

But the secretly elected Bishop Montgolfier had not forgotten. In fact, he thought that it would be imprudent to invest postulants with the habit of the Grey Nuns just at this critical period

in the affairs of the Church in Canada, and he advised delay.
Mother d'Youville, having received his decision, replied with her customary gracious acquiescence.

I thank you for the trouble that you have taken to answer me, and I shall abide by what you have decided on the subject of novices and postulants. . . . I take this opportunity to assure you of my most humble regards, and to express my gratitude for your kindnesses to our whole house and particularly to me. . . . All of us together offer our poor prayers to the Lord for your safety, the success of your journey, and your prompt return.

In London at last, Bishop Montgolfier found the situation less favorable than he had hoped. His election as bishop was acceptable only on certain conditions, among them the approval of Governor General James Murray.

This approval having been refused, another election was held in the following year, and Father Jean-Olivier Briand, Vicar General of Quebec, was chosen bishop and officially received.

Father Montgolfier must at least have succeeded in convincing authorities that religious communities were far from useless in Canada, for Mother d'Youville wrote to one of her relatives on August 20, 1766:

There is great hope that our Communities will be sustained. Our Bishop has allowed the profession of a novice at the General Hospital. . . . Things seem to be taking a good turn for our holy religion. Several young people are coming forward to resume their studies. One must hope that God will shower His blessings on this poor country.

Who could know during these troubled years how great were the blessings that God had already showered on this poor land, even though the blessings were made with the sign of the cross? Who could know then the deadly blow that the French Revolution only a few years later would deal to religion even in the mother country?

Not only did Mother d'Youville maintain extraordinary equanimity during all these years of grave financial and religious uncertainty, keeping her soul in grace and gratitude, in courtesy and courage; not only did she uphold all the work of the General Hospital with an invincible quality of perseverance that brought it back eventually to prewar development. Trusting in God, she also went forward to higher achievement.

In fact, at the beginning of 1760, as a gesture of complete abandonment to Divine Providence—some might call it extravagance—she spent 1665 pounds for a beautiful new altar dedicated to the Eternal Father and set up in the left transept of the chapel. On the base of this altar, elaborately constructed according to her own artistic ideas, two invocations were carved in relief: *Pater aeterne Deus, miserere nobis!* and *Pater aeternus benedicat nos!* This white-and-gold shrine, made in the midst of suffering and insecurity, is now carefully preserved in an oratory of the community room in the General Hospital. Above it hangs the memorable painting of the Eternal Father which Mother d'Youville purchased from France in 1741.

An altar dedicated with great sacrifice to the fatherhood of God was not the only active, substantial, and enduring prayer that Mother d'Youville offered to Divine Providence at the time of the capitulation of Canada. In the right transept of the chapel she erected a shrine to the Sacred Heart, the personification of charity. Could the Father of mercy and the Son of His love resist her trust?

Yet Mother d'Youville did more in these critical years than erect two shrines in the transepts of the chapel. To these two attributes of God, mercy and love, she raised a living altar—her home for abandoned babies, the first of its kind in North America. This was her dearest work, the crowning tenderness of her maternal heart, her most precious offering to the Creator and the Redeemer of human souls.

Long before the letters patent of 1753 guaranteed the stability of the General Hospital, Mother d'Youville's very soul had ached for the little ones abandoned by heartless parents to a governmental system almost as unfeeling. Under the old French regime, foundlings were turned over to a midwife who assigned them to paid nurses. When they were eighteen months old or younger, they were distributed to families who received subsidies for the care of them. As soon as the little outcasts were old enough to work, they were often retained as servants until they reached the age of eighteen or twenty. Not at all secret was the stigma of their birth.

In spite of the good intentions of the government, many revolting abuses crept into the system. Very often it was only the money that mattered. Rarely did the unfortunate children receive the love and protection that their little hearts craved, much less the religious training that their souls needed. Sometimes unscrupulous nurses, greedy for money, even sold the babies to the Indians. More than once the government had to act against such cruelty.

That Mother d'Youville seriously thought of adding the care of foundlings to the work of the General Hospital is evidenced by a memorandum among her papers, written at the time of negotiations for the letters patent. It reads:

If the Court approves our remaining here and if it should be disposed to uphold us in the good that God inspires us to do, we shall take care of foundlings. They suffer so much through the little care that is given to them. Out of twenty that are baptized, only two or three are raised. Indeed they reach the age of eighteen without learning the rudiments of religion. I know some of them twenty-three years old who have not made their First Communion!

It was never Mother d'Youville's way to develop in words any expression of her deepest personal feelings; but, from a study of her statement of facts in this memorandum, it is easy to conclude that for many years she had been following the unhappy fate of foundlings with a motherly compassion that had to be expressed in action sooner or later.

Six times she had herself known the blessed actuality of motherhood; six times she had received into her arms the helpless little body of a newborn babe. But she had also known the anguish of seeing four of her babies die in spite of her tender care. How could her maternal heart, denied again and again the living love of her children, help but be drawn to little ones unwanted and unloved? Comprehending the Mystical Body of Christ, as undoubtedly she did, she must also have seen again in the pitiful foundlings of the street her first little François and tiny Ignace, sweet Madeleine Ursule and baby Louise. Her mother heart could never forget, but it could open wide to other children of God.

Even though the Court made no mention of the care of foundlings in granting letters patent to the hospital, Mother d'Youville did not let the matter drop. She could not. Acting on the approval of Father Normant and trusting solely in Divine Providence for support, she received seventeen abandoned babies from 1754 until the fall of New France in 1760.

After the cession of Canada two tragic factors made the problem of foundlings very much more serious: first, the usual effect of war on the morals of a people; and secondly, the decision of the English government to make no appropriation for illegitimate children.

Now, in the midst of poverty and confusion, there were more abandoned babies than ever. Shameless mothers indifferent to their children, or despairing mothers unable to take care of them, simply disposed of them in whatever ways they chose. One found tiny infants in doorways or alleys, in open streets or lonely paths, exposed to prowling animals as well as to inclemencies of climate.

Mother d'Youville learned one day that someone had found two of these babies drowned in the river that ran close to the walls of the hospital. A few days later she herself came upon the body of a newborn child half buried in the mud of the street.

The climax of her horror in these inhuman happenings came one bitterly cold day in the midst of winter. Crossing the St. Pierre River on their way into the city, Mother d'Youville and her companion suddenly stopped short. There, frozen in the ice at their feet, lay a tiny dead baby with a cruel knife in its throat. Its little arms were stretched stiffly upward as if pleading for mercy.

Heartbroken at this terrible sight, the two Sisters knelt and tried to detach the little naked body from the ice. Mother d'Youville, convinced now that it would be another kind of cruelty to neglect any means of preventing such inhumanity as this, resolved then and there to give herself completely to the care of foundlings. A special department would be opened for them at the hospital, and everyone would know that here these most needy of the children of God would find a home and a mother's heart.

The other Sisters could not but follow Mother d'Youville's lead in this specific charity. Father Montgolfier, now their ecclesiastical superior, could not but approve. He even suggested that they should withdraw from the city nurses all children no longer in need of their care, and arrange for the nursing of newly found infants at the customary price. What if their funds were almost exhausted? What if their future was insecure? Divine Providence would find a way to supply for the needs of these helpless little beings blessed with immortal souls. "Suffer the little children to come unto Me." Had God not said it? Would He not provide for those who came?

It was certainly under circumstances of utmost adversity that Mother d'Youville began this most delicate and most exacting of her many works. How the Sisters were able to give the time and labor that it demanded is another miracle of Divine Providence. The foundress herself admitted the magnitude of this problem when she wrote:

The care of foundlings will keep at least three Sisters busy: one for the newborn, another for those who are beginning to walk, and a third for those who must be instructed and shown how to earn their living. Indeed I believe that only one Sister in each of these offices would be insufficient.

233

The financial aspect of this work was not any more encouraging. The nurses had to be paid promptly. The little ones needed not only food but also warm clothing and, often, medical care.

Yet from many sources aid did come. When General Gage learned from Father Montgolfier of the great charity undertaken by Mother d'Youville for foundlings, he was so glad to have this immense civic problem taken out of his hands that he allocated to the work all fines received for infractions of city laws. The civil government that succeeded his rule did not, however, share his benevolence, and the hospital gained only 288 francs from this source.

Occasional donations and bequests helped further to defray current expenses; but some of these, made in Canadian paper money, were greatly depreciated by the extraordinarily high cost of living and, later, by the King's decrees.

It would seem that the Eternal Father wished Mother d'Youville to leave entirely to His Providence the support of this work of heroic charity. Never did He fail to provide for the needs of the least of His little ones, even though numerous were the occasions when all human resources seemed at an end and nothing more could be done.

Early one morning, while checking accounts in her office to see just what her assets were, Mother d'Youville discovered, with quite natural dismay, that she had one silver coin to her name—only one, worth about a dollar. At that moment a poor woman came in to claim her payment for nursing one of the babies. She asked for exactly the amount of the silver coin. Instantly, for this was a just charge and the woman was in need, Mother d'Youville put her hand into her pocket to draw out the one coin. To her ineffable amazement, her hand closed on several, as many as she could grasp. Involuntarily she reached into her other pocket and brought forth another handful.

"O my God!" she exclaimed in humble abasement. "I am a wretched creature!"

Perhaps that was exactly the reason why Divine Providence came to her aid. After all, what are a few silver coins to the Creator of the world?

With the help of God, and in spite of all obstacles, the work went on. In the first year after the surrender of Montreal, Mother d'Youville found place for thirty more foundlings. At the time of her death, ten years later, 318 had been received, and nurses had been paid 9300 francs!

By no means did the care of foundlings end with Mother d'Youville's life. On the contrary, so completely had this blessed charity become a part of the spirit of the community under her influence, that the Sisters of Charity, the Grey Nuns, continued to support it with greater devotedness than ever, at a cost sometimes that only God could record.

Today, at beautiful Côte de Liesse, not far from Montreal, a magnificent five-story building, the D'Youville Crèche, stands as a living monument to the valiant Mother who received Christ in a little child. Constructed of steel, concrete, and light yellow brick; entirely fireproof; modern in every detail, it provides complete facilities for the care of 780 foundlings, of whom at least half are usually infants less than a year old. Here the children are kept—unless adopted—until they reach the age of five years, when they are transferred to orphanages also maintained by the Sisters.

This great institution, the development of the first foundling home in North America, inaugurated by the first North American-born foundress of a religious community, is not only the last word in scientific organization; it is also a beautiful and inviting home. Ten bright, sunny nurseries, each equipped with forty bassinets marked with pink or blue ribbon rosettes, complete departments for older children, operating rooms and dispensaries, laboratories, offices, immense kitchen, bakery, laundry, and sewing room, playrooms, enclosed sun porches, and pavilions— all preserve the happiness and health of smiling, rosy-cheeked children rescued from disgrace, destitution, and death.

The actual services of six medical specialists from the University of Montreal, 70 Grey Nuns, 80 secular nurses trained in pediatrics, and 150 employees make possible the operation of this vast institution. For a number of years the government has made partial appropriations for expenses, which are further discharged through voluntary donations and the faithful work of the Sisters.

Statistics record that since 1754 more than 57,000 children have been received at the foundling home begun by the foundress of the Grey Nuns. Who can tell how many have become useful members of society and citizens of heaven?

But Mother d'Youville, two centuries ago, could not foresee the Liesse of today. Lifting up her first little foundling from the streets of old Montreal in 1754, she saw only this most needy of the children of God, and simply trusted in Divine Providence for everything else.

In the year following the surrender of Montreal, Mother d'Youville began another great work of charity which has been faithfully preserved by her religious daughters to this day—assistance to young men studying for the priesthood. This undertaking was certainly a holy challenge to Divine Providence, for the total income of the General Hospital for 1761 was 9000 pounds, as compared with 60,000 pounds in the good years before the war. Yet, on March 30 of that year, when funds had reached bottom, Mother d'Youville sent fifty pounds to Father Villard, in charge of foreign missions, to help pay the expenses of a young seminarian named Pierre Menard.

One may imagine her joy and gratification when Father Menard himself called upon her at the General Hospital early in June of 1764, bearing the following letter from the Abbé de l'Isle-Dieu:

It is young Father Menard who is charged with my letter, and whom we are sending back to you as a priest. He was ordained last Saturday, the eve of Passion Sunday. He seems to have a very great

236

eagerness to give himself to his native land, where, I believe, people will be pleased with him. He is a very good subject; but since you are taking an interest in him, encourage him to particular prudence, respect, and discretion in dealing with the new government. Under the circumstances we must not expose ourselves to the slightest attack or criticism, if we wish to keep the freedom of religion which has been granted us. . . .

The interest that Mother d'Youville manifested in this young priest has borne blessed fruit throughout the years. At the General Hospital, in a separate building managed by the Sisters, six seminarians are now always lodged and supported during their preparations for the priesthood. How many "other Christs" have raised consecrated hands in thanksgiving for this aid since the day when Mother d'Youville, in blind trust, inaugurated it!

On the whole, 1764 was a comparatively hopeful year for the General Hospital. The tide seemed to be turning a little in favor of religious interests; at least conditions were not worse. Although death claimed two of the Sisters, Catherine Dulude, a novice only twenty-three years old, and Sister Agathe Véronneau, already mentioned, Mother d'Youville was greatly consoled when Father Montgolfier allowed two others to make profession. Sister Thérèse-Geneviève Coutlée, destined to be the third Superior General, pronounced her vows on October 24; and Sister Madeleine Pampalon, on the twenty-second of February in the following year. A few promising candidates were in the novitiate.

Spring smiled more brightly that year. The farms took on new life in abundance. Mother d'Youville, responding to the good signs of the times, just about made up her mind to launch out into the deep once more by purchasing a vast and beautiful seigniory at Châteauguay that one of her boarders, Marie-Anne de Lanoue, had offered at a bargain. It seemed too good an opportunity to neglect. It would provide security for the future.

But the future took a sharp and sudden turn! At half-past two in the afternoon of May 18, a basketful of smoldering ashes, carelessly deposited in the loft of a frame building on the corner of Notre Dame and St. Francis Xavier streets, burst into flame. In a few moments a strong wind roaring down from the mountain to the river had picked up the fire and hurled it mercilessly at every home in its path.

Mother d'Youville, hearing the terrible news and believing her property to be perfectly safe on account of its location, immediately sent her able-bodied men and women, as well as some of the Sisters, to fight the disaster as best they could and give aid to the stricken victims.

But nothing could stop the roaring wind and the flaming brands that leaped the walls of the city. Before Mother d'Youville had time to realize what had happened, the cedar shingled roof of the old General Hospital had caught on fire. It was unbelievable!

"I could hardly make myself believe," Mother d'Youville wrote later to a friend, "that God would not save this house which was, as you know, the refuge of the poor!"

There was no way to fight the flames that ate down quickly from the upper floor. There was nothing to do but pull out to safety first of all the poor people trapped in the building—old men and women, the helpless sick, and frightened little children.

Meanwhile the Sisters who had hurried to help in the city came running back, hardly believing their eyes, to their own burning home, followed by many citizens who seemed to forget their own loss in this tragic climax of the great fire. Some of the priests from the seminary were soon on hand. All together, frantically, they saved what they could—Mother d'Youville's box of precious documents, among them the letters patent signed by the King; furniture, bedding, clothing; valuable vestments and other chapel goods. Father de Féligonde, the chaplain, stumbled out of the suffocating holocaust holding in his arms the beloved painting of the Eternal Father.

But many piles of rescued possessions were dropped too close to the burning building, and before long these, too, caught fire.

Worse than that, a few vandals, on the pretext of saving hospital property, carted it away, never to be seen again.

All too soon nothing more could be done. Now the floors were crashing down into the blazing inferno; now great red tongues of flame were licking all the window frames, so lately renewed at so great a cost. Could this possibly be the end of the General Hospital, so dearly bought, so needed?

Poor Mother d'Youville stepped back at last from the terrible heat and the blinding smoke, her eyes burning, her hands blistered, her heart broken. As she made her way toward a corner of the great stone wall where her Sisters, the poor, and her little ones were gathering, her thoughts took their accustomed course —the mystery of the cross, this mystery of love, the treasure of grace hidden in this mystery!

She understood the outburst of human anguish that greeted her as she approached, the bitter tears, the broken crying of these poor afflicted ones. Her arms ached to enclose them all in loving comfort. But she knew a better way to help them, a way that would lead them straight into the arms of their Eternal Father.

"My children," she said, in a tone that touched their souls, "we are going to say a *Te Deum* on our knees to thank God for the cross that He has just sent us."

Irresistibly impelled by her spiritual strength, they all knelt together; and through the black smoke that billowed above their heads there ascended to the throne of God the fragrant incense of their hearts' oblation.

Then, rising quickly, this strong Mother spoke again. "Take courage, my children," she consoled them tenderly, her tired face lighting up in a beautiful smile, "our home will never burn again!"

And to this day it never has! Surely one whose trust was heroic could dare to prophesy!

Night was falling now, and some shelter would have to be found at once for these 118 persons left without a home. Having talked the matter over with the Sisters, Mother d'Youville announced that they would all go to Point St. Charles to crowd into the house and barns there until better arrangements could be made.

"But you, dear," she remarked with delicate consideration to a young novice, Sister Barbe-Françoise Prud'homme, "you may, if you wish, remain with your own family until our troubles are over, and then returning to us, you will make profession."

"Please, Mother," pleaded the little Sister, "please allow me to remain with the Sisters!"

Comforted by her generous spirit, Mother d'Youville permitted her to share with the Sisters the trials and privations that for many months were to be their lot.

Just then Father Montgolfier appeared. "The Sisters of Hôtel-Dieu will receive you all," he said. "They have made places for you and they want you to come."

Instantly obedient, though deeply reluctant to impose upon the generous Sisters, almost as poor as themselves, Mother d'Youville abandoned her plans and made known to her sorrowful and bewildered family the course that they would take.

It was a pitiful journey that they now made. Leaving behind them the smoldering ruins of their home, they straggled over the little river, choked with debris, and along St. Paul Street to Hôtel-Dieu. All the way on their left was the charred, still burning horror where only that morning more than 215 families had known security and peace. And yet many of these people, completely destitute, wept to see the Grey Nuns and their poor once more on the way of the cross.

It was eight o'clock when the poor sufferers, with Father de Féligonde at their head, arrived at Hôtel-Dieu. With tender sympathy and affection the good Sisters received them all. In the infirmary beds were ready for Mother d'Youville and her seventeen Sisters. In the apartments usually reserved for royalty accommodations were somehow provided for the lady boarders who preferred to remain with the Sisters, sixty-three poor men and women, and sixteen little children.

240

The night so blessed by the charity of the Sisters of Hôtel-Dieu did not, however, hold very much rest for the exhausted victims of the disaster. It was a long time before the fires died down; now and then barrels of powder exploded violently. "We thought that our last hour had come," Mother d'Youville wrote to Madame de Ligneris, one of their friends in France. "I consider it providential that the whole city was not destroyed."

Nevertheless, invigorated by Mass and Holy Communion the next morning, Mother d'Youville and the Sisters prepared to clear away the ashes of catastrophe and begin at once the reconstruction of the General Hospital. God had supremely tested their faith and their love. They would meet the test; they would forge ahead in greater fidelity, more ardent charity, unlimited confidence. Could there be the light of trust, anyway, without the burning fire of adversity?

Yet it was an undertaking of immeasurable magnitude that faced these poor women. Financially, these were bitter times. The total loss of the hospital amounted to more than 91,045 pounds. Everything they had was gone—furniture, clothing, supplies. In her letter to Madame de Ligneris, Mother d'Youville summed up the situation: ". . . on all that huge piece of land, only our brewery and our mill remain. . . . We are daring enough to try to recover a corner of the house where the walls are still good."

"We have not saved one eighth of what we had," she also wrote. "God has permitted it so. May His Holy Name be blessed!"

Perhaps to reward and encourage the Sisters, God also permitted a great joy to be given to their submissive hearts a few days after the fire. Some workmen, raking away the debris that glutted the interior of the hospital, came upon a brightly shining object. It was the precious little brass statue of Our Lady of Providence before which Mother d'Youville and her first companions had made their act of consecration on October 30, 1738. The base of the statue, also made of brass, had melted away in the intense heat of the fire, but the figure of the Blessed Virgin and her Child had remained in perfect condition. This little statue, only five inches high, is now one of the greatest treasures of the Grey Nuns. What a message of hope it must have brought to the Sisters that day, straight out of the ashes of their home!

Mother d'Youville lost no time in organizing the work of reconstruction. A few days after the fire she quartered in the brewery some of the poor men able to help in clearing away debris. In order to relieve even further the crowded condition at Hôtel-Dieu, she sent others to Point St. Charles.

It was necessary first of all to get funds to start the work. Father Montgolfier advanced 15,000 pounds, in partial payment for which Mother d'Youville immediately asked Father Cousturier in Paris to keep a bill of exchange for 7620 pounds, so eager was she to reduce her indebtedness as much and as quickly as possible.

Even though a fourth of Montreal was destroyed in the terrible fire of 1765, the poor people of the city showed extraordinary generosity in giving both money and labor to the rebuilding of the hospital. By orders of the Vicar General, special collections were taken up in all the parishes of the district, and workmen engaged in reconstruction were permitted to labor on Sundays and feast days, provided they first attended Mass.

Even the Indians, remembering Mother d'Youville's care during the smallpox epidemic of 1755, sold their treasured possessions—silver trinkets, cloth, knives, blankets—and gave her more than 460 pounds!

On the ninth of June, Mother d'Youville wrote to the Abbé de l'Isle-Dieu to ask him to obtain nine or ten thousand pounds on credit "for the rebuilding of our house which it has pleased God to take away from us by fire." Very simply she added, "We have begun and we shall try to go on, hoping that Divine Providence, which has always upheld us, will continue to do so."

The greatest financial aid came eventually from the people of London, who made public collections for the benefit of the sufferers of Montreal. From this source Mother d'Youville received 19,407 pounds, truly a considerable sum, of which she made grateful mention in a letter to the Abbé de l'Isle-Dieu in 1768.

I attempt this little note to thank you for your kindness and to beg a continuation of it in our great need, for our affairs are not going well: to lose what we are losing in France, to have endured a fire which has drowned us in debts, of which we could never be relieved without the alms that we have received from public collections made in London, easing our burden a little. Divine Providence is wonderful! It has inscrutable ways of relieving those who depend on it. It attends to everything! In it is my confidence!

If there was one subject on which Mother d'Youville could grow eloquent at any time, but particularly in times of privation and suffering, that subject was certainly Divine Providence. Then she opened her heart!

Surely something more than human sympathy inspired the supernatural charity given to the Sisters and their poor during the months of heroic struggle that followed the fire, something more than human effort that made it possible for them to be together again under their own roof before the year was over! During all this time food for every one of them was most generously supplied by the seminary, the religious of the Congregation of Notre Dame, and many citizens. Governor General James Murray must also have been one of the first to come to their aid, for only three weeks after the fire Mother d'Youville wrote to him:

I have the honor to present to you my most humble regards and to thank you for the rations that you have had given to me. I earnestly beg the continuation of your bounty. We are offering all our poor prayers to the Lord for the preservation of your health; and may He grant you all prosperity!

Who would not want to help a poor woman so humbly and so promptly grateful for every favor? It would seem that not even Heaven could resist her.

One day, shortly after the fire, workmen found in the cellar vaults of the old hospital a large barrel two thirds full of ordinary wine. It was served to the poor (who needed, goodness knows, this simple, sustaining pleasure) until the barrel was nearly empty. Then the Sister in charge thought that she ought to mention the matter to Mother d'Youville.

"Only a trickle as thin as a straw is coming out of that barrel now, Mother. What shall I do?"

"Keep on drawing it out, Sister," Mother d'Youville returned quite confidently, "and do not get tired of drawing it!"

The fact remains that the wine lasted—and tasted very good —until mid-December, when enough of the hospital was repaired for Mother d'Youville and all her family to be together again. It may be that Our Lady of Providence had repeated her Cana reminder.

It was actually on the twenty-third of September that quarters were ready for the poor men of the hospital. Two of the Sisters also moved in that day to take care of them. On the fifth of December the remaining Sisters and the resident boarders were able to return, but the rest of the women had to wait patiently for two weeks longer.

What a joyful, thankful Christmas they all celebrated that year; truly a Bethlehem Christmas, for they had little more than shelter—shelter and the ineffable warmth of love!

Mother d'Youville, however, had already said to the Abbé de l'Isle-Dieu, "We shall be very badly off, but we shall be at home. We shall not lack the means of doing penance, but we have need of it. We shall try to profit by it."

This heroic Mother had also written, "To adore the designs of God and to submit to His will—that is what we have all tried our best to do!"

CHAPTER FIFTEEN

CHÂTEAUGUAY

I T WAS usually under the most precarious circumstances that Mother d'Youville took the longest steps forward. Her purchase of the seigniory of Châteauguay three weeks after the fire of May 18, 1765, is an example of high courage in the depths of disaster, of farsighted progress in spite of insecurity and want.

Several months before the fire she had entered into tentative negotiations with Mademoiselle Marie-Anne de Lanoue, sole owner of the property, whose only surviving brother, having decided to leave Canada after the war, had surrendered to her his share of the vast estate. It was too much for a woman to handle alone, particularly for a woman whose only desire was to spend her last years at the General Hospital in peace.

Mother d'Youville, already with her eye on several of the great estates that were being sold for a song because the owners had only a limited time to dispose of them before going to France, welcomed the offer of her boarder, Mademoiselle de Lanoue, to sell her seigniory on easy terms.

Herself a daughter of the seignorial system, she knew the substantial economic advantages of living on the land. The war had taught her also that she could no longer depend principally on the Sisters' sewing for the subsistence of her large family, nor on the numerous but transitory methods of making money to which they had devoted themselves. No longer, moreover, could she count on the contributions of the wealthy, for the most comfortable families had gone to spend the rest of their lives under the flag of France.

It was the future that she had to consider, the future security of her community and the future well-being of her poor.

Strictly speaking, the disastrous fire might have been a good excuse for Mother d'Youville to withdraw her consideration of the purchase, leaving Mademoiselle de Lanoue to find another buyer. Too delicately honorable for that, however, she sought advice from the right authorities, raised her heart to Divine Providence, and signed the contract on the eighth of June.

By the terms of the purchase, Mother d'Youville was committed to the payment of a principal of more than 15,000 pounds, besides a life annuity of 900 pounds to Mademoiselle de Lanoue. To meet this obligation, she obtained permission to sell property at Chambly. Later, she drew also upon her own family inheritance, left to her at the death of her mother, and upon that of Sister Thérèse Despins.

Mother d'Youville now found herself in legal possession of a great seigniory on Lake St. Louis, about twenty-one miles southwest of Montreal. On St. Bernard Island, nearly 650 acres in area, stood the manor house, a low wooden structure twenty by fifty feet in extent, a stone stable and barn, and an old windmill. Not more than eighty acres of land were in cultivation.

Now she also held seignorial rights over the tenants already on the land; and to them she had specific obligations. It was her duty to see that they had what they needed to live in decent prosperity and comfort.

One would think that the supervision of the rebuilding of the General Hospital would be enough to occupy a woman already sixty-four years old, at the same time that she provided for 118 dispossessed persons dependent upon her care and authority. But to these duties, and many a lesser one, Mother d'Youville added, in that summer of 1765, the work of putting Châteauguay on a paying basis and of making necessary improvements there. One must not forget, however, that she could depend magnificently on the co-operation of the Sisters. She knew how to delegate authority for the good of all. Her problems were family problems, and every member cared.

One of Mother d'Youville's first projects at Châteauguay was the construction of a large water mill to replace the windmill already there, which was too small and too difficult of access for the tenants who had to use it. She herself selected a fine spot for it—the best on the land, according to an expert surveyor many years later—about two and a half miles from the old manor. To provide sufficient water power, a canal two hundred feet long had to be dug, and a dam four hundred feet long had to be constructed.

In the course of time, Mother d'Youville also had a bakery built for general use. She repaired the stable and barns, had more land put into cultivation, and planted an orchard. Clearing the land of forest growth was a major operation in which everyone shared. Sister Louise Thaumur herself wanted to cut down the first tree. This she did with extraordinary vigor after she had several times recited aloud, *O crux, ave, spes unica!*

Many a trip to Châteauguay did Mother d'Youville make in a heavy, jolting, two-wheeled wagon! Seasons made no difference to her if she had to go there. She was always at the manor house on St. Martin's Day in November to receive the rents of her tenants and to hear their requests. When her work was over and carefully recorded in her book of accounts, she would gather the little children of the neighborhood about her and teach them the beautiful truths of their religion. Those who learned the best were always rewarded with cookies drawn from the mysterious pockets that hung at her side. How many little eyes were fixed on those pockets during the beautiful lessons!

Many years later, in 1850, a venerable old man named Etienne Duranceau stopped to listen to Mother Deschamps as she taught catechism at Châteauguay to the little ones of her day. Just then she produced some cookies for the best ones in the class. The old man laughed.

"I, too!" he said. "I learned my catechism here. It was a very long time ago! It was Mother d'Youville who used to teach us, and she used to reward us just as you are doing, when we had been smart!"

Mother Deschamps, to test his memory, thought that she would put to him a question or two.

"What height was Mother d'Youville," she asked, "and what was her complexion?"

"She was tall," he answered quickly, "light tan and ruddy!"

"And what color were her eyes?"

"Oh, well, as for that," the old man smiled, "I wouldn't know how to say!"

Mother Deschamps was convinced of his truthfulness, however, and quite delighted to record his reminiscence.

In memory of their beloved foundress as a teacher, the Grey Nuns of Montreal opened a free elementary school at Châteauguay in 1884. This little school, fully approved by the Catholic Scholastic Commission, is still in operation.

Today St. Bernard Island at Châteauguay is not only a highly productive farm. It is also a delightful vacation spot where the Sisters, surrounded by natural beauty and heavenly peace, may in well-ordered rest periods renew their strength, both physical and spiritual. There, too, when the labors of life are over, they are laid to rest in the Sisters' Cemetery, a beautiful haven on the highest part of the island.

But the Sisters of Charity, the Grey Nuns of Montreal, do not keep Châteauguay all to themselves. In the spirit of their foundress, they are hostesses every summer, in co-operation with the Daughters of Wisdom, to the poor and crippled children of the city.

During the crowded months in which the indefatigable spirit of Mother d'Youville brought Châteauguay up to her standards, the reconstruction of the General Hospital continued. By 1767 the building was once more complete, and the chapel was blessed in August of that year.

Untold were the hardships of the Sisters and their poor during these months, almost unbelievable the physical work that they all had to perform. To do their washing, for example, on the banks of the river, beating the clothes with smooth, round rocks in order to get them clean, might have been an active form of recreation in warm and sunny months, but what must it have been in the winter when the wet garments froze and icicles hung from their clothing! Although this was only one of the labors that they had always had to perform, it was harder now because of so many privations.

Think of the furnishings that had to be supplied all over again for this poor house—beds and bedding, clothing for old and young! But Mother d'Youville wrote to the Abbé de l'Isle-Dieu: "Always on the threshold of want and yet we are never in want, of necessities at least. Every day I marvel at Divine Providence, who wishes to use subjects so poor in order to do some little good!"

As soon as the rebuilding of the hospital was well under control, Mother d'Youville set out to make improvements also at Point St. Charles, having in mind a better stone residence for the farmer who lived there as well as new quarters for the Sisters charged with supervision. She thought, too, that in this quiet, secluded place, removed from the work and hardship of Pointe-à-Callières, a peaceful and prayerful retreat could be provided. A little stone house not far from the main building proved to be such a retreat.

Here, when possible, Mother d'Youville also gave herself those precious moments of leisure in God alone which everyone needs at times in order to bring body and soul into more even balance and more pleasing harmony.

Confiding as she always did in the bounty of Divine Providence, Mother d'Youville did not by any means neglect any resource at hand in order to meet her enormous expenses. Particularly in the years after the war did she follow up very closely whatever might be a means of paying her debts. Her letters make frequent mention of attempts to collect bills due to the hospital and to have justice done for the sake of the poor.

No case gave her so much trouble for so many years as that involving Madame Péan, the celebrated Angélique des Meloises, for whose fascinating sake the miscreant Bigot had committed memorable extravagances. Now her husband, fallen with the unhappy Intendant, was paying in prison for his share of crimes against France.

Had this case been a matter of charity needed by Madame Péan herself, there is no doubt that Mother d'Youville would have given such charity with an open heart.

But it seems that in 1761, Madame de Laronde, the lady's aunt, had died at the General Hospital after an illness of more than six months, and that Madame Péan, responsible for her aunt's money, had not acknowledged the bill duly sent to her in accordance with the wishes of the deceased.

On July 16, 1764, Mother d'Youville made the following observation to the Abbé de l'Isle-Dieu:

I am very much surprised that Madame Péan has not yet cleared the bill of exchange for 1050 pounds drawn on her to the account of Madame Laronde, her aunt, since she had some money for her, and since this sum is due to the hospital for her board and funeral expenses. In this case she does not have to wait until her husband gets out of prison in order to find the money, for the deceased said that she had 21,000 pounds of her own on hand and many bills of exchange.

Two years later Mother d'Youville, having received an indirect but unsatisfactory answer to her inquiries, wrote to Madame Péan herself, for this was the year after the fire, and the need was very great.

I learn from Monsieur Daine that only in coupons that the King has granted for bills of exchange can you discharge the draft which he drew on you for the amount of 1050 pounds for the board and funeral expenses of Madame Laronde. You will please me, madame, by remitting this sum to Father Savarie, procurator of our hospital, at the Seminary of the Foreign Missions, in coupons of equal value. Madame de Laronde told me several times that she had the money on hand in France and that the hospital would not suffer on account of expenses incurred for her. However, it is now six years since we paid everything for her in specie, which was very rare in this land. . . . I beg you, madame, to finish up this matter. We are more than ever in need.

Three years later the invincible Mother d'Youville, persistent in the cause of justice, again observed to the Abbé de l'Isle-Dieu:

I have already written to Madame Péan about the bill of exchange . . . furnished in fine specie to Madame Laronde. She has not answered me. She [Madame Laronde] has a daughter a religious in France. I am going to write to her so that she may finish this affair.

That very day Mother d'Youville did write to the religious daughter of Madame Laronde, appealing to her influence to have the money paid. "You will render us the greatest of services," she explained, "for we are in extreme need."

Not even this appeal was effective. A year later Mother d'Youville had recourse again to her procurator. ". . . it was fine silver money that we had loaned for that lady," she mourned, "to take care of her for six and a half months of illness, to furnish her food, and to have her buried honorably, as was suitable."

In 1771, a few months before Mother d'Youville's death, there was a ray of hope that the just debt to the hospital would be paid, for Madame Laronde's son had put in an appearance; but nothing more definite was ever said on the subject. The recording angel could hardly have accused the poor directress of not doing her utmost to win justice for the hospital that she served!

Another case, just as unsatisfactory in her lifetime, and far more painful, involved Mother d'Youville's own son.

When Father François d'Youville was assigned to the country

parish of St. Ours, he felt that the poor little mission chapel there ought to be replaced by a suitable church. He did not have sufficient funds for this undertaking, but he did have his mother, who always found a way to help those in need. In 1759 he appealed to her for aid.

Mother d'Youville, having nothing of her own, loaned him 9000 pounds from the resources of the General Hospital, on condition that he would very faithfully repay this sum; and the zealous priest promised to do so.

The church was duly built and the lean years passed, but, sad to say, Father François d'Youville made no move to reimburse the hospital. In fact, he reminded his mother that she had always given bountifully to the poor and ought therefore to donate something to him for his good work. Anyway, had she not kept him from receiving an inheritance from his father? And had she given him even an account of his maternal grandparents' bequests?

Strangely, Father François d'Youville remained deaf to his mother's explanations and repeated appeals to repay the money that belonged not to her but to the poor. He continued to insist that she had given to the poor what belonged to him.

Undoubtedly she knew that the late war had created financial hardships for him as well as for everyone else. She knew that he was poor, too; but that was not the point. She expected him to be his mother's son in the best sense of the term, to make an honest effort to repay the money in the spirit of his promise, no matter how long it took.

After the fire had reduced the hospital to extreme need, poor Mother d'Youville informed Father Montgolfier of her son's refusal to clear up his indebtedness. The whole matter was then submitted for arbitration to three disinterested persons chosen by Father d'Youville himself. However, when they decided that he should make restitution, he refused outright to abide by their decision.

Now the poor mother had to suffer the painful humiliation of reporting the unhappy affair to the Bishop. It was a question of justice, of goods belonging properly to others. Natural love for her son had to be supernaturalized by the demands of equity.

Bishop Briand, thoroughly annoyed by Father d'Youville's action, wrote him a severe letter, which he enclosed in a message to the saddened mother.

The rest of the affair can best be told by Mother d'Youville herself in her sincere, forthright account to the Bishop early in 1769. There are no unnecessary preliminaries. She plunges straight into the matter closest at the time to her maternal heart.

I received your letter and one that you wrote to my son that I have not sent to him, first, because of the accident which happened to him on the second of February. While accompanying a visitor to the door, he fell and broke his left arm about four fingers from the shoulder. He has enough trouble for the present. I learned this news on Saturday. I left on Sunday to go to see him. I found him well enough: no fever, no swelling. I returned on Thursday, promising to send him company. Mademoiselle Legardeur left and one of our Sisters, who are still there.

In between the staccato sentences of this account, which outlines in sharp, incisive strokes the good mother's instant response to the misfortune of her erring son, one can detect compassionate understanding, ability to sacrifice a point of honor for sweet charity's sake, clarity of vision free from sentimental illusions, unreserved and even delicate attention to one in trouble, no matter what his faults. She would not break the bruised reed!

The rest of her letter to the Bishop is a detailed repetition of the whole affair, in case His Excellency had not clearly understood; and it closes abruptly with a single sentence: "There are a great many things to say which would be too long to write." Yes, the thoughts of a mother's heart would indeed be too long to write!

Although Mother d'Youville did not in her lifetime have the consolation of seeing the disputed 9000 pounds returned to the treasury of the hospital, she did by her charity win a greater victory over her son's heart. After her death Father François d'Youville began to reimburse the institution. He succeeded in repaying 7000 pounds of his debt, and his brother, Father Charles Dufrost, supplied the rest.

It was at the General Hospital, under the devoted care of the Grey Nuns, that Father François d'Youville spent his last years, in long and intense physical suffering. He died there on April 10, 1778, and was buried in the crypt at his mother's feet.

If Mother d'Youville was persistent in pursuing justice for the hospital, even at a great personal cost, she was not less fearless in her efforts to seek the happiness and comfort of individuals residing there. In August of 1764, she wrote in polite but unmistakable terms to Madame Mercier:

You do not know that your mother has been living in this hospital for ten years. That is why, madame, I hope you will not take it amiss that I describe for you her condition, which is pretty sad. She is without linen. It is more than ten years since she has been given a hand towel. She owes 1800 pounds here for her board, although she makes very small expenditures. For four years she has drunk only water, which is very hard for a person who never lacked wine and a good many little comforts that a person of her age really needs. For her total resources she has only a principal of 4000 pounds and an income of 150 pounds on her dowry. You see that she has not the means to take care of her needs, honor her debts, and pay her board. . . . That is why, madame, I join her in asking you to give up your share of the dowry which you will not be able to enjoy at her death, since it will revert to the King of England. Be assured, madame, that I am telling you nothing but the truth, and that I would be very sorry to impose on you in anything.

Although Mother d'Youville considered it an obligation to collect all money honestly due to the hospital, and to promote the well-being of those who lived there, she never allowed herself to exaggerate the claims of justice or violate even the least requirements of charity.

When, in 1764, the Abbé de l'Isle-Dieu discovered an error of four or five hundred pounds, to the disadvantage of the General Hospital, in the accounts of the late Father Nicolas de Paris, procurator of the seminary, he was seriously disturbed and thought that the heirs of Father de Paris should make good the loss. But Mother d'Youville wrote:

The dear deceased did his best to render us service, and we would be most ungrateful if we attempted to embarrass his family. No, Father, assure them of the contrary . . . for we consider him clear before God and before men, and we pray for the repose of his soul.

Accompanying this letter was a written statement freeing the heirs of Father Nicolas de Paris from all responsibility for the error. As far as Mother d'Youville was concerned, the "dear deceased" should have the benefit of the doubt.

Evidently the Abbé de l'Isle-Dieu did not dismiss the matter quite so promptly, for two years later Mother d'Youville remarked to him in polite and praiseworthy impatience: "To what purpose can you be disturbed by an error of four or five hundred pounds, perhaps not made at all, since you have rendered us priceless services which neither we nor our successors ought ever to forget?"

No matter what kind of letter Mother d'Youville had to write, she could not help revealing her simple, sincere, and very grateful heart. Over and over again she slipped graceful expressions of gratitude into her business letters; services to her were indeed repaid in golden words. On one occasion she wrote to Father Savarie:

I have many thanks to express to you for having accepted the procuration of our house, particularly since you are so busy with the affairs of other communities. But this one is all for the poor; you will have double reward: you will share in their prayers and those of all our Sisters, who ask me to tell you of their appreciation for rendering us this service.

In letters to the Abbé de l'Isle-Dieu, there are many variations of the motif of thankfulness which runs like a delightful melody through all her messages to this eminent benefactor: "I cannot express my gratitude and that of my Sisters for all your kindnesses, which I never stop proclaiming and admiring!" "You carry your kindness to a degree without parallel, and God alone can reward such attention. He will be your recompense!" "Our whole community, as well as I, is imbued with a thankfulness that my pen cannot compass." "We ask the God of all bounty to shower you with His graces in time and in eternity."

When Governor General Guy Carleton, successor to James Murray, made a special donation to the hospital in June of 1770, he must have felt himself richly rewarded by the courteous message that Mother d'Youville immediately sent to him:

Sir, in the need wherein our hospital finds itself, I admire Divine Providence for having inspired you to the charitable gift of twenty-five quarters of pork, for which I express my most humble thanks. I would never have dared to ask you for anything, knowing that you have much to give to different poor people in great need. We shall, all of us in this house, offer our poor prayers to the Lord for your safety, the success of your undertakings, and a happy journey.

The refreshing charm of Mother d'Youville's letters, simple and few as they are, comes not only from felicitous expressions of gratitude; in her messages to relatives and friends little personal touches and delicate signs of affectionate interest also reach the heart.

"I was at Gamelin's house when Carignan brought your letter," she wrote to one. "He could not read it; his tears choked him. Everyone felt the same, so happy were we to know that all had arrived safely. That is all we wanted, having no way of seeing one another again, except in heaven."

To a solicitous guardian she sent a cheerful assurance: "Catherine is doing wonderfully well. She comes every day to see if I am writing to you, and to ask me to send you her love."

Less than a year after the terrible fire of 1765, Mother d'Youville wrote to her niece, her dear Josette: "I know your kind heart too well to doubt your concern about our accident. It is over with; one must think no more about it!"

This swift dismissal of an event so important left room for matters of more personal interest to Josette, for her aunt continued:

I shall do nothing to oppose the departure of your family, but to tell you the truth, if it happens, it will not be soon; at least that is what I think. Their absence will be your cross for some years. Time will tell when you will be reunited. . . .

I cannot describe the joy that spreads through the community when we receive news of you. Everyone pays you a thousand compliments. . . . I cannot end without mentioning our little Benac [Josette's godson, aged four]. He is too sweet; he has a fine figure and is a handsome boy and not a bit bad for being spoiled.

Whenever there were children in the family to which she wrote, Mother d'Youville never failed to send them "embraces," and other little greetings.

It was not at all her practice to suppress lively interest in her good friends. Especially of those who had left Canada for France did she often ask for news. "I shall be delighted to learn news of my old friend through Monsieur Le Moyne," she assured Madame de Ligneris. "He has not yet arrived. He is passing through New York. They do not expect him until next month. Let me always know the news about your family, which will ever be very dear to me."

To Dr. Ferdinand Feltz, with whom Mother d'Youville maintained a faithful friendship dating from his attempt to cure her infected knee with live toads, she wrote on August 25, 1768:

We have not yet had any news of you. How is Madame Feltz? Is she having as hard a time of it in not seeing her friends as they are having in not seeing her? All our Sisters assure her of their regards, above all, Sister Despins and I. . . . I had the sorrow of seeing my sister Clemence die on the twenty-second of March after fifteen days of illness, almost always in agony, without losing speech or consciousness. My comfort is that she had the death of one predestined . . . Poor Gamelin worries me. He fails astonishingly. He has grown thin beyond recognition since my sister's death.

Dr. Feltz received another friendly assurance in July of 1770, and further family news in which he was personally and professionally interested.

I shall never forget the friends from whom I have received a thousand kindnesses and as many courtesies; and I assure you that your absence and that of your wife cost me very much. We often speak of you among ourselves. . . .

Poor Gamelin is always in the saddest condition: he is deaf, speechless, almost blind, and almost completely paralyzed. My sister [Louise, his wife] and Lajemmerais have been taking care of him every day, and a man, with one here, every night, for nearly six months.

Sometimes in her letters Mother d'Youville had to convey news sadder than illness; but she did so simply and gently. To Madame de Ligneris she wrote on July 23, 1770:

I wish indeed that I had something pleasing to tell you, but on the contrary, I have the most sorrowful news, occasioned by the death of Madame Mackay, your dear daughter, at noon on the thirteenth of this month. Our consolation is that she suffered with heroic patience, that she received all the sacraments and asked for Extreme Unction herself, after which she wished to make a general confession. Her husband and her brother were all ready with what was necessary, so that she would not lack anything, spiritual or temporal.

As Mother d'Youville's years grew close to threescore and ten, she continued to give evidences of kindly human interest in everyone. "I see by your accounts," she wrote to her procurator in 1771, "that Brother Joseph Dellerme is still living. According to the age that he gave when we entered the hospital, he must be ninety years old. I should indeed be delighted if you could go to see him and let me know where he is."

There is never lacking in any letter, no matter what its purpose, that wholesome tone which could only be the expression of a very candid and very affable personality. Particularly good-humored is this little note addressed to Father Villard: "I learn through Monsieur Boirette that you are a Superior and that you are ill. I am very sympathetic for the one as for the other. I pray the Lord to help and sustain you in both."

Mother d'Youville had no secretary to help her with correspondence; and of course she had no typewriter, no carbon paper. Nevertheless, in large, strong notebooks, admirably suited to the purpose and faithfully preserved to this day, she carefully inscribed a copy of her letters. Sometimes, just to be sure, she made two copies. Only a person who had reduced all her duties to a well-ordered system could have accomplished a task so time consuming, to say the least.

For she was an exceedingly busy woman, particularly throughout the years in which most of her letters were written. These were years of great responsibility and development, years heavy with material burdens though bright with spiritual joy. But Mother d'Youville had lost no time after the fire in restoring the order and spirit of prayer which had characterized her establishment from the beginning. In no other atmosphere could harmony and success be achieved; in no other way, surely, could only eighteen Sisters, "half of them no longer good for anything," have taken care of a hospital that now sheltered 170 persons.

It was certainly a trial of major proportions that death claimed three of the Sisters during the last years of Mother d'Youville's life, just as affairs at the hospital seemed more promising for the future.

Sister Thérèse Beaufrère, only forty-three years old, went to her eternal reward on April 28, 1769, after sixteen years of hidden but devoted care of the poor. One year later, on April 15, Sister Antoinette Arelle died in Mother d'Youville's arms. For twenty-nine years she had shared the fortunes of the foundress whom she dearly loved.

These deaths came at a time when the hearts of all the Sisters were aching because of the tragic loss of a young and very promising novice.

Sister Madeleine Céloron was the daughter of the celebrated Pierre Céloron de Blainville, a knight of the Order of St. Louis, who had been sent to the Ohio valley in 1749 to strengthen French influences among the Indians. Her mother, now a widow, was a comfortable boarder at the hospital.

The young novice had completed her novitiate after a number of trials and was on the threshold of religious profession when an act of grave imprudence cut short her life.

Mother d'Youville had sternly forbidden the Sisters to carry baskets of wet clothing alone. They were always to ask assistance in lifting these particularly heavy burdens. But one day, Sister Madeleine Céloron, ardent, generous, full of zeal, forgot the rule. Not seeing anyone near on whom she could call for aid, she took a chance and tried to lift a heavy basket by herself. It was too much and she collapsed under the load. A serious internal rupture resulted, which all the medical care of the time failed to repair, and in a few days she was at the point of death.

Now she begged for the privilege of pronouncing her vows; and Mother d'Youville had to make a decision which might have serious consequences in the future. The young novice had meant well; but she had been disobedient, so gravely disobedient that by her premature death the Community and the poor would forever be deprived of her services.

After long and fervent prayers, and with the advice of her councilors, Mother d'Youville sadly but firmly decided that the dying novice could not pronounce her vows publicly, that is, in the presence of the Sisters.

It is a gracious tradition, however, that Mother d'Youville, always the tender mother, understanding the frailties of our nature, received the vows of the poor little Sister privately, thus giving her sweet consolation and peace before her death on October 18, 1768; but her name does not appear in the Register of Professed Sisters.

There were objections, of course, to the decision that the foundress had made. This young Sister was the daughter of the great De Blainville. Her mother, influential and wealthy, was here in the house. What would the people say? No matter, thought Mother d'Youville. Obedience was greater than sacrifice. Discipline in the house was far more important than the approval of the people.

Madame Céloron, far from resenting the course of action that Mother d'Youville had felt justified in taking, asked for the privilege of replacing her daughter in the novitiate. Although she was forty-seven years old, she was accepted on account of her unusual virtue. "She is not young," wrote Mother d'Youville, "but she is good."

Sister Catherine Céloron pronounced her vows on July 3, 1771, only a few months before the death of the foundress herself. It is a coincidence that this last Grey Nun to be admitted to profession by Mother d'Youville was a widow like herself. She gave valuable service to the Community for twenty-six years, of which the last fourteen were spent as mistress of novices.

God seemed pleased to make good the loss of the other two Sisters, and at the same time to balance the forty-seven years of good Sister Catherine Céloron, by sending Mother d'Youville two excellent young candidates, both of them under twenty years of age. Sister Marie Elizabeth Bonnet was professed on October 27, 1769, and Sister Suzanne Benoit, Mother d'Youville's last postulant, was admitted to the novitiate on May 29, 1771.

In all the years of her life, Mother d'Youville had never had time or inclination to review the sorrows and trials of the past. "One must think no more about it," was her terse comment on the great fire only a year after it had happened. It is not unlikely, however, that in her seventieth year she checked over the work that God had given her to do. She was too wise not to make sure that her accounts were in order.

She, too, like the valiant woman of Holy Scripture, had "considered a field, and bought it . . . put out her hand to strong things . . . opened her hand to the needy, and stretched out her hands to the poor . . . opened her mouth to wisdom . . . looked well to the paths of her house."

CHAPTER SIXTEEN

IN THE SPIRIT IS LIFE

IN ALL the vicissitudes and misfortunes that followed close upon one another in Mother d'Youville's work for the poor, there was one development that suffered no interruption, that knew no change. This was her religious life among her Sisters. Founded on solid principles of utter simplicity and self-sacrificing charity, this religious life could only become deeper and stronger as sufferings and trials exercised the virtues essential to its growth; for the cross is the sign of spiritual vitality.

Yet unswerving fidelity to these fundamental principles involved interior conquests far greater than the victories won over François Bigot and the antagonistic elements of Montreal, far more difficult building and rebuilding than the old General Hospital had ever required. For Mother d'Youville and her Sisters to adhere faithfully to the first simple rules outlined for them by Father Normant, and to do so all the days of their lives under the most challenging circumstances, was an achievement in the spiritual realm infinitely beyond the material progress of their works.

During all these years of trials so great that today we wonder how a frail woman could have borne them, Mother d'Youville laid the foundations of a religious community that has never lost her spirit. Natural gifts of personal charm and adminis-

263

trative ability—and with these the great foundress was unquestionably endowed in high degree—could never alone have achieved this remarkable result. It is the spirit that is immortal; it is the supernatural that endures.

Thus at the same time that Mother d'Youville preserved and fostered works of charity at the General Hospital, she solidified with equally heroic fortitude the religious spirit of her Sisters: exquisite discretion, born of family love for their community; perfect union of heart and soul; entire poverty; profound humility; obedience to authority; simplicity in speech and conduct and flawless courtesy; attention to one's own work and scrupulous respect for the work of others; openheartedness; continual mortification; unlimited charity for the poor; purity of heart; fidelity to rules.

To list these virtues was one thing; to practice them day in and day out was another; but it was yet more to establish them as a way of life for the Grey Nuns of the future. This was the work of God, in which Mother d'Youville co-operated with all the powers of her soul.

By Divine Providence her whole life was a preparation for this work. There was nothing sudden about it; nor was there anything constrained or unnatural. For her faithful, sometimes heroic practice of the cardinal virtues of prudence, justice, fortitude, and temperance, God manifested in her soul the supernatural beauty of lively faith, cheerful hope, and ardent charity. She was a valiant woman who fulfilled the will of God to the best of her ability with the help of His grace. In her fulfillment lay the abiding strength of her community.

Among her Sisters, Mother d'Youville was essentially maternal. It was natural for them to call her Mother; they did so long before ecclesiastical approval confirmed her in office. She was the heart of their religious home, loving each one as faithfully as the physical heart beats for each organ of the body; and this love, truly radiant, extended through and beyond them to every person under their care, even to this day.

Refreshing simplicity and openheartedness always characterized her relations with her Sisters. Although she habitually ac-
commodated herself to them, as to everyone else, she was so
frank and straightforward that they had to be the same. Her
discernment of reality was instant and accurate.

Like a true mother, she was personally interested in the affairs
of each of her Sisters. Her burdens were never so heavy that
she could not help them to carry theirs. She understood that the
power of endurance is not the same in all individuals, that souls
are as different as bodies, that sympathetic love is the only key
that will open all hearts. Whenever her Sisters went to her with
their problems—and each one had many in the great work that
they all shared—she received them lovingly, listened to them
sincerely, and helped them generously out of the abundance of
her spiritual treasury. Her door was always open to them.

They loved to gather close around her during their hours of
recreation. Seated on their heels, they would listen as rapt as
children to her stories, but above all to her spiritual discourses.
Ordinarily a woman of few words, she would on these intimate
occasions open wide the channels of her heart and mind, so that
upon those who loved her and whom she loved her dearest gifts
could freely flow.

Filial love for the Eternal Father; unlimited trust in Divine
Providence; devotion to the Sacred Heart of Jesus, and tender,
womanly confidence in the Immaculate Heart of Mary, whom
she invoked on awakening every morning; trust in St. Joseph and
the dear guardian angels; the ineffable mystery of the cross;
the happiness of complete dedication to the poor and abandoned;
the strength and consolation of perfect union of heart and soul
among themselves; the riches of poverty and the freedom of
obedience—these were the favorite topics of her talks to her
Sisters.

She was not always serious in these family gatherings, however; and yet, even while discoursing on the most serious subjects, she lifted up the souls of her Sisters to regions of pure

spiritual happiness by the power of her own unchangeable joy of heart. Each one became her best self as she listened—and one's best self is always happy!

Mother d'Youville encouraged gaiety and good humor and bright liberty of spirit. She certainly gave a consistent example of cheerfulness herself, never allowing her sorrows and anxieties to overshadow the lives of those around her. Once in a while she wisely provided special recreations for her Sisters, all the more enjoyable and relaxing because they were unexpected. In the delightful simplicity of their intercourse with one another on these pleasant occasions, their mutual affection was strengthened and their union intensified. Indeed, it was their greatest pleasure to be together, sharing little intimacies and rendering little services that other hours of the day were too full to hold.

In one of these happy interludes, Mother d'Youville, chatting amiably in the midst of the Sisters crowded around her, stopped rather suddenly and remarked to Sister Coutlée, "You will be the one among us to live the longest, and you will survive us all!"

Was this just a fleeting thought that the good Mother expressed? Was her unexpected comment just another pleasant diversion for her Sisters? Uttered in a tone half serious, half humorous, it made a deep impression on them, nevertheless; for they heard the undertones of prophecy in her words.

Strange to say, Sister Coutlée did live the longest of the happy group gathered around Mother d'Youville that day. Having survived them all, she died on July 17, 1821, in her eightieth year.

If Mother d'Youville shared wholeheartedly in the recreations of her Sisters, she was in the midst of them also in complete fidelity to every other part of their rule. She knew that example is more eloquent than precept, that the corporate perfection of her institute demanded a stable union of its spirit with a tangible pattern of observance.

Filial dependence on the fatherhood of God for the management of their work among His children, the suffering poor, and unbounded trust in Divine Providence for the material support of this work, demanded something more than Mother d'Youville's own interior devotion. She put this devotion into practice. While making every human effort to build up the hospital and provide for the poor, she sincerely manifested unchanging self-possession and serenity, without which exterior signs her declaration of trust would have been an illusion.

Moreover, in order to perpetuate in her Sisters this essential attitude of trust, she conferred long and earnestly with Father Pierre de Lavalinière, one of the Sulpician Fathers, for the composition of invocations to Divine Providence. Her Sisters, daily repeating these confident praises, could not but become permeated with their spirit. "Divine Providence, Thou art the source of all good. . . . Thou art our protector. . . . Thou art the provider of all things. . . . Thou art the support of the poor. . . . Thou art the bread of the hungry!"

At Mother d'Youville's request, Father de Lavalinière composed a similar but much longer litany of invocations to the Eternal Father. This litany, a daily prayer of all Grey Nuns since April 4, 1770, is more than an expression of filial praise and love; it is also a profession of faith and a beautiful summary of Christian belief.

Our Father, Who art in heaven,
Hear the voice of Thy children on earth. . . .

O Father of all eternity,
Show Thyself our Father. . . .

O Father, Source of all love,
Multiply our works of charity and render them fruitful unto eternal life. . . .

O Father, Source of all power,
Render us capable of undertaking all things for Thy glory. . . .

O Father of our Lord Jesus Christ, Who art pleased likewise to be our Father,
Grant that we may always remain Thy faithful children!

Thus, slowly but surely through two hundred years and more, the essential spirit of Mother d'Youville's daughters has been developed by means of one of the most potent pedagogical principles: repetition; repetition of a basic truth—the brotherhood of man in the fatherhood of God. No stronger foundation could her institute have had for the support of the works of charity to which it was dedicated. In the spirit is life!

It may seem a paradox that deliberate poverty should have shaped the vessel which Mother d'Youville and her daughters confidently expected the Eternal Father to fill with the riches of His bounty. On the contrary, emptiness attracts divine beneficence. When, figuratively and literally, they sold all that they had and gave to the poor, they did so because of their trust in the divine promise of treasures in heaven. By personal poverty they made God alone the support of all their works, never relaxing, however, in the human efforts to which He would give the increase.

In the simplicity, frugality, and vigilance that this poverty implied, Mother d'Youville herself gave the most perfect example. Her apartments contained only those furnishings required by practical common sense and necessary to the pursuance of her work. They were plain, but solid and substantial; for poverty does not mean destitution and disorder, nor the cheapness that demands frequent replacement. Her furniture, still preserved, will last for several more centuries, if pious admirers can be kept from cutting chips out of it!

Mother d'Youville took care of everything that she used. She mended her clothing over and over and rejoiced to wear a habit that showed repair. So simply did she preserve the spirit of poverty in these little practices that her Sisters found a true interior joy in following her example. Like her, they wasted nothing.

She never allowed herself to be served food different from that of her Sisters. The simple breakfast that they all shared standing in the community room, where in the early days this meal was taken, was exactly the same for her as for the others: a cup of cold water and a piece of bread cut from the loaf according to each one's need. Butter or cold meat for their bread was festal fare! Hot barley coffee was served three times a week until after the great fire of 1765, when Mother d'Youville decided that the Sisters needed it every day because of their excessive work. She took her place in line with the others while the Sister in charge for the week poured the hot beverage into each one's pewter cup.

Ordinarily the Sisters had meat only at the noon meal, which, like the evening collation, was served in the refectory. On fast days only vegetables and milk foods appeared. Very seldom did Mother d'Youville buy fish for her large family.

No one ever knew Mother d'Youville's likes or dislikes with regard to food. If she had to make a choice of servings, she would take the least. The principles of mortification that she practiced herself she applied also to others, with kindly discernment of circumstances, of course, but without respect of persons. She would never permit the slightest remark about the preparation or seasoning of the food that was served. Once she overheard two or three Sisters expressing their personal feelings on this subject.

"You are not mortified," she reminded them very frankly. "You do not know well enough how to practice different kinds of self-denial."

Unfortunate was the Sister who would take a larger serving of any dish than she really needed and then leave the superfluous portion on her plate! Mother d'Youville would have this remnant served to her at the next meal, without anything else. If to those who now enjoy an era of abundance this correction seems somewhat severe, let them remember that the first Grey Nuns lived in days of dire want; in days, too, when the religious foundation of the Community was being laid by one to whom God had entrusted this work.

Mother d'Youville was too kind, both by nature and by grace, to correct harshly; too just to reprove where reproof was undeserved. Her Sisters, for the most part, accepted her reprimands gratefully, for they trusted her leadership and loved her with a love in which holy fear had a salutary share. They knew that austerity strengthened their souls and freed their hearts for truly spiritual joy.

It was certainly not only at mealtime that Mother d'Youville led the way in self-renouncement. This practice became second nature to her in all the actions of her life. Her strong sense of duty provided innumerable opportunities; for the exact performance of one's duty at all times is indeed a mortification having many aspects. Fine in her perceptions, moreover, and exquisite in her sensitivity, she undoubtedly had to do great violence to her feelings in her work among the sick and the poor. Yet in this realm of charity, her realization of the Mystical Body of Christ swept aside whatever repugnances she might have experienced, as reactions completely unworthy of recognition.

Whenever she went into the wards of the poor, she made it a practice to take a drink of water from the cup for general use. She would do this quite simply, without showing the least aversion or fear of results. There was a lovely element of positive charity in this little custom; she did it to show her beloved poor that she was one of them and that they were all at home together. For the same reason she would never allow the Sisters to have more conveniences than the poor enjoyed. They were all to consider themselves as members of one family, united by the bonds of charity.

One day on a visit to Châteauguay, where Sister Louise Thaumur was in charge, Mother d'Youville noticed a little wooden bracket fastened inside the door of the community room, just above a jar of water for the use of the Sisters. On this nice little convenience, instead of on the cover of the jar, stood the cup to be used.

But Mother d'Youville was not favorably impressed by this modern improvement; it was a superfluity.

"Who put that there?" she asked.

"I did, Mother," admitted Sister Thaumur promptly.

"Take away that board, Sister," Mother d'Youville directed in a gentle tone. "The poor have none in their room, and we ought not to be more comfortable than they are."

By examples such as these, the foundress kindly but firmly encouraged her Sisters in the exercise of that self-effacement which is absolutely necessary for effective work among the needy—the poor, the sick, the aged, the lonely, the ignorant. Depending on the grace of God to enlighten her, she taught them how to endure whatever was crude or unfeeling or selfish in others, because "they know not what they do." Without nourishing pride in one of its most subtle forms, she made the Sisters realize that the more delicate their own feelings were, the more they could offer to God.

Through her constant teachings and example in self-denial and the spirit of religious detachment, Mother d'Youville also impressed upon her Sisters the importance of little things for the enkindling of a great love for God and the poor. She believed, rightly, that only by faithful attention to details could the perfection of the whole work be attained. Nothing was too small for her notice, and nothing too great for her courage.

But she was so gentle and direct in her guidance and corrections that the Sisters were doubly benefited: as their faults became fewer in number, their love increased, for she never suppressed their liberty of spirit. She knew how to fit her remarks to the size of the offense, with due regard for circumstances of time and place and human frailty. Conscientiously fearful of the least implications of detraction, she carefully protected from the notice of others the little failings in her Sisters that no one but herself had observed. Public faults, however, she publicly corrected.

One day the Sister in charge of a ward noticed that the wood piled in the refectory for the fireplace there was drier than that in her department. Thoughtlessly she took it. When Mother d'Youville found out what had happened to the supply intended for the refectory, she openly reprimanded the guilty Sister in that very place and told her to restore immediately what she had taken. She took the occasion to remind all the Sisters then and there that they should respect one another in all things. "A Sister should never take anything from any department," she said, "without the permission of the one in charge."

Mother d'Youville looked upon mutual respect as one of the strongest safeguards of that unity of heart and soul which she desired so ardently in her Sisters. "All the riches in the world," she once wrote, "cannot equal the happiness of living together in unity."

How earnestly she counseled vigilance against unkind thoughts, gentleness in judgments of others, the mutual exchange of loving sentiments and thoughtful services! Nothing pleased her more than to see her Sisters trying to please one another. "Have only one heart and one soul among yourselves," she would say. "Rival one another in respect and attention. Support most charitably the faults of others, seeing with surprise how others support yours!"

Contention she would not tolerate, nor mockery, nor unkind criticism. Against these violations of mutual charity she was constantly vigilant.

One afternoon, just as she unexpectedly entered a room where several of the Sisters were working together, she noticed that their unusually animated conversation suddenly stopped. An unmistakable tension seemed to charge the atmosphere.

"What is the matter?" she asked. "Why have you suddenly stopped talking?"

There was nothing to do but tell her that one of the Sisters, in the course of the conversation, had spoken too sharply to her companions. Understanding perfectly that the fault sprang from weakness rather than from ill will, but desiring above all things "to keep the unity of the spirit in the bond of peace," Mother d'Youville quietly but firmly told the impatient Sister immediately to kiss the feet of her Sisters. Although they all begged that she be spared this humiliation, the wise Mother insisted that the penance should be performed. And that was the end of it, except that the momentary resentment of the offended Sisters was changed to deeper affection for their hasty companion, and she was strengthened in her guard for the future. It is not unlikely that Mother d'Youville had a special smile for her erring daughter before the day was over.

In spite of the courageous and constant efforts of the foundress to preserve charity and the blessings of fraternal union, the last year of her life was cruelly saddened by one of the greatest trials that a religious Superior could experience—the persistent insubordination of one of her own Sisters. To continued patience and gentleness on the part of Mother d'Youville, this Sister returned only treachery, disobedience, and the most extravagant worldliness. As time passed, she lost her fervor and religious spirit completely, thus weaving for her long-suffering Superior a final crown of thorns.

At first thought, one would naturally regret this grievous trial just at a time when difficult adjustments were being made to the reverses suffered as a result of the war and the disastrous fire; just when the religious foundation was paramount; just when Mother d'Youville herself seemed most in need of relief.

But, in the Providence of God, this trial also had its purpose, happening as it did through His permissive will. In all things mortal there must be shadow where there is light, if only to call attention to the shining. Contrast intensifies effect. Undoubtedly the other Sisters, while exercising forbearance and other aspects of charity, worked harder for the poor and also practiced their rules more perfectly. The dear foundress, afflicted in heart and soul, bore her sorrow with sweeter patience, creating in this circumstance, as in all others, a Christlike pattern for the future.

After Mother d'Youville's death, the Community was obliged to dismiss the unhappy Sister in question. Several years later, subdued and repentant, probably through her spiritual Mother's continued intercession, she sought to return, but was admitted only among the poor, with whom she lived in humble reparation until her death on May 22, 1813. Whenever she would see a novice admitted to the Community, she would exclaim, weeping bitterly, "Oh, there is another in the place that God had reserved for me!"

The example that Mother d'Youville gave her Sisters in their life together was effective also in their common labors among the poor. Although the responsibilities of administration rested upon her, she performed her share of work in the house, sewing, caring for the sick, attending to the needs of the poor, maintaining pleasant and courteous associations with the resident boarders, showering upon the poor little abandoned babies the gifts of her maternal heart.

Her capacity for work was extraordinary. Through the pervasive power of love and personal interest, she knew every detail of all the activities of the General Hospital, even though she carefully left the management of each department to the one in charge. She moved among her Sisters as one who served.

As often as possible she visited the poor, the sick, and the aged, lavishing on them the sympathy and delicate attentions that so relieved their deeply human needs. How they loved to see her come cheerfully into their wards! Each one would try to capture her first smile. She always had kind words of consolation for them and spiritual reminders for the goodness of their daily lives. As if she had nothing else in the world to do, she would listen to their stories, sometimes lengthily reminiscent, sometimes querulous and unreasonable; but she was always patient, always sympathetic. With their occasional rebuffs or ill humor she was most gently understanding. Their lives had been hard, she would say, excusing them; they did not know any better; only God could read the hidden goodness of their hearts. There was no one among them so wretched that she could not see in him the image of God.

The light of resignation and joy always shone more brightly

upon these needy ones during her visits. When she finally had to leave them, they would try to keep her from going by catching hold of her dress, just as children would restrain their dear mother.

Whenever the little ones of the house saw her coming, they would run to her, stumbling over one another, pure delight vibrating through their small bodies. They would crowd around her, each one grasping as much of her as his tight little arms could hold. She was their mother, the only one they knew, and her heart had room for them all.

What was the secret of Mother d'Youville's power over all these poor and abandoned ones? It was the charity of Christ that radiated from her heart, the charity that would heal the sick, relieve the destitute, understand and pity moral weakness; the charity that would look at the faults of others and even at their most repellent characteristics without seeing them; the charity that could sympathize, forgive, and then forget. She was a human mother, fashioned by the Eternal Father on the pattern of His Son, Who said, "I am the way, and the truth, and the life."

But Mother d'Youville's heart was larger than her hospital in 1769. On July 22 she wrote to the Bishop of Quebec:

There would certainly be a great deal of good to do if we only had the means. Every day poor come to us who are really in need. We have no more room and I cry bitterly in sending them away, but it must be done. . . . If I knew where there was so much money that I could take it without stealing, I would soon have a building that would hold almost two hundred, but I have nothing. God will be satisfied with my good will.

Considering, however, all the reverses and expenditures that Mother d'Youville had been obliged to meet, she certainly had done very well in her affairs. By 1769 all her debts were paid except seven thousand pounds which she had borrowed for the repair of buildings.

Poor as she was, she managed, moreover, to afford little gratifications from time to time for those who rendered service to the hospital. Her book of accounts faithfully records them. Sometimes these gifts were made by the Sisters and were therefore of double value to the recipients. On New Year's Day she always remembered friends and benefactors with a gracious courtesy that made her remembrances priceless.

Besides, she dared to give thought to the finishing touches of artistic beauty that raise the heart to God. "Let me know what it would cost to have a picture of St. Joseph with a gold frame," she wrote to her procurator in 1771, "the Holy Child Jesus caressing St. Joseph, with his table and carpenter's tools, and a cross a little more than his height."

It was not until fifty years later that Mother Lemaire succeeded in having a picture of St. Joseph made according to Mother d'Youville's specifications. Now it hangs above the main altar in the great chapel of the General Hospital, a magnificent painting twelve feet high and nine and a half feet wide.

The last letter inscribed by Mother d'Youville in her copybook was addressed to Governor General Guy Carleton in behalf of the foundlings dearest to her heart. On July 23, 1771, she wrote:

Your absence and the fear of losing you make the news of your return even more welcome. I hope that the good will that you have shown toward Canadians will accompany you in your return. I ask it, sir, for our house and in particular for the foundlings that we have taken since we came under English domination. I beg the honor of your influence with His Britannic Majesty to obtain some help for these unfortunate little ones. I am afraid of being obliged to give up this work for lack of means to support it. You can surmise, sir, how much cruelty that would cause in those persons who would want to bury their shame with their children. This consideration is strong enough to make an impression on a compassionate and charitable heart. I hope that you will not refuse me this favor.

There was nothing more that she could do. This letter to the Governor General was the beginning of an appeal that, resounding through many years, finally brought government aid to the most helpless of her needy; not much, it is true, but enough to assure the continuance of her work.

As Mother d'Youville silently marked her seventieth birthday on the fifteenth of October, she probably recalled that her sister Louise, residing at the hospital, was the only one left to her of the large and happy family that had once been united in Varennes.

But the full years had given her two other families: her beloved needy and her Grey Nuns. These two would remain. Christ Himself had said, "The poor you have always with you." As long as there were poor in this world to be cared for, her daughters would live.

As autumn came to a close that year, the Sisters noticed a gradual change in their Mother. Her spirit seemed to be losing its strength, just as a beautiful elm lets fall its golden leaves, silently, surely. Her step was often unsteady; her speech became slow and uncertain. A quiet kind of anxiety began to pervade the old hospital as she appeared less frequently among her poor and her little ones. Something seemed to be going away from all of them.

Early in December continued weakness obliged her to remain in her room, but her interest in the affairs of the house did not diminish. All day long, as the Sisters slipped in to see her, she expressed her maternal concern for them and for the needs of the poor. Nothing else mattered. How she wanted to be sure that all went well with those whom she loved!

On the ninth, while she was talking over business matters with one of the Sisters, she suddenly stopped speaking. Her companion, glancing up in surprise, had time only to stretch out her arms as Mother d'Youville collapsed, her face white and distorted.

Dr. Landriaux, summoned at once, only confirmed what the

heartbroken Sisters had already guessed: a stroke had paralyzed her left side and taken away her speech.

While they tried to make her as comfortable as possible, someone notified Father Montgolfier, who, as their ecclesiastical superior, had reason to be seriously concerned. Temporarily suspending the rule of enclosure for Hôtel-Dieu, he sent Sister Martel, renowned for her skillful care of the sick, to take charge of Mother d'Youville.

Day and night this devoted nurse, the best in Montreal, lavished her expert care upon the beloved patient, who gradually regained consciousness and the use of speech. In a few days, supported by her Sisters, she was even able to take several steps in her room. Her mental faculties seemed in no way impaired, though at times she spoke with more or less difficulty.

Sister Martel need remain no longer, the Sisters thought; they could take care of their Mother now, since she had recovered so quickly. "If God would be pleased to leave her even in this condition, we should consider ourselves blessed," they said to one another. "We would do our best to care for her in order to keep her with us."

So Sister Martel went back to her cloister and the Sisters surpassed themselves in their devoted ministrations. Masses were offered for her complete recovery; prayers and sacrifices ascended to heaven in continuous impetration.

But Mother d'Youville herself was not deceived by her improvement, almost as sudden as the attack had been. She felt that it was only a respite. In between the solicitous visits of the Sisters, who ran in to see her every chance they could get, she prepared her soul yet more for the moment when it would appear before God. Gently she tried to prepare her Sisters also for the inevitable separation.

At noon on the thirteenth, however, she felt so much better that she thought it unnecessary for anyone to remain with her while she had her dinner. Always considerate of others, she turned to her nurse and said in a very positive tone, "You do not need to bother about me. I shall get along easily without you. You go and have your dinner."

The Sister noticed that the good Mother had already taken her soup without any trouble and was about to help herself to the two other dishes before her; so, promptly obedient, she went to the refectory for her own meal.

Uneasy, however, she ate very little and then hurried back to her precious patient. Not a moment too soon! Mother d'Youville had fallen sideways against her little table. Her face was deathly white and twisted. She was motionless, speechless, almost lifeless.

The Sisters, hastily summoned by their companion's sharp cry of alarm, sent at once for Sister Martel. In a remarkably short time Mother d'Youville responded to treatment; her consciousness returned; she seemed completely in control of her mental faculties, but her speech continued to be affected.

There was something, however, that she wanted to say to her Sisters, something that was not too hard for her to articulate, because her whole life had been formed by the principle that it contained.

"It is the will of God, my dear Sisters," she finally managed to say to those kneeling around her. "I must submit to it. You, too, submit with all your hearts to the Divine Will. It is God Who asks this sacrifice of you."

When Father de Ligneris, a very close friend, came to see her and the Sisters that evening, they begged him to pray fervently for the cure of their Mother.

"I assure you that I shall do nothing of the kind," he declared with unmistakable emphasis; "nothing of the kind! Certainly I shall pray to God for your Mother, but not that He will keep her here for you. It is time that she went to heaven!"

As the Sisters seemed somewhat rebuffed and disheartened by his blunt words, he added in a gentler tone, "What does it matter if she dies? She will protect you just as much from heaven, and she will obtain for you the help and the graces that you need."

The next morning then—December 14—Mother d'Youville received the Last Sacraments. What a solemn moment it was, too solemn to be broken by any sounds of grief, too precious to hold anything but prayer. All the Sisters were kneeling there in her little room, reverently silent, sharing with their Mother as much as they could this last ineffable experience. There she lay, in serene and perfect peace.

All at once she opened her eyes and looked around at each of them with deep and personal tenderness. Close beside her were Sister Louise Thaumur and Sister Catherine Demers, faithful companions since their very first day together; gentle Sister Thérèse Despins, truly a Grey Nun after her spiritual Mother's own heart; little Sister Suzanne Benoit, her postulant, so young for this trial; and there, with all the others who loved her was the one who would not serve! Softly, but very clearly, Mother d'Youville began to speak.

"My dear Sisters," she began, her beloved voice distinct in the silence, "be constantly faithful to the duties of the state that you have embraced. Walk always in the path of regularity, obedience, and mortification; but above all, let the most perfect union reign among you!"

The most perfect union! This was her last request.

Before she had finished speaking tears were flowing freely down the cheeks of her Sisters. They understood that her words were a prayer, not a farewell; a summary of all her teachings, a précis of all her life. They were overcome by the poignant beauty of her last gift to them, a gift that every Grey Nun has treasured in her heart.

Before noon that same day Mother d'Youville made her last will and testament, final this time, dictating its simple terms to Pierre Panet, the royal notary, in the presence of Father de Féligonde, confessor for the Sisters, and Father Claude Poncin, chaplain to the poor.

Having recommended her soul to God, she requested that her body be buried in the crypt of the General Hospital, in the place and with the ceremonies that the Superior of the seminary judged fitting; that her debts be paid, and that her wrongs, if any, be righted; that thirty Masses be offered for the repose of her soul; that her Sisters remember her in their prayers. She declared that everything in the hospital and in her room belonged to the institution. Of personal family property belonging to her by rule, she gave half to her sons, Father François d'Youville and Father Charles Dufrost; the other half she gave to the poor, with a request that her sons, if they should ever be in need, would be lodged and cared for, with the permission of the Bishop, according to their state, that state to be determined by the Bishop or by the Superior of the seminary.

Everything now was done, except to wait in prayer and peace for the final summons. She continued to encourage her Sisters cheerfully, allowing them to render her all the little services that their love inspired.

One day Father de Féligonde took it upon himself to remark, with solicitude kindly enough, that Mother d'Youville would perhaps sleep better at night if Sister Coutlée did not remain in the room with her in order to take care of her least needs; and he suggested that the devoted Sister should move elsewhere.

"Oh, Father, she will not do it!" Mother d'Youville hastened to assure him out of the depth of her human understanding. "I assure you that she would not have the strength to do it!"

On another occasion, observing her Sisters all around her, as if they simply could not bear to be anywhere else, she smiled and tried to stretch out her hands to them.

"Oh, how happy I would be," she exclaimed, "how happy I would be if I could see myself in heaven with all my Sisters!"

On Monday morning, December 23, the dear patient seemed very much better. The Sisters were delighted and began to hope that even if she were not cured, they might be able to keep her with them a little longer. Late that afternoon she went to Confession, in preparation for receiving Holy Communion the next morning. Shortly afterward her devoted niece, Madame Louise Porlier Benac, came to see her; for although the Sisters did not customarily admit secular persons to her room, they did not exclude her relatives. On the contrary, in a spirit of charity, they made it a point to keep them closely informed of her condition.

Madame Benac, encouraged by the improvement in her aunt and hoping to relieve the Sisters a little, offered to spend the night taking care of her.

"Tonight!" Mother d'Youville suddenly exclaimed. "Oh, tonight I shall no longer be here!"

But the Sisters, too optimistic on account of her apparently excellent condition, could not take her words seriously.

That evening, during the recreation hour, the Sisters assembled in her room for a happy little visit and then retired to the community room for night prayer, leaving their Mother in the good care of her nurse.

Shortly before half-past eight Mother d'Youville stirred uneasily in her bed and tried to speak to the Sister instantly beside her, but she could not make herself understood. She gestured, however, that she wished to get up. Scarcely out of bed, she made a sign that she wanted to return. Gently and patiently helped in again, she suddenly collapsed. Her face became deathly white; her eyes grew dull, her head fell forward. A third stroke had come, the worst and the last.

To the instant alarm, Sister Thérèse Despins ran into the room just in time to take her in her arms. In five or six minutes Mother d'Youville was dead.

All the Sisters had hurried in and had knelt down, praying, unbelieving, unable to grasp the sudden and terrible truth that their Mother was gone.

The news spread like fire through the whole house. Sobs and cries rose uncontrolled from the bereaved hearts of the poor, who gathered in the halls in shocked and confused groups. "Oh, how terrible this loss is!" they exclaimed on all sides. "There will be no more Mother d'Youville for us!"

Sister Despins, in an account to Madame de Ligneris a few months later, described the sorrowful reaction in these words:

I leave you to imagine the desolation of this poor house, madame; the cries, the tears, the lamentations of such a great number of children who have lost their most tender mother. I cannot express to you the overwhelming natural anguish that this sudden death has caused us. We weep and mourn her for ourselves, for I believe that she is in heaven to receive the reward of her labors.

There was a certain amount of natural comfort for the desolate, however. After death, Mother d'Youville's face lost all signs of suffering and settled into an expression of serenity so lovely that the Sisters and all who came could scarcely stop looking at her. Her features appeared clear-cut and perfect, her complexion softly pink. Never before had she seemed so beautiful.

The Sisters, having no picture of her at all, called on Philippe Liébert, the best artist available, to make a painting of their Mother as she lay so beautiful in death. But no sooner had the artist begun to work the very next day than her features changed. So suddenly was her expression transformed that he could not capture for this earth the spiritual beauty that her Sisters had vainly hoped to retain. The picture that he made gives only a fleeting suggestion of the secret reserved for heaven.

And yet heaven itself seemed not to keep secrets. On the night of Mother d'Youville's death, at exactly half-past eight, Jean Delisle, a physician renowned for his integrity as well as for his knowledge of the physical sciences, happened to be walking outside the city walls on his way to Pointe-à-Callières. Suddenly he saw a great luminous cross, perfectly formed, shining brightly above the old General Hospital. Startled, hardly able to believe his eyes, he called the attention of a passer-by to the phenomenon, exclaiming, "Oh, what cross are the poor Grey Nuns going to have now!"

The next day, when the news of Mother d'Youville's death spread through the city, many other witnesses of the brilliant

283

cross came forward with their account of its appearance. The Sisters, however, inside the building and all too deeply concerned with the reality of their loss, did not see it.

It was indeed a cross that the poor Grey Nuns had suffered, but its luminous rays have never ceased to shed blessings on their work.

Sad hearts celebrated Christmas as best they could that year. In the evening of the great feast the Sisters carried Mother d'Youville's body to the chapel, where it lay in state for the night.

The next morning, the feast of St. Stephen, the funeral Mass was celebrated by Father Montgolfier, assisted by Father de Féligonde and Father Poncin. The chapel was crowded to the walls with many priests and friends from Montreal and nearby towns.

Father François d'Youville was present, but his brother, obliged to perform parish duties for his people on Christmas Day, was too far away to reach the hospital in time for the funeral. Always tenderly devoted to his mother, he felt this sacrifice very deeply. Father Gravé, a professor at the Seminary of Quebec, and a close friend of Father Charles Dufrost, wrote to Sister Thérèse Despins on January 5, 1772: "I told him of his mother's death. I wanted to go to spend a few days with him to console him. He needs all his faith to bear this blow."

By Father Montgolfier's arrangement, Mother d'Youville was buried in the crypt of the General Hospital, opposite the window through which her beloved poor could look into the chapel. It was fitting that she should rest in death nearest to those for whom she had given her life.

The next day, December 27, all the Sisters assembled in the presence of Father Montgolfier to elect a successor to their great foundress. But first they settled a very important matter dear to her heart.

Up to this time, by the letters patent, only twelve professed Sisters, as administrators, wore the silver cross designed by

Mother d'Youville. The others, though professed, were known as lay Sisters and wore a cross of wood. Now it was decided that this second group should be called *associate* instead of *lay*, that they should have the silver cross, and that they should be entitled to vote.

These changes having been established, the Sisters proceeded at once to the election. Sister Thérèse Despins was unanimously chosen to succeed her beloved Mother d'Youville.

Father Gravé, in a letter to the new Superior General a few days later, said very simply, "I do not congratulate you on succeeding her. It is not pleasant immediately to succeed a foundress, a Mother so tenderly loved, one whose merit was so high above the average; in a word, to succeed another Chantal, for I do not fear to make the comparison."

As a faithful, loving daughter; a dutiful wife, a devoted mother, a perfect religious, Marguerite d'Youville was indeed "another Chantal." As a valiant daughter of the Eternal Father, she was the channel of His providence to the needy; she was His apostle to the poor.

CHAPTER SEVENTEEN

IN THE LIGHT OF THE CROSS

FOR seventy years after the death of Mother d'Youville, her Grey Nuns labored faithfully and fruitfully in the old General Hospital of Montreal, seeking no renown, asking no reward. No farther than Châteauguay had they extended their activities.

During this period of discipline and perseverance in her principles, the "mustard seed" of charity that she had planted grew steadily in the mystical light of the luminous cross that had appeared at her death.

But never did this cross shine more brightly than in the decade between 1840 and 1850, the era of foundations, the planting season for seeds from the parent growth, seeds which would themselves become strong trees, shading the earth with their luxuriant branches.

What surprise, not unmixed with sorrow and elation, struck the little Community at Montreal in 1840 when Father Edouard Crevier, trusting in Divine Providence, asked for Sisters to take care of the poor and needy and sick in St. Hyacinthe, also in the Province of Quebec! It took long deliberation and many fervent prayers before the administrators decided that God wanted them now to spread His work.

Four Sisters were chosen for the new foundation—Sister

Marie-Michel Thuot as Superior, who had been the first to volunteer, and three young Sisters, formed by herself in the religious life, who had expressed a desire to accompany her. The decision of Bishop Ignace Bourget of Montreal that this establishment would be completely autonomous doubled for these brave Sisters the acute pain of sacrifice that they all experienced when they left their dearly loved Motherhouse on the sixth of May.

Although St. Hyacinthe is only thirty miles distant from Montreal, the pioneers of 1840 took just thirty-six hours to make the trip! Toward evening on the eighth, they drew near their destination. Suddenly the bells of the little city rang out in joyous welcome; the carriages bearing the Sisters passed between lines of happy people—students, teachers, priests, officials —all rejoicing that at last God had sent Sisters to take care of their poor.

With hearts not yet empty of old and dear associations, yet open to the new, they stopped before the big yellow building that would henceforth be their home. Having responded graciously to the warm welcome of Father Crevier and his reception committee, they crossed the threshold of Hôtel-Dieu.

There before them, clothed in rags, was a poor deformed idiot, scratching on a broken violin his own discordant greetings!

Trained in heart and soul to see Christ in the person of the poor and afflicted, these daughters of Mother d'Youville reverently bowed to the pitiful creature and saluted in him the Master Whom they had come to serve.

During the passage of another century, the Grey Nuns of St. Hyacinthe flourished in the shining of the cross. In 1886 an autonomous foundation was made at Nicolet, Province of Quebec, which in 1940 became a province of the Montreal establishment.

Today, in twenty-six large institutions in Canada, New England, and Haiti, more than eight hundred of these Grey Nuns of St. Hyacinthe are caring for thousands of poor, sick, aged, and orphaned members of society. Only in these works of charity are they by rule engaged. In the light and in the shadow of the cross they have labored; and God has blessed their labors.

In 1845, five years after the foundation of St. Hyacinthe, the life-giving rays of the luminous cross fell upon the planting of another "mustard seed" in Bytown, now Ottawa, the capital of Canada. For the first time the work of the Grey Nuns was carried into the Province of Ontario, then known as Upper Canada.

At the urgent request of Bishop Patrick Phelan and of Father Pierre Telmon, Superior of the Oblates of Mary Immaculate and parish priest in the needy locality, the Motherhouse in Montreal agreed to send four of Mother d'Youville's spiritual daughters to care for the poor and the sick as well as to provide for the education of French-Canadian and Irish girls.

With accomplished young Sister Elizabeth Bruyère as their Superior, the brave little group of pioneers left Montreal on February 19, in the depths of winter, for fields of activity hitherto unknown.

For them, as for their Sisters of St. Hyacinthe, the journey was very long, and, because of the season, it was also extremely difficult. Yet all hardships were forgotten in the warmth of the extraordinary welcome that began for them as soon as they approached their destination. In a glad procession of eighty carriages they entered the little city of Bytown. Bells rang jubilantly, and happy, curious children ran along the streets to see what the Sisters were like.

It was in two little wooden houses on St. Patrick Street that these Grey Nuns of the Cross, as they came to be known, began their work. On the third of March they received 120 little girls in the first bilingual school of Ontario; and the day that they welcomed the first poor patient under their roof was an occasion for special joy. In poverty and suffering, in trials and disappointments, but always under the superb guidance of Mother Bruyère, the mission flourished. For reasons judged best by ecclesiastical superiors, this foundation also was completely autonomous.

A century of progress now finds more than 1500 Grey Nuns of the Cross in 83 establishments, teaching over 35,000 pupils in all kinds of schools, caring for more than 38,000 patients in hospitals, sheltering 700 aged men and women and over 400 orphans in homes for the needy. Not only in Canada and the United States do they labor, but also in Basutoland of distant South Africa, where a novitiate for native Grey Nuns of the Cross has, with the help of the white Sisters, staffed seven flourishing missions.

From the parent tree of Ottawa two autonomous branches have grown. The Grey Nuns of the Sacred Heart established their Motherhouse in Philadelphia, Pennsylvania, in 1921, in order to maintain schools as well as other works of charity in the United States. In twenty-one establishments, more than three hundred of these daughters of Mother d'Youville perform the works to which she dedicated her Congregation over two hundred years ago.

Five years later, the Grey Sisters of the Immaculate Conception, now also more than three hundred in number, formed a separate Motherhouse at Pembroke, Ontario, in order to support works of charity and of education among English-speaking Canadians. To twenty-three different mission fields, including far western Canada and even distant China, they have carried their apostolic activities.

In 1849, a full century after Mother d'Youville took possession of the General Hospital in Montreal, Bishop Pierre-Flavien Turgeon, coadjutor of the Archbishop of Quebec, appealed to the Motherhouse for Sisters to carry on works of charity hitherto supported by the Charitable Society of Catholic Ladies of Quebec.

This was an appeal that the spiritual daughters of Mother d'Youville could not refuse. Cholera was still ravaging the old city, and the need was very great. After united prayer and long deliberation, the administrators chose five Sisters, under the superiority of Mother Marie-Anne-Marcelle Mallet, for the new foundation, which would, like the others, be entirely autonomous.

It was with sad hearts that these pioneers left the Motherhouse so dear to them all, but it was also with generous and noble hearts, eager to do the work to which Divine Providence had called them.

On August 22, 1849, Mother Mallet and her five companions arrived in old Quebec. There were no bells to greet them, no joyous procession to escort them along the streets, for this was a stricken city. But from the Bishop and the Ladies of Charity there was a fervent welcome, and in the hearts of the people who saw these Grey Nuns for the first time there was assurance and relief.

A small orphanage sheltering 25 children, where also 250 little girls received free education, was the field where these foundresses, known henceforth only as Sisters of Charity, planted their "mustard seed."

The years that followed were years of extraordinary development, blessed by the sign of the cross. On May 3, 1854, the feast of the Finding of the Holy Cross, the orphanage, now enlarged and greatly improved, burned to the ground. But these heroic daughters of Mother d'Youville, in unison with the Bishop and priests who shared their sorrow, lifted their hearts in the *Te Deum*, just as the foundress had done.

The centenary of this great foundation of Sisters of Charity records sixty-four establishments grouped into five provinces dependent on the Motherhouse in Quebec. Almost 1800 religious are active in the different branches of this flourishing community, wherein are relieved the helplessness of children, the sorrows of orphans, the loneliness of the aged, the sufferings of the sick, and the misfortunes of the mentally afflicted. The young are educated in forty-three schools of all types—primary, secondary, normal, domestic, commercial, nursing. In twenty-five institutions 2250 orphans and 1530 aged are sheltered; and in nineteen modern, fully equipped hospitals, both general and special, the sick are tended. But the greatest service to suffering humanity is rendered by these Sisters of Charity of Quebec in immense hospitals for the mentally ill, where more than five thousand patients receive devoted care and expert treatment.

Living faith, consoling hope, abiding charity—these are the virtues that have animated the spiritual daughters of Mother d'Youville in all the foundations inspired by Divine Providence, "but the greatest of these is charity."

During the century of development that followed the first planting in 1840, the Motherhouse in Montreal also put forth branches of extraordinary vigor and fecundity; but the establishment of the Sisters of Charity of Quebec was the last autonomous foundation by Montreal. To cut forever the actual ties that bound the Sisters to their Motherhouse had proved too painful. Henceforth, no matter how distant the missions, they would always be united to the parent stem, through groupings into provinces responsible to the General Administration.

It was on September 13, 1843, that Bishop Norbert Provencher, of the Red River region of the far West, stood before the thirty-eight Grey Nuns of the Montreal Community, with an appeal for missionaries among the Indians. At a word from the Superior General, who uttered for them the will of God, all thirty-eight immediately volunteered. Four Sisters were chosen from the generous group, with Sister Valade in charge.

On April 24 of the following year, these four true daughters of Mother d'Youville set out for St. Boniface, Manitoba, on a journey of over 1400 miles that would take them 59 days, following the trail made by La Vérendrye more than a century before.

Through fires and floods, through hunger and cold and privations almost unbelievable, these pioneer Sisters laid the foundations of missionary activities among the Indians and Eskimos that are today compassed by thirty-nine missions in three great provinces of the Grey Nuns of Montreal. Fearful of being recalled from labors that they loved for God's sake, they hid their sufferings from the Motherhouse! Farther west they went, then farther north, until they stood on the edge of the Arctic Circle. Here, in the Land of the Midnight Sun, is now their most distant mission, Aklavik, on the delta of the Mackenzie River, 4127 miles from Montreal.

Not only by foundations were the ranks of the Grey Nuns of Montreal depleted in the decade between 1840 and 1850. In 1847 the tragedy of famine in Ireland threw hundreds of Irish immigrants, stricken with typhus, on the shores of Canada. In sheds at Point St. Charles they lay, the dying with the dead. What could be done for them?

When Mother McMullen, then Superior General, appealed to the Sisters for volunteers to care for the victims of the highly contagious plague, twenty-three responded at once and eight were chosen. Before a month was over, all the Sisters, professed and novices, were engaged in the terrible work; some in the filthy sheds where hundreds of men, women, and children writhed in agony; some caring for their own Sisters, of whom thirty were stricken. Of these, seven consummated the offering of their lives. Yet their sacrifice bore fruit; for, from that time, vocations increased in number and missions developed.

In Bytown, the Grey Nuns of the Cross, under the leadership of Mother Bruyère, were equally heroic in meeting the scourge of the typhus epidemic. In less than a year they took care of 573 victims. Of 21 Sisters, 17 contracted the disease, but fortunately no one died.

In 1851 the Grey Nuns of Montreal opened their first separate orphanage, St. Patrick's, chiefly for Irish children bereaved by the plague. Four years later they established their first hospital in the United States, St. Vincent's, in Toledo. This great institution has been followed by others in New Jersey and New England, the most notable being the Holy Ghost Hospital for Incurables, in Cambridge, Massachusetts, where these Sisters also have a novitiate for English-speaking candidates.

Today 1981 Grey Nuns of Montreal, grouped into six provinces, are nursing about 85,000 patients a year in 34 hospitals, of which 10 are among the Indians and Eskimos; taking care of 11,119 children and 3513 aged men and women in 32 orphanages and homes; and teaching 13,000 pupils in 30 schools, of which 15 are for Indians and Eskimos.

The bright rays of the luminous cross that shone over the old General Hospital on December 23, 1771, have fallen upon uncounted hundreds of achievements, spiritual and material, that Mother d'Youville's daughters have offered to God in her spirit. Many books have been filled with the history of these achievements, and even in these all that could be told has not been fully recorded. This brief chapter cannot, therefore, relate what has been written in heaven.

But here and there upon the three continents where the Grey Nuns have tried to fulfill the traditions of their venerable foundress, in the different sister Communities that Divine Providence has inspired them to establish, the lovely radiance of the cross particularly attracts our attention.

Only these rays could penetrate the soft shadow of humility in which good Mother Mary of the Nativity worked exclusively for the poor of the city of Quebec from her profession as a Sister of Charity of Quebec in 1852 until her holy death on March 4, 1917. Among the rich she fostered the joy of giving; to the poor she taught the higher art of being happy in the midst of want. In her hands she carried material aid; from her lips poured healing, consoling words.

Two works she loved above all others—preparing first communicants and assisting needy aspirants to the priesthood. For these latter she obtained scholarships or episcopal patronage; she sought and found allowances, benefits, assistance of every kind. Through her help many a young priest ascended the altar of God. How surprised good Mother Mary of the Nativity would be today to hear herself called the hidden beginning of the present Apostolic School!

Her blessed apostolate, sustained through more than sixty

fruitful years, derived its power from a spirit of prayer to which a high degree of asceticism was constant companion. "Behold, the enemy is I!" seemed to be her watchword. Sleep and meals were almost obstacles to her zeal for works of charity among the poor of Quebec.

Venerated by the unfortunate to whom she revealed Divine Providence, admired by her Sisters for whom she continues to be an example of high virtue, this humble Sister of Charity of Quebec, from her shining place in heaven, still faithfully responds to the trust of those who invoke her aid.

On March 11, 1920, His Eminence, the late Cardinal Louis-Nazaire Bégin, Archbishop of Quebec, in approving the following prayer, was pleased to predict the canonization of good Mother Mary of the Nativity, beloved now as in her lifetime by the people of Quebec.

O God, Father of the poor and Protector of the humble, glorify Thy servant, good Mother Mary of the Nativity, whose whole life was consecrated to serve Thee in the person of the poor and to glorify Thee by helping priestly vocations.

We beg this of Thee through the Immaculate Heart of Mary.

May good Mother Mary of the Nativity pray for us and obtain for us the grace that we seek. Amen.

(Six Pater Nosters, Aves, and Glorias for her deceased protégés and for young seminarians.)

May the radiance of the luminous cross become for her someday the bright aureole of sanctity!

In 1902 four Grey Nuns of the Cross began a special apostolate, not in surroundings familiar and dear, but among the Cree Indians at the fur trading post of Albany, on the shore of James Bay. Here they would educate the young, nurse the sick, care for poor orphans, and shelter the aged.

Eight hundred miles from the Ottawa Motherhouse that had protected them in peace and security, these brave daughters of Mother d'Youville lived in a poor little cabin until the building was ready that would serve for them as residence, school, and hospital.

To the meager help granted by the government was added the immense charity of friends, all of whom made possible the development of this mission and that of two others at Fort George and Moosonee. Who can estimate the work of the Sisters in educating young Indian girls for Christian family life, and in caring for the sick in hospitals visited by a doctor only once a year?

For fifteen years Sister Marie Elmire, the "White Angel" of the Albany mission, gave extraordinary service to Indian patients, particularly in cases of grave emergency when no doctor could be summoned in time. Besides treating countless medical cases, she performed twenty-five surgical operations, including amputations, and more than five hundred dental extractions. To this humble, reserved Grey Nun of the Cross, there was nothing unusual in her heroic attempts to save lives.

Nor do Grey Sisters of the Immaculate Conception, Mother d'Youville's youngest daughters, consider it unusual that at Vancouver, British Columbia, on the Pacific coast, they conduct the only all-Chinese grade school in Canada. The initial registration of fifty-five pupils in 1939 has constantly increased, in spite of opposition from various nonsectarian agencies.

This school is the latest development of an apostolate in Canada which began in Vancouver's Chinatown on December 3, 1933, with the opening of a kindergarten in St. Francis Xavier's Chinese Catholic Mission. At first there was only one pupil in the kindergarten; then two, then three. Fifty is now the regular enrollment.

Not only among the Chinese of Vancouver have the Grey Sisters of the Immaculate Conception carried out Mother d'Youville's injunction "to undertake all good works that Divine Providence presents to them and in which they will be authorized by ecclesiastical superiors." In distant China the cross shines brightly on their missionary labors—the education of Chinese girls and the care of the sick poor.

Lishui has been the headquarters of their work in the Orient since 1932. A second mission was opened in Lungchuan in 1939 and a third at Sungyang in 1941. All three, however, had to be abandoned at the time of the Japanese invasion in circumstances thrilling enough for a book of their own; but the return of the Grey Sisters to these missions at the end of 1946 was an event that can best be related through excerpts from Sister Mary Angela's own day-by-day account.

December 21—This is our Happy Day—how we dreamed of it, hoped for it, and longed for it! We are at home, and there cannot possibly be any happier hearts than ours in God's big, beautiful world. The little town is all agog with excitement. Church bells and firecrackers announced our arrival, and Chinese were popping from everywhere to greet the *Mo Mo* again. . . . Entering the Lishui City Gate, we intoned the Magnificat.

December 22—We were up early, exploring our convent and having a look at the neighborhood by daylight. . . . It is very cold and a white frost covers the tiled roofs and the ground. Father Venadam said Mass at seven. We tried so hard to be recollected, but the sight of the church was a terrible distraction. Our once lovely and well-cared-for church is now little better than a barn. The main altar has been badly battered. . . . During both invasions the Japanese used the church as a stable and the sanctuary as a kitchen. The pews were used for firewood and even parts of the altar, too. There is not a pane of glass in any of the windows; they are boarded up with old lumber to keep out the rain and wind. Nothing remains of our lovely French statues; and of the Stations, only the third is left. The sacristy was bombed, the altar rail taken away. . . . The Compound has been crowded since Mass time. Christians and pagans have been swarming in, all as happy and excited as ourselves. Please God, we shall never have to leave these poor people again. Right after breakfast a man came, begging us to visit his sick baby.

December 23—Our Venerable Mother d'Youville's feast. We celebrated it by caring for the many patients who came for treatment, and by visiting others in their homes. . . . We have only four chairs in the house. They make quite a quartette, all battered, rungless, and one, the best, has a chicken-wire seat. A cupboard and table complete the furniture. . . . The only other furniture is our six beds. The mattresses are not in yet, but, as Sister Mary Catherine says, "The boards get softer every night." Poor and all as our convent is, it is Home to us, and we love every square inch of it.

December 24—Christmas Eve! A heavy frost greeted us this morning. We washed the altar linens and tried to tidy up a bit in the church. The boys are decorating, and so far have twelve large paper angels hovering above and around the altar. Two of the angels are hugging teddy bears and two more are blowing horns.

December 25—Christmas Day. Christmas greetings are sent out over the miles to all of you. We are having a really grand day. There was a great crowd at Mass. Sister Mary Genevieve was organist and Sister St. Martin and I, the choir. Our pagan friends crowded around the organ and pushed in so close that at times Sister could not keep her hands free enough to play, and our singing was drowned by their comments and chatter as well as by the noise of firecrackers at the church door. . . .

Our dinner was very good. A woman had given us a Mushori duck, and Father Venadam donated four chickens. Our cake was the gift of a gentleman in New Orleans. Besides, we had tomato soup, Jello, and chocolate bars, all saved from Canada. Cooking dinner was a picnic in itself. Lacking pots and pans, we had recourse to our washbasins. One must improvise in China!

December 28—Today we were asked to visit the Christian mother of three of our former pupils. The woman is dying. She recognized us but was unable to speak. Our walk out—five miles up and over the mountains—did not seem to tire us, but when we reached the first mountain on the homeward trip, our feet began to whimper. . . . Our two years at home softened us up a bit too much, but we shall soon get our Chinese feet again. . . . Sister Mary Catherine and I went across the river on a sick call. It was a twenty-six-day-old baby, waiting only for a ticket to heaven. I baptized him Gabriel, our first baptism since our return.

January 2—A letter from the Motherhouse—nothing more precious—and we nearly ate it up. Another baptism today too.

January 3—It will take some time to get the church in order, but we will do a little each day. The boy said today, "Even God is happy to see the Sisters back."

Indeed the rays of the luminous cross reach gloriously to distant China where the spirit of Mother d'Youville is still living in her daughters.

But not less gloriously do they shine with the light of heroic charity into the mental darkness that shrouds St. Amable Refuge in Canada. Here, in memory of the poor idiot boy who played his broken violin to welcome the Grey Nuns to St. Hyacinthe in 1840, the Sisters have made a permanent home for about thirty like him, the most mentally afflicted, the most pitifully unwanted victims of physical and intellectual disorder.

With infinite patience the Grey Nuns of St. Hyacinthe try to draw these poor human beings gradually into a gentle discipline that seems to improve their condition. They study their capabilities, less to receive the benefit of the work they might do than to keep them busy and to give them the satisfaction of being useful in their environment. Many can help in housework, in the laundry, or in the workshop, but only the Sisters can handle them or keep them employed.

To the Sisters engaged in this heroic work constant vigilance is necessary to guard against accidents and to detect the strange tricks of these sufferers; solid virtue to support their instability and their abusive language; robust health to endure unending physical strain.

Yet among the daughters of Mother d'Youville—these Grey Nuns of St. Hyacinthe who render immeasurable service to humanity by caring for these unfortunates and by making them happy—is one who has spent twenty-five years among them, loving in each one the soul that is made to the image of God.

Here at St. Amable Refuge the glory of the cross is in its hidden sanctity.

Dispelling darkness of another kind, the bright rays of the cross have fallen since 1861 into Nazareth, the only Catholic institution for the blind in all Canada. Founded by Father Victor Benjamin Rousselot, of the Society of St. Sulpice, and confided by him to the Grey Nuns of Montreal, this great institution is unique also in its reflection of Mother d'Youville's spirit; for it was a blind woman whom the foundress first received into her home.

It is an unforgettable experience to make a tour of the beautiful, thoroughly modern, completely equipped building where Mother d'Youville's daughters, by means of the Braille system, teach two hundred boys and girls the standard courses of primary and secondary education, train them in arts and crafts, and even prepare them for liberal professions. One marvels that a little blind girl, charming and sensitive, can play a difficult classical selection on piano and on violin with as much ease as she solves an arithmetical problem on her Braille slate.

Because the senses of touch and hearing are highly developed in the blind, music is a specialty in this school. The Normal School and the Academy of Music of Quebec have paid special tribute to its graduates. Some of them have received distinguished European awards. Several are renowned organists in the city of Montreal.

Even after the pupils of Nazareth leave the school, they share the advantages of a circulating Braille library of more than ten thousand volumes. A kindly Sister, whose love and understanding of the blind has been exercised for many years, supervises the distribution of these precious books. Thus has the light of learning been diffused among those who might otherwise have spent their lives in darkness.

Such light has fallen also on the shores of Lake Erie, where in 1907 the daughters of Mother d'Youville established their first liberal arts college for women. D'Youville College, in

Buffalo, New York, now directed by the Grey Nuns of the Sacred Heart, began its actual history on March 25 of that year with the blessing of the Apostolic Delegate, Diomede Cardinal Falconio. His Eminence wrote: "I wish to join with you on this occasion in praying God to shower down upon you and your works His choicest blessings, so that your work may be blessed with success for His greater glory and for the advancement of Catholic education."

On that very day the Most Reverend Charles Henry Colton, Bishop of Buffalo, ceremoniously broke ground for the new institution. On the second of April workmen arrived.

In the meantime, a group of women, enthusiastically interested in the new project, formed for its support the D'Youville Association, under the patronage of the venerable foundress.

On March 25 of the following year, His Excellency, accompanied by the dearly loved Father Nelson P. Baker, blessed the completed building.

Application to the State Legislature for a charter brought from a member of the Board of Regents a frank statement that he would use all his influence to oppose it. He believed, he said, that it would but open the way for a flood of similar applications. The cross shone more brightly!

Through the efforts of courageous benefactors, distinguished for their knowledge and for their appreciation of higher education, the bill granting a charter was passed by the State Legislature and signed by Governor Charles Evans Hughes on April 5, 1908.

Nine young women presented themselves for the formal opening early on September 27. Bishop Colton blessed the occasion with the celebration of Holy Mass, while a choir of students from Holy Angels Academy provided singing worthy of their Grey Nun teachers.

Four years passed, as college years do, quickly and happily, until there came, on June 8, 1912, the beautiful evening of the first graduation. Long before the appointed hour friends and relatives of the graduates filled the auditorium, lovely with ferns and flowers. Four young women, taking the places assigned to them, waited until the distinguished dignitaries of the occasion had assembled on the stage. There in the center was His Eminence, John Cardinal Farley. Bishop Colton smiled his gratification. The Most Reverend Thomas F. Hickey of Rochester was there, and the Most Reverend Joseph Henry Conroy, beloved Bishop of Ogdensburg. Many other eminent friends were present, and members of the faculty.

A short greeting to His Eminence by Bishop Colton, chancellor of the college, was followed by a scholarly address, "The Aims of D'Youville," delivered by Professor William Martin. While the choir chorused a triumphant "Magnificat!" the first diplomas of the college were awarded to the four graduates who had successfully completed the course of study. Bishop Conroy congratulated these happy young women with his customary grace and eloquence, and then His Eminence closed the significant occasion with a broad and beautiful blessing.

Hundreds of graduates have carried the torch of learning from the halls of D'Youville College since that first happy evening, and the light therefrom has mingled with the shining of the cross.

Not only light but also warmth, the warmth of heroic charity, spreads over the cold, bleak moraine of Chesterfield Inlet, close to the northwestern shore of Hudson Bay. Here the Grey Nuns of Nicolet devote themselves to a mission field called by His Holiness, Pope Pius XI, "the most beautiful, the most difficult, the most meritorious" in the world. "If We could see only one mission," the Holy Father declared, "that is the one We would want to see."

It was on June 21, 1931, in the stately Cathedral of Nicolet, Province of Quebec, Canada, that four spiritual daughters of Mother d'Youville dedicated themselves to that mission in an apostolate offered by Divine Providence through the Most Reverend Arsène Turquetil, O.M.I., Vicar Apostolic of Hudson Bay.

In the Mass of that memorable morning His Excellency consecrated four small hosts with the large one of the Holy Sacrifice; and these he gave in Holy Communion to the four privileged missionaries kneeling in the sanctuary.

A few days later, fortified by the special graces of their dedication and by the prayerful love of their Sisters, they left their beautiful Hôtel-Dieu for the barren lands of Chesterfield Inlet. On October 3, the feast of St. Thérèse of the Child Jesus, they crossed the threshold of the little red-trimmed white hospital that bears her name.

To the nomadic Eskimos of that vast and desolate area the small white hospital standing three stories high on the frozen ground has become a beloved refuge for the poor, the sick, and the abandoned. Drawn to this haven by the outstretched arms of a great bronze statue of the Sacred Heart rising also from the rock, they quickly find the fulfillment of the Eskimo words engraved there on its base: "Sacred Heart of Jesus, bless the Eskimos and those who bring the Gospel to them."

The evangelists here mentioned—Oblates of Mary Immaculate and Grey Nuns—enjoy God's benediction in proportion to the immense hardships and privations of their daily lives. They endure long months of darkness, bitter cold, almost complete isolation, the special self-annihilation of conformity to Eskimo ways of life. Raw fish, dried potatoes, canned vegetables, fats, bread, occasional sweets are their ordinary foods; and blubber, a spongy, white substance fishy in flavor, enjoys the prestige of the staff of life!

And yet the lack of material comfort in Chesterfield is more than balanced by the spiritual vitality of the mission, just as the frozen, treeless, twisted terrain intensifies by contrast the pageant splendor of sunrise and sunset, the majestic beauty of the rolling sea, the diamond brilliance of low-hanging stars. Conversions are very numerous among the Eskimos, who foster their faith in simple fidelity to liturgical devotions. To the Sisters who patiently teach them—men and women, young and old—it is a consoling reward to hear them chant the parts of the Mass by memory, or break into a glad "Magnificat!" in Latin as an act of welcome or of thanksgiving.

It is another reward, perhaps in the natural order, for the Grey Nuns of Nicolet to find among the Eskimos of Chesterfield that quality of ingenious inventiveness which is for the Sisters themselves a special expression of their supernatural spirit of poverty, a part of their heritage from Mother d'Youville, who knew how to make good use of everything!

While God undoubtedly reserves for eternity the supernal reward of heroic missionary activities at this desolate post, He has been pleased on certain occasions to manifest through His representatives the consolation that the Grey Nuns of Nicolet daily give to His Divine Heart. One of the most significant of these occasions was in August of 1944, in the visit of the Superior General, Reverend Mother Marie Evangéline Gallant. In a special way the joys and sorrows of this mission, the activities and heroic virtues of the Sisters were revealed to her mother heart during the brief and blessed days of her visitation. On one side were the solemn High Mass chanted in perfect unison by the Eskimos and the great banquet afterward for all to enjoy; on the other, the death of a little child and the tragic wreck of the good ship, *Thérèse*, with the loss of all supplies for the year; and over all, like the brilliance of the luminous cross, joyful self-sacrifice and holy resignation!

What summary of the spirit of this mission could be more complete than Mother Gallant's farewell message, registered on a phonograph record before her departure? Thanks to a faithful transcription made at the time by her secretary, Mother Léonie Ferland, we also may read:

On this fourteenth day of August 1944, I address to my beloved Sisters at Chesterfield a message of congratulations and maternal affection.

Having seen you at work for several days, I have found in each one of you, my dear daughters, the regularity, self-denial, and apostolic zeal of our Venerable Mother d'Youville. I congratulate you, for you are, dear missionaries, the purest glory of our Community! I thank you, for the real wealth, the true value of an institute is found in the sanctity of its members.

When you hear this message, I shall be far, very far from you, but I shall keep you, as I do today, in my heart and in my thoughts. Yes, in hours of sacrifice, remember that in Montreal as in Nicolet, Mothers and Sisters love you and pray for you every day.

Remain faithful, fervent, generous. May fraternal charity reign among you; always more and more let your devotedness to your dear Eskimos support that of the Reverend Fathers and the Brothers. Be apostles, souls of prayer—above all, souls of prayer! Be saints according to the spirit of our venerable foundress.

I bless you, I thank you, and I love you.

Your Mother,
SISTER EVANGÉLINE GALLANT,
Superior General

Blessed and beautiful is the light of the luminous cross at distant Chesterfield Inlet, the light that is shining now in special glory on a little novice there, Sister Pelagie Innuk, the first Eskimo nun in the world.

How brilliant must have been the rays that illuminated the arrival of the first Grey Nuns of the Cross at Basutoland, in the mountains of South Africa, early in November of 1931! Little did they guess that the thunder, lightning, and pouring rain that greeted them were good omens to the natives, who depend upon rain for the abundance of their daily bread.

Good omens indeed! Storms more destructive than productive were followed by epidemics of typhus and influenza, and then by a famine of terrible proportions. Only the Sisters had corn in their reservoir—by the Providence of God and the foresight of Mother Louis-Gérard, Superior and foundress.

But one day, after having supplied the personnel of the mission and neighboring sufferers for many weeks, the good Mother Superior sent one of her Sisters up the ladder to see how much corn still remained in the reservoir. The Sister promptly obeyed.

"Why, Mother," she exclaimed from the top of the ladder, "it is full!"

And it was! Only when the new harvest had begun to come in did the supply in the reservoir begin to diminish.

"Miracles?" says Mother Louis-Gérard with a shrug. "There was nothing but miracles!"

One should write quickly of the phenomenal development of five flourishing missions sprung from the original foundation at Pontmain: a boarding school at St. Paul of Butha-Buthe; another at Paray, besides a hospital; a house of studies for native Sisters at Roma; a mission at Seboche. Mother Louis-Gérard has prepared a course of study for industrial schools that is now followed in all Basutoland. Native teaching Sisters are equipped with Normal certificates; four, called "the smiling Sisters," are preparing to become registered nurses in the Glen Grey Hospital of Queenstown.

This remarkable expansion has been made possible through the establishment of a novitiate for native Sisters, of whom there are now forty-eight. What an event it was in the history of the Community when seven perfectly black aspirants, braving parental anger and worse, traveled on foot from the mountains of Basutoland to become Grey Nuns!

Six months later, on June 13, when the favored candidates received the holy habit, Queen Angelina was present to hear the first novice called by her name. The principal chiefs of nearby localities were there, and parents glowing with extraordinary pride. Admiration passed all bounds when the novices appeared, clothed in grey just like the white Sisters. Tears ran freely down shining black cheeks, while eager hands clapped in unrestrained excitement.

On November 11, 1936, six native novices, thoroughly and sympathetically trained by Mother Louis-Gérard, pronounced their vows in the presence of the Reverend Mother St. Bruno, Superior General. Six black Grey Nuns, the vanguard of many more, took their places in the ranks of Mother d'Youville's daughters.

Ten years later came a glorious event—the presence of Reverend Mother St. André-Corsini in her African missions for almost a year. Accompanying the Superior General on this trip were four Sisters on the way to Nyasaland to open another African field of missionary activity.

Thirty days on the ocean, three hundred days on land, thirty hours in the air—this is the Reverend Mother's succinct summary of her visit. What it meant to her daughters there is best expressed in the reception address written and read on February 22, 1946, by the second oldest native Grey Nun, significantly named Sister Marguerita d'Youville, the accomplished daughter of a mountain chief. Thus gracefully she greeted the Superior General:

Reverend and dear Mother,

Certainly we have no words to express our feelings to such a grand visitor as you are. Allow us therefore to approach thee with the children's simplicity and love for their dear mother.

Though St. Paul is not the first mission of the Grey Nuns, nevertheless today we are the first native Sisters to receive you in this country, all along the valleys of our small mountainous land. Therefore we have all the reasons to be proud, for ours is the best part.

Therefore we welcome thee, Most Honorable Mother. We greet thee, the brave and noble heart. Your motherly love has bound you to such a long, tiresome and perilous journey. Truly the love has conquered thee. To think that you have come for your Canadian children shows your love, bravery and courage; but to believe that you did not come for them only, rather for these poor darkies of Africa, sounds so strange, yet true, that we cannot help to gaze and admire at such generosity and self-denial of our dear Mother.

Today our dear Mother Louis-Gérard is glad to put in your hands a group of her little native Sisters, her spiritual daughters. These are the fruits of her work during fifteen long years in Africa. She and all the Sisters have tried their best to make us real Grey Nuns of the Cross. We hope through our good will that God will give us the strength to be real religious, fervent souls who shall only work for His glory, by practicing to be saints every day.

Dear Reverend Mother, we are aware that we owe a great deal to Canada for having given us her daughters for our mothers, especially our Mother Louis-Gérard. We dare not tell of her works in Basutoland, her noble deeds, what sacrifices she has made daily; through what great difficulties she did pass only God knows, and He alone has counted the prize.

We welcome thee, kind and good Mother: in the name of all the African Sisters of our Congregation, in the name of our Mother Louis-Gérard, the Provincial, and in the name of our dear Superior, and finally in the name of all the pupils of the St. Paul Mission. May our heavenly Mother Mary, Queen of heaven and earth, bless your days in Africa, guide you back as you return to Canada, and through her powerful prayers may we be united at the feet of the Savior forever. "Long live our dear Reverend Mother!"

How beautiful is the setting of this welcome in the light that falls upon it from the luminous cross!

Not only in darkest Africa but also in the little black Republic of Haiti do the daughters of Mother d'Youville reflect the glory of the cross.

In 1940 good Father Alix, chaplain to the Grey Nuns of St. Hyacinthe at Berlin, New Hampshire, listened quietly to some visitors from Haiti as they deplored the condition of their people. "Do you know what you need down there?" he remarked. "Grey Nuns!"

The tiny seed sown by these simple words began to be a flourishing tropical growth in 1943 in the little village of Dame-Marie. Now six Grey Nuns of St. Hyacinthe—"white nuns" there, because of the climate—conduct a school for native children and a dispensary for the sick. Only their own hearts know what it meant to become familiar with the needs, customs, language, and mentality of a people so different from themselves. Yet in the kingdom of the soul there is no nationality, and only one language—the language of charity.

Among these people, intelligent, trustful, and very poor, the Sisters were soon at home. Little children are lovable all over the world; and to a Grey Nun anywhere the suffering poor are dear. Four times a week the doors of the dispensary are opened wide to the sick—twenty, forty, sixty a day—who come from all directions and all distances to be treated by the good Sister nurse. Very often she proceeds tactfully from the care of the body to that of the soul; and soon another penitent is at peace with God.

To nourish the spiritual nature of the natives of Haiti, to care for the sick in their poor little huts, to respect their inborn pride, their simple courtesy—these are the privileges of the Grey Nuns of St. Hyacinthe, privileges that could be trusted only to those gifted with the comfort touch bequeathed by Mother d'Youville and illumined by the light of the cross.

Indeed, there was no light at all except that of the cross to guide the two Grey Nuns of the Sacred Heart who knocked at the door of the Griffin Memorial Hospital in Kodiak, Alaska, at one minute past midnight on the eleventh of November in 1944. Yet in the blackness of the night and in the deeper darkness of bigotry and opposition, these daughters of Mother d'Youville stood strong and valiant in the rays of the cross that shone upon them from afar.

The will of God had brought them to this place. For several months negotiations had been made to transfer the hospital from secular management to the care of Sisters. Early in October five Grey Nuns had left their Motherhouse in Philadelphia to carry the traditions of their great foundress to an Alaskan island where Sisters had never before been seen.

Delays and disappointments, unfriendliness and resentment lay heavily on the hearts of the valiant five who finally waited in Kodiak for word to take possession of the little hospital that they had come to serve.

At last Father Edgar Gallant, responsible for their coming, brought the awaited message. At half-past eleven that night, in

308

thick, black darkness and pouring rain, Sister Mary Monica and Sister St. Hilary, led by Father Gallant, splashed along the middle of the muddy street to the cold white building that would become their home.

No welcome awaited them. The night nurse and the supervisor explained that the former staff would continue to occupy their rooms for a day or so. Nevertheless, the Sister Superior donned her white uniform and proceeded to study the patients' charts, while Sister St. Hilary studied the confusion in the office.

The rest of the night wore on. At five o'clock Sister St. Hilary descended to the kitchen to prepare breakfast for the patients—eight adults and two babies. The former cook appeared in the door, somewhat curious, but offered no assistance whatever.

Shortly after daylight the other three Sisters, having attended Mass after a very anxious night, came to relieve the situation and permit their companions to receive Holy Communion.

Then the work began, the Grey Nun way in good earnest, according to Mother d'Youville's own principles of order and the spirit of prayer. The room chosen for the chapel was cleared of debris and thoroughly cleaned. The altar, which had been brought in once before and hastily removed under threat of its being used as a bar, was now installed, and Christ the King took up His residence, too, on the island of Kodiak.

But every member of the former staff refused to remain; and to the five Sisters fell the management of all the departments—kitchen, laundry, laboratory, office—besides the care of the sick both day and night. Nevertheless, they met the emergency quietly and effectively.

Before many months had passed, the white light of charity had dispelled the dark shadows of resentment and opposition. Enemies became friends, and friends multiplied. To the care of the sick has been added the teaching of catechism to the little ones of the town. As the list of conversions grows longer each year, the cross shines more brightly on faraway Kodiak.

It was in 1938, during the bicentennial celebration of the

founding of the Congregation, that the cross diffused its most beautiful radiance, for this great celebration had but one end: the happiness of the poor.

"We shall feast the poor," wrote Reverend Mother Marie Evangéline Gallant to her Sisters, "because they are the reason for the existence of our institute, because it is for them that we have been given our special vocation as Sisters of Charity."

With this one end in mind, preparations were intensified for a year in a twofold manner: first, by prayer, in the secret garden of each Sister's soul; then, by the making of clothes, knitted goods, and other needed articles during the hours of recreation that the Sisters spent together. With the help of the St. Vincent de Paul Society they became acquainted with 155 poor families —775 men, women, and children—for whom they made 6694 articles of clothing.

A glorious triduum of charity began on September 27, 1938, with a Pontifical High Mass of thanksgiving, the ultimate of majestic beauty in Sacrifice, setting, and song. The great Chapel of the General Hospital was filled with priests, nuns, friends, the aged men and women of the house, employees—all whom gratitude had united in Mother d'Youville's heart. Delegates from the sister Communities of St. Hyacinthe, Ottawa, Quebec, Nicolet, Philadelphia, and Pembroke joined the Grey Nuns of Montreal in a *Te Deum* that certainly symbolized the perfect union for which their great foundress had pleaded.

About three o'clock that afternoon the guests of honor, the beloved poor—old men and women, the unfortunate young, little children—began to arrive in groups of thirty, brought to the General Hospital in busses from different parts of the city. Each group was graciously received by a committee of four Sisters and conducted first to the tomb of Mother d'Youville before proceeding to the chapel, where, at four o'clock, Benediction of the Blessed Sacrament filled all hearts with ineffable joy.

Then all these guests were taken to the Sisters' refectory,

transformed for this event into a splendid banquet hall. Several bishops were present, a number of priests, and his honor, the Mayor of Montreal. What a sumptuous feast was laid before them all, served with exquisite attention by Reverend Mother Gallant, other members of the General Administration, and assisting Sisters! Who can doubt that the gracious spirit of Mother d'Youville moved among them all, reflecting on each kindly countenance the heavenly light of her charity? Did not this good Mother rejoice to hear the comments of all these happy guests of her Sisters?

"I am thirty-two years old," remarked one poor man, "and this is the first time that I have tasted chicken."

"Do you not think," whispered another to his wife, "that this is even finer and better than our wedding dinner?"

"How true it is," sighed a poor mother, watching her little ones completely enjoying themselves, "how true it is that the Grey Nuns are good Sisters!"

At last the time came when not even the children had room for another piece of candy. Then Mayor Raynault addressed the satisfied assembly, concluding his good-humored discourse with two points of advice: never to be discouraged; never to speak ill of the clergy or of religious communities. On the hearty invitation of Bishop Deschamps, everyone joined in the singing of gay Canadian folk songs until it was time for the final surprise of this very happy occasion.

Directed again by committees, all the guests proceeded in groups to the Sisters' community room, where ten beautifully decorated booths, each dedicated to a different Community of Grey Nuns or to a charitable association connected with the work of the Sisters, had been erected. In these booths were all the gifts destined and marked for each member of each family —hats, coats, shoes, stockings, underwear, dresses, suits—enough to last for two or three years. There were also baskets of candy and fruit, and little gifts dearer sometimes than essentials.

Finally, when hearts and arms could hold no more, these be-

311

loved poor were returned to their homes, where the Reverend Mother General and members of the administration personally visited them the next day, to make doubly sure of their happiness and satisfaction.

The second day of the triduum was also devoted to demonstrations of glad appreciation on the part of the Marguerite d'Youville Alumnae, graduates of the highly qualified School of Domestic Arts conducted by the Grey Nuns at the General Hospital.

The third day of jubilation began with a Solemn High Mass attended by all the lay employees of the hospital and by the aged men and women, about two hundred in number, permanently residing there. It was an unforgettable feature of this event that the employees and the old men, perfectly trained in Gregorian chant, alternated with the Sisters' choir in the singing of the Mass.

At dinner that day all these groups were served by the Sisters, whose joy in this privilege was but one of the highlights of the celebration.

At three o'clock in the afternoon 1500 children from ten orphanages conducted by the Grey Nuns in Montreal and environs began to arrive in busses for their share in this great bicentenary of charity. In perfect order they marched four abreast into the chapel until every possible place was occupied. Then all these children sang solemn Benediction, directed by a Sister from the front of the chapel. What hours of careful training had achieved this triumph of pure harmony and perfect unison!

After the *Laudate,* six representatives of the orphanages conducted in the United States by the Grey Nuns of Montreal marched up the center aisle preceded by a standard bearer carrying the American flag. They advanced to the left transept, where they proudly laid a magnificent wreath of roses upon the tomb of Venerable Mother d'Youville. As they did so the immense chapel rang with the jubilant singing of a prayer for the beatification of this great mother of the poor and of the orphaned.

Again in perfect order, these children assembled in the Sisters' community room, where a little girl closed a graceful program with these words, addressed to Reverend Mother Gallant:

May this sheaf of roses be a token of the loving sentiments of the little children of the Boston Province. Each petal is a heartfelt prayer that our Venerable Mother d'Youville will soon be adorned with the halo of the blessed, thus realizing the ardent desire of your maternal heart and adding a new luster to this wonderful Community.

Needless to say, this happy feast for the children came to an end with mountains of sandwiches and ice cream!

The next morning in the chapel, from which every vestige of festal decoration had been removed, a Solemn High Mass of requiem was celebrated for all deceased Grey Nuns, their benefactors, and their poor. No one was forgotten in this unique bicentennial demonstration of charity.

The crown of the whole glorious event was yet to come. His Holiness, Pope Pius XI, through the Papal Secretary of State, Eugenio Cardinal Pacelli, now gloriously reigning as Pope Pius XII, sent to the whole Congregation of Grey Nuns a great Apostolic Benediction.

Moreover, His Holiness, in supreme recognition of Reverend Mother Marie Evangéline Gallant's extraordinary leadership in the charity of Venerable Mother d'Youville's spiritual daughters, bestowed upon her the highest papal award granted to a woman—the gold medal, "Bene Merenti."

The bright rays of the luminous cross have fallen not only upon outstanding achievements in the history of Mother d'Youville's daughters. They have pierced obscurity also, shining softly upon hundreds and hundreds of Grey Nuns—the hidden saints who generate the light—spending their lives in quiet fidelity to the duties of their state. Into crowded parochial classrooms; into cheerful hospital wards; into happy homes for the aged, the orphaned, the abandoned, the incurable; into work-rooms of every kind, these blessed rays have fallen, touching with heavenly radiance the countenances of those who quietly enkindle in the souls of God's needy ones the soft light of His love.

All these humble unknown have their part to play also in the beautiful symphony of praise that ascends to the Eternal Father for their foundress, the Venerable Mother d'Youville, apostle to the poor.

And all together, many daughters have risen up to call her blessed, for her works praise her.

APPENDIX

APPENDIX

Extracts from the official report of the exhumation of the body of the Reverend Mother d'Youville, foundress of the Sisters of Charity of Ville-Marie, made December 7, 1849.

We, the undersigned, Etienne Michel Faillon and Mathurin Bonnissant, priests of the Seminary of St. Sulpice, commissioned by Most Reverend Ignace Bourget, Bishop of Ville-Marie, to proceed to the recovery of the body of Madame Marie Marguerite Dufrost de Lajemmerais, the widow d'Youville, foundress and first Superior of the Sisters of Charity of Ville-Marie, deceased on December 23, 1771: wishing to acquit ourselves of our commission with all the exactitude and fidelity possible, went several times to the General Hospital of this city, where they say the body of the said foundress rests, and began to question the Sisters as to the place where she was buried.

By the uniform answers that they gave us, we were certain that since the death of Madame d'Youville, the Sisters had always transmitted the tradition from one to another that the body of their foundress was buried in one of the vaults which divide the length of the Chapel of the General Hospital, and which, having been meant at first for the burial of the Brothers of the Cross, called the Charon Brothers, served later for that of the Sisters of Charity who succeeded them in the direction of this hospital. . . .

We learned also, by the same tradition, that Father François d'Youville, pastor at Saint Ours and son of the said foundress, had been buried on April 12, 1778, at the feet of his mother. . . .

To draw down the blessing of Heaven on this . . . search, the Community of Sisters wished to make a novena of prayers. . . . The event soon justified the pious intention and gentle confidence of the Sisters. For scarcely had the men dug four or five feet when they found a casket enclosing a whole body which they believed to be that of the foundress and which they transported to a room in the hospital on December 7, in order to examine it at leisure. . . .

After what has been said above, the body of Father François d'Youville, pastor of Saint Ours, should be found at the feet of that of his mother, and found there in such a way that his feet touch those of his mother, because of the inverse position in which they should have been buried, the mother having her feet turned toward the altar, and the son, as a priest, having his turned toward the door. And that is precisely what was revealed in the discovery of the body of Madame d'Youville, for they found at the feet of her casket another which had its end adjoining hers and which evidently held the remains of a priest, as it seemed by the position of the body, proper to priests in burial, and then by the parts of shoes in which he had been interred— another circumstance entirely unwonted in the burial of Sisters of Charity and in that of the Charon Brothers who preceded them. Should one not marvel at Divine Providence, which, in allowing the casket and the body of Father François d'Youville to be dispersed in the disturbance of the earth, wished, however, that the feet of this body, which would be useful some day for the recognition of that of the foundress, should be preserved intact with their shoes?

Thus, a great many details met together to confirm the authenticity of the body of Madame d'Youville. First, it was noticed that the casket in which it was enclosed had been found perfectly intact, and that the surrounding earth had not been disturbed; and it was exactly in this state that the body of the foundress should have been found, in accordance with a recommendation made by the Sisters never to bury anyone in the place where she was. Secondly, Madame d'Youville's casket is different from all the others ever seen in these vaults in that each of the two large sides was composed of two parts, which formed at their meeting a small angle corresponding to corners; and that, moreover, the four corners of the casket were trimmed with iron squares meant to strengthen it and allow it to be carried easily. These details, entirely unusual in the burial of Sisters, openly indicate that a casket made with so much care enclosed remains dearer to the Community than those of other Sisters, and more worthy also of being preserved in the future. Thirdly, the place where the casket was found was the middle of the chapel at the time of Madame d'Youville's death; that is, the most honorable place. . . .

Even the examination of this body confirms the authenticity of it more and more. First, although all the clothes have been destroyed, with the exception of the scapular, one recognizes, however, the head-gear of the Sisters of Charity by the two crossed pins which they have on the forehead, even in their burial. They also judged that this body had belonged to a person advanced in age, by the lightness and color of the bones. Moreover, Madame d'Youville was very tall, as it is said in her *Life*, and that is another detail which confirms the identity of her body. For the casket, although it was five feet two inches long, would have been too short if the body, which touched both ends, could have been stretched out in it and had not been paralyzed. It is to be observed that Madame d'Youville, at the end of her life, was stricken with paralysis which affected the left side of her body, of which she gradually lost the use, as is said in her *Life*. Now, the body found in the casket is exactly in the position of a person who died paralyzed on the left side. . . .

Consequently, for all these different reasons put together, of which we declare that we have ourselves examined the foundations and the certainty, and in order to conform to the desires of His Excellency, the Bishop of Ville-Marie, who has commissioned us to get information on the aforesaid matter, we think that it is certain and that it is proved that the body found opposite the window for the old men is the real body of Madame Marie Marguerite Dufrost de Lajemmerais, the widow d'Youville, foundress and first Superior of the Sisters of Charity of Ville-Marie.

In belief thereof we have signed the present official report, this twenty-second day of December, 1849.

FAILLON, *priest*

M. C. BONNISSANT, *priest St. S.*

SOEUR HARDY, SOEUR SEGUIN, SOEUR CHERRIER, SOEUR CHENIER

B. H. CHARLEBOIS, M.D.

MANDATE OF BISHOP IGNACE BOURGET
ON DECEMBER 23, 1849.

Ignace Bourget, by the mercy of God and the favor of the Apostolic Holy See, Bishop of Montreal, et cetera.

To all who witness these presents: Greeting and benediction in Our Lord.

Considering the permission given by us on the fifth of this December to exhume the body of the Reverend Mother Marie Marguerite de Lajemmerais, the widow d'Youville, foundress and first Superior of the General Hospital of this city, so that it could be put and kept in a more becoming place; which permission has been approved by his honor, the Chief of Justice in Montreal, the twentieth of the same month;

Considering also the official report of our dear Fathers Faillon and Bonnissant, priests and directors of the Seminary of St. Sulpice, dated the twenty-second of this month and approved by us today, by which it is evident that the body that we have permitted to be exhumed is truly that of the said foundress;

Considering, moreover, the request made to us by the said Sisters of Charity, administrators of this hospital, to move and preserve respectfully the precious remains of their foundress in a reliquary kept for this purpose, to which request we have already done justice, as is evident by our act of approval above mentioned relative to the authenticity of the body found and recognized to be that of the said foundress;

We went today to the chapel of the said General Hospital to proceed to this pious ceremony according to the ritual approved by us yesterday.

There, after having chanted a Pontifical High Mass over the said body, covered with a wax mask and with the special habit of the Sisters of this institute, to celebrate her seventy-eighth anniversary, we transported and placed it in the reliquary which had been prepared for it, offering the prayers of the Church and assisted by Father Billaudèle, one of our Vicars General and Superior of the Seminary of St. Sulpice of this city; by Fathers Faillon and Guitter, directors

320

of the said Seminary of St. Sulpice of Paris; by Father Bonnissant, confessor of this Community; by Fathers Barbarin, Toupin, and Chalbos, priests of the said seminary; by Father Pinsoneault, priest of the Bishop's palace; by Reverend Fathers Havequez and Larcher, of the Society of Jesus; by several ecclesiastics of the great seminary and by Brothers of the Society of Jesus and of the Christian Schools, and in the presence of the whole Community and the poor together, which reliquary we have closed and sealed with our seal, so that no one may take anything from the body or add anything foreign to it.

We leave to God, Who has promised to exalt the humble, the responsibility of glorifying His Servant; and to the Apostolic Holy See the exclusive right of examining and judging the deeds which can turn to the glory of this pious foundress. Only, we beg this faithful Servant of the Lord, if, as we can hope from the divine goodness, she is in heaven, to make us feel her influence before God, by obtaining for us the grace to guide, according to her spirit and her rules, the daughters that she has left to our care. She has seen us at her feet with her beloved flock, exposing to her with confidence our personal needs and those of the whole diocese. May she deign to relieve them with that tender charity which always characterized her great heart.

We should like to do something that could express all the gratitude that the pastors and faithful of this diocese owe to her for all the generous sacrifices that she made for the glory of God and the relief of the poor. But not being able to do this worthily, we beg her to consider as acceptable the efforts, however small they may be, that each one has made on this occasion to prove his good will.

Given at the General Hospital of Montreal, the twenty-third day of December, one thousand eight hundred forty-nine, under our signature and seal and the countersignature of our secretary.

✠IGNACE, Bishop of Montreal
J. O. Paré, chancellor secretary

DECREE
for the Beatification and for the Canonization
of the Venerable Servant of God
Marie Marguerite Dufrost de Lajemmerais
the widow d'Youville
foundress and first Superior of the Sisters of Charity of Ville-Marie

321

APPENDIX

ON THE QUESTION
Should the Commission for the Introduction of the Cause be signed, in the present case, and for the purpose of which there is question?

The Servant of God, Marie Marguerite Dufrost de Lajemmerais, the widow d'Youville, born in the year 1701, in the village named Varennes, in Lower Canada, was certainly a valiant woman, burning above all with the fire of charity toward the poor.

In the various states of life through which Divine Providence caused her to pass, she gave an admirable example of all the virtues. She founded an institute of women for the purpose of constantly helping the poor, and of procuring for them the benefits of merciful charity. This institute, with the help of God, has not ceased to produce abundant fruit.

Adorned with heavenly gifts, the Servant of God drew her last breath on December 23, 1771, leaving behind her a glorious reputation for holiness.

Now this renown for holiness, supported by prodigies considered to be divinely wrought through the intercession of this Servant of God, for a full century, far from becoming eclipsed, has only increased from day to day. Whence it came about that the Most Reverend Archbishop of Montreal decided to begin the ordinary proceeding for information on the reputation for holiness, on the virtues, and on the miracles of the Servant of God.

The investigation, concluded according to regulations, has been referred to the Sacred Congregation of Rites, and Our Holy Father, Pope Leo XIII, has kindly agreed that the question of the signature of the Introduction of the Cause of the aforesaid Servant of God should be discussed in the usual assembly of the Sacred Congregation, without the intervention and the vote of the consultors, and before the passage of the required ten years since the day when the process for information was laid before the Secretary of the Sacred Congregation.

That is why the undersigned Cardinal Prefect of the Sacred Congregation of Rites, on the entreaty of the Reverend Father Arthur Jules Captier, Procurator General of the Seminary of St. Sulpice, Postulator of this Cause, having considered the supplicatory letters of several Most Reverend and holy bishops and other illustrious men, invested

322

with dignity both ecclesiastical and civil, proposed to discuss the following question in the usual assembly of the Sacred Congregation of Rites, held in the Vatican on the day set: Should the Commission for the Introduction of the Cause be signed, in the present case, and for the purpose for which there is question?

And the Sacred Congregation, having thoroughly examined all points, having agreed, by word of mouth and in writing, with the sentiment of the Most Reverend Father Augustin Caprara, Promoter of the Holy Faith, has now thought that "Affirmatively" should be answered; that is, that the Commission should be signed, if that is agreeable to His Holiness, March 27, 1890.

The faithful report of all that precedes having been made, by the undersigned Secretary, to Our Holy Father, Pope Leo XIII, His Holiness has ratified and confirmed the decree of the Sacred Congregation, and with his own hand has signed the Commission for the Introduction of the Cause of the Venerable Servant of God, Marie Marguerite Dufrost de Lajemmerais, the widow d'Youville, on April 28 of the same year.

C. Card. Aloisi Masella, Pref. of the S.C. of R.
Vincentius Nussi, Secretary of the S.C. of R.

BIBLIOGRAPHY

BIBLIOGRAPHY

Archives of the General Hospital of the Grey Nuns of Montreal
  Documents
  Registers
  Letters
André-Corsini, Mère St., S.G.C., *30 Jours en Mer, 300 Jours sur Terre, 30 Heures dans l'Air*. Montreal: Imprimerie Populaire, 1947.
Angela, Sister St., "A Refugee's Diary," *China*, XXIV (December 1943), XXV (January, February, March 1944).
Atherton, William Henry, *Montreal under the French Régime*, 2 vols. Montreal: S. J. Clarke Publishing Company, 1914.
———, "The Foundation of the *Soeurs Grises*," *Deux Cents Ans*. Montreal: Imprimerie Modèle Limitée, 1938.
Auger, Soeur, "Les Soeurs de la Charité de St. Hyacinthe," *Deux Cents Ans*.
Beston, Henry, *The St. Lawrence*. New York: Rinehart, 1942.
Blanche, Soeur Ste., *Une Disciple de la Croix*. Quebec: Tremblay, 1932.
———, *Une Fondatrice et Son Oeuvre, Mère Mallet et l'Institut des Soeurs de la Charité de Quebec*. Quebec: L'Action Catholique, 1939.
Brown, George W., *Building the Canadian Nation*. Toronto: Dent, 1942.
Chafe, A., S.F.M., "A Grey-Clad Legion of Mercy," *China*, XIX (December 1938).

327

Code, Joseph Bernard, *Great American Foundresses*. New York: Macmillan, 1929.

Colby, C. W., *Canadian Types of the Old Régime*. London: Bell, 1908.

Drouin, Soeur Clementine, *Mère d'Youville*. Montreal: Soeurs Grises, 1921.

Dubois, Emile, *La Vénérable Mère d'Youville*. Montreal: Soeurs Grises, 1921.

Duchaussois, P., *The Grey Nuns in the Far North*. Toronto: McClelland and Stewart, 1919.

Duffin, Mother Mary Gertrude, *A Heroine of Charity, Mother d'Youville*. New York: Benziger, 1938.

Dufrost, Charles d'Youville, *Vie de Madame d'Youville*, manuscript in the archives of the General Hospital; reprint, Levis, 1930.

Faillon, Etienne Michel, *Vie de Madame d'Youville*. Montreal: Soeurs Grises, 1854.

Fauteux, Soeur Albina, *Vie de la Vénérable Mère d'Youville*. Montreal: Soeurs Grises, 1929.

Ferland, Mère Léonie, S.G.M., *La Devotion à St. Joseph chez les Soeurs Grises de Montreal*. Montreal: Soeurs Grises, 1941.

———, "Madame d'Youville, Première Fondatrice Canadienne Française," *Album Souvenir* de la Société S. Jean-Baptiste, Montreal, 1938.

———, *Sentinelles du Christ: Les Soeurs Grises de Montréal à la Baie d'Hudson*. Montreal: Soeurs Grises, 1944.

———, *Un Voyage au Cercle Polaire*. Montreal: Soeurs Grises, 1939.

———, "Veillards et Orphelins," *Deux Cents Ans*.

Ferland-Angers, Albertine, *Mère d'Youville*. Montreal: Beauchemin, 1945.

———, "Mère d'Youville, la Grande Réalisatrice," reprint from *Le Devoir*, Montreal, 1910.

———, *Pierre You et Son Fils, François d'Youville*. Montreal: Soeurs Grises, 1941.

Grey Sisters of the Immaculate Conception. "Twenty Years After" (pamphlet), Pembroke, Ontario, 1947.

Hélène, Soeur Sainte, *Profils et Croquis Haitiens*. St. Hyacinthe: Soeurs Grises, 1945.

Hutchison, Bruce, *The Unknown Country*. New York: Coward-McCann, 1942.

BIBLIOGRAPHY

Jetté, Berthe Laflamme, *Vie de la Vénérable Mère d'Youville*. Montreal: Cadieux et Derome, 1900.

Keefe, Sister St. Thomas Aquinas, G.N.S.H., *The Congregation of the Grey Nuns (1737–1910)*, doctoral dissertation, Catholic University of America, 1942.

Krumpelmann, Cosmas, *In This Sign Thou Shalt Conquer*. Muenster, Saskatchewan: St. Peter's Press, 1938.

McDowell, Franklin Davey, *The Champlain Road*. Milwaukee: Bruce, 1939.

McFarland, L., S.F.M., "Shock Troops of Christ," *China*, XXIV (November 1943).

Marion, Seraphin, *Pierre Boucher*. Quebec: Proulx, 1927.

Moore, Irene, *Valiant La Vérendrye*. Quebec: Proulx, 1927.

Parker, Gilbert, *Old Quebec*. New York: Macmillan, 1903.

Parkman, Francis, *Old Régime in Canada*. New York: Little, Brown and Company, 1922.

Paul-Emile, Soeur, "Les Soeurs Grises de la Croix au Basutoland," Causerie à la Semaine Missionnaire de Noranda, Ottawa, 1940.

———, *Mère Elisabeth Bruyère et Son Oeuvre*, Hull, P.Q.: L'Opinion Limitée, 1945.

———, "Nos Missions de Canada," Causerie à la Semaine Missionaire de Noranda, reprint, Ottawa, 1940.

Ramsay, D. S., *Life of the Venerable Marie Marguerite de Lajemmerais, Madame d'Youville*. Montreal: Soeurs Grises, 1895.

René, Soeur M-Carmen, "L'Institut des Soeurs de la Charité de l'Hôtel-Dieu de Nicolet," *Deux Cents Ans*.

———, *Soeurs Grises Nicolétaines*. Trois Rivières: Bien Public, 1949.

Repplier, Agnes, *Mère Marie of the Ursulines*. New York: Doubleday, Doran and Company, 1931.

Riley, Sister Mary Gabriel, G.N.S.H., *The Social Thought of the Venerable Mother d'Youville, with Emphasis on Child Care*, typescript, master's thesis, Catholic University of America, 1942.

Sattin, Antoine, p.S.S., *Vie de Madame d'Youville*, manuscript in archives of General Hospital of Montreal, reprint, Quebec, 1930.

Soeurs Grises de Montreal, *Cinquantenaire de l'Institution des Jeunes Aveugles de Nazareth*. Montreal: Soeurs Grises, 1911.

———, *Fêtes Jubilaires*. Montreal: Soeurs Grises, 1938.

————, *La Crèche d'Youville et l'Adoption des Enfants.* Montreal: Soeurs Grises, 1933.

————, *L'Hôpital Général,* 2 vols. Montreal: Soeurs Grises, 1915 and 1933.

————, *Souvenir d'un Evénement Mémorable.* Montreal: Soeurs Grises, 1934.

Soeurs Grises de St. Hyacinthe, *En Feuilletant les Chroniques.* St. Hyacinthe: Soeurs Grises, 1940.

Staub, M. Clement, *Mère et Modèle.* Montreal: Soeurs Grises, 1912.

Talbot, Francis, S.J., *Saint Among Savages.* New York: Harper, 1935.

Tessier, Albert, "Servir Sans Faiblir," *Deux Cents Ans.*

Wallace, William S., *The Dictionary of Canadian Biography.* Toronto: Macmillan, 1926.

Wittke, Carl Frederick, *A History of Canada.* Revised edition. New York: Crofts, 1933.

INDEX

INDEX